Carol

In a wonderful day.

and the smiles

December 08. 2011

Past into Print

Past into Print

The Publishing of History in Britain 1850-1950

LESLIE HOWSAM

THE BRITISH LIBRARY
and
UNIVERSITY OF TORONTO PRESS

First published 2009 by
The British Library
96 Euston Road
London NW1 2DB

British Library
Cataloguing in Publication Data
A catalogue record for this title is
available from The British Library

ISBN 978 0 7123 5027 3

First published in North and South America
in 2009 by University of Toronto Press
Incorporated

Library and Archives Canada Cataloguing in Publication
A CIP record for this volume is
available from the University of Toronto Press

ISBN 978 1 4426 4057 3

University of Toronto Press
acknowledges the financial assistance
to its publishing program of
the Canada Council for the Arts
and the Ontario Arts Council

University of Toronto Press
acknowledges the financial support
for its publishing activities of
the Government of Canada through the
Book Publishing Industry Development Program
(BPIDP)

Designed by John Trevitt
Typeset in Scotch Roman by
Norman Tilley Graphics Ltd, Northampton
Printed in Great Britain by
MPG Books Ltd

Contents

List of abbreviations — *page* ix
Preface: Narrative and discipline — x

1 Every Schoolboy Knows: Publishing the Narrative of England's Liberty, 1850-1863 — 1
The life cycle of the history-book reader — 3
The agency of the publisher — 5
Tension between professional and popular accounts of the past — 6
History books as material objects — 9
Nursery histories and their competition — 10
New editions of old titles — 18

2 Quality and Profit: New Histories of England, 1863-1880 — 24
Alexander Macmillan and the historians — 26
The Clarendon Press (Oxford) and the historians — 40
The Pitt Press (Cambridge) and the historians — 44

3 Breaking the Drowsy Spell of Narrative, 1880-1914 — 49
Seeley and the reading public — 50
Browning and the publishers — 54
New formats for history: periodicals and series — 59
Acton and the Cambridge Modern History — 62
New blood at Oxford — 71

4 Historians and Publishers in an Age of War and Revolution, 1914-1929 — 76
Revisions and reiterations — 79
Ernest Barker at Oxford — 81
Belligerents and ex-belligerents, a series — 84
Imagining an Oxford History of England — 86

More histories at Cambridge 89
The Cambridge collaborative histories 92
The Power sisters and Cambridge Histories for Children 95
London publishers 1914-29 96

5 Knowledge in the Marketplace, 1930-1950 100
The Cambridge collaborative histories 102
History from the Oxford University Press 104
History books: text, object, context 113
History as text 115
History books as material objects 115
The social and cultural processes of book-making 117

Epilogue: History, out of print 122

Notes 129
Chronology 155
Bibliography 162
Index 178

Abbreviations

CMH	*Cambridge Modern History*
CUP	Cambridge University Press
EHR	*English Historical Review*
ODNB	Oxford Dictionary of National Biography
OUP	Oxford University Press

Preface

Narrative and discipline

PAST INTO PRINT is about the publishing history of history; it tells a story of how knowledge of the past was captured in books and periodicals, in Britain between 1850 and 1950. Its human protagonists are historians and publishers and its theoretical concerns lie with historiography and bibliography. It teases out some of the implications of two unstable terms – history and the book – whose several meanings are complicated by the way each modifies the other. *The book* is a material object or a written text, but the term can also encompass the cultural transaction wherein object and text together are composed and circulated, received and replicated. *History* can refer to the literary genre or to a specific narrative, or it can be conceptualized broadly in terms of practice and discipline. The book itself has a history, which like other histories is recorded in books.

Research into the history of authorship, publishing and reading has addressed a wide range of practices and institutions in book culture. But most such studies have been concerned with the publishing histories of canonical or popular literature, or of science. The publishing history of history has been neglected even though history, like science, flourished in the later nineteenth century as both a burgeoning academic discipline and a popular narrative form. Unlike the history of science, historiography has not benefited from the insight afforded by an alternative academic perspective, and it can be difficult for practitioners to recognize how much their discipline is shaped by the contemporary book culture. Scholars have been reluctant to acknowledge the influence of publishers upon not only the history we read, but also the history we write.

This reluctance is not only about the materiality and commercial aspects of books. The intellectual culture of the historical discipline has been inimical to recontextualizing the work of its forebears. We warn students to avoid consulting works published more than a decade or two ago, and advise them to seek out innovative methods and theoretical approaches. Although this way of thinking is unexceptionable, in that it promotes rigorous research, the practice has had unintended consequences, both historiographical and bibliographical. Older works of history have been neglected – seldom valued as literature, and not often collected as artefacts. Unlike the culture wars associated with a body of imaginative literature, the history wars have not been fought over a canon. New studies of medieval England or of imperial Britain need not trace their lineage to William Stubbs or J. R. Seeley. But old works of history survive, despite the neglect and disdain of contemporary practitioners. They are consulted in libraries and on-line; sometimes they remain in print. They are read and remembered, and even taught and studied, long after they disappear from academic conversation. They provide entertainment, patriotic inspiration or escape and contribute to the formation of personal and national identities.

To recognize the survival of old history books is one thing, but to put them in context for contemporary readers is quite another. This is where historiography and cultural history meet bibliography and the history of the book. A study of the history of the historical discipline that includes its publishing practices can overcome that unintentional anachronism dictated by the practical needs of historians. Superseded history books are immensely valuable artefacts for interpreting the times in which they were written, published and first read. *Past into Print* suggests some themes and sets out a chronology for developing such interpretations.

The chronology is based on a coincidence that was not an accident. Towards the end of the nineteenth century and the beginning of the twentieth, something happened to history and something happened to books. At the same time as the discipline was being made scholarly, quasi-scientific, and ultimately academic, the publishing business was flourishing, using new technologies like electrotype and photography to supply a reading public much better equipped with literacy and leisure than earlier generations. Popular print and rigorous history came together; and both discipline and narrative were transformed by the encounter. I do not define *discipline* here in Michel Foucault's terms, and nor do I use *narrative* in the context of postmodern debates, whether within literary criticism or historiography. Rather, I am concerned with the beginnings of history as an academic discipline, and with the kind of narrative that purports to tell people a true and compelling story about their past.

It is difficult to reconstruct just how excited that small band of serious historians were about their discipline and its possibilities in the days when Leopold von Ranke's writings were first being read in England and being interpreted by scholars like Stubbs at Oxford and Lord Acton at Cambridge. We might compare it to the enthusiasm for Foucault and Derrida that recently seized some parts of the academic world, were it not so ironic that those postmodern questioners of objectivity and truth in scholarship were setting themselves up in opposition to the very ideology that had likewise – only a century earlier – proclaimed an exclusive vocabulary and an austere critical stance. Perhaps it would be more useful to compare the Victorian and Edwardian historians to Darwin and Huxley, who also confronted readers with carefully-documented evidence, and challenged them to abandon a deeply entrenched belief system. To believe in the indisputable truth of England's liberty and King Alfred's experience with the cakes was perhaps less profound than to accept the biblical account of creation. Still, the loss of faith could be a powerful experience in both cases, an experience shared by a reading community. And as with the tension between religion and science, the uneasy co-existence of a traditional narrative and documentary scholarship was mediated to that community largely by the entrepreneurs of print culture.

My approach has built upon the importance of history and history books in Victorian and Edwardian culture and asked, first, what contemporary publishers made of the historians' new commitments, and then how the successors of both groups handled their continuing encounter in the wake of two world wars. Historiography offers little in the way of answers, and nor do most biographies of well-known historians or the house histories of publishers; but valuable sources have nevertheless survived. The chief source for *Past into Print* is letters, some written by historians to their publishers, and others by publishers to their historian-authors. These letters include reports, written at the request of publishers, passing judgement and criticism on the work of others and in the process revealing the reporters' (and perhaps also the publishers') understanding of what readers were looking for when they encountered a work of history. Such letters and reports are abundant in the archives of Macmillan and Company, of Cambridge and Oxford University Presses, and of several other publishers. They are also to be found in archival collections of the papers of historians. With the use of a database computer-program, extracts and summaries of large numbers of these documents can be organized in chronological order so that patterns begin to emerge. Sometimes both file copy and original of the same letter might be traced; quite often both request and reply survive in separate collections. An author identified throughout his or her career with one publisher is found submitting work to another. Gaps in historians' correspondence as published in their Lives and Letters are now filled in, with useful details of royalties or revealing observations about audience. Rivalries between publishers show up, as one firm's profitable series of Epochs is emulated by another's Heroes of History. In many cases, the letters raise questions which can be answered only by a look at the book that eventuated from the correspondence. An examination of that book, however, whether by reading the text or analyzing its 'Paratext' (preface, acknowledgements, illustrations, binding, advertising material and so forth), would disclose nothing of the story found in the correspondence. These are revealing documents, most of them meant to remain private and confidential. They expose some of the commercial and career motivations that lay behind public statements of intellectual and pedagogical purpose. Sometimes utterly scathing and often very funny, correspondence and reports also reveal something important about the intellectual and political culture of their time.

The idea for reading these letters, and investigating these problems, was inspired by my reflections on how historians write the history of the book, and in particular the way my own experience with the discipline has shaped the way I think about the study of book culture. I've written elsewhere about the significance of different disciplinary approaches to the interdisciplinary subject of book history. Beginning in the mid-1990s I noticed how much book history was written by literary scholars, about the authorship, reading and publishing of novels and poetry, and by historians of science about the way in which scientific knowledge was mediated to the reading public. As a historian, I decided, I ought to investigate history books. Funding from the Social Sciences and Humanities Research Council of Canada allowed me to visit the archives and to engage student research assistants, and the invitation to deliver the 2006 Lyell Lectures in Bibliography at the University of Oxford determined the shape of the present book. The Oxford title was 'Discipline and Narrative: Historical Knowledge and British Publishers, 1850-1950'. The lectures in this volume constitute a first instalment on the subject of the publishing history of history in Britain between those dates. They set out a chronology and identify a number of themes, but they do not exhaust even my own research of the past ten years. I expect to return to the subject, and very much hope that my ideas and arguments will inflect the research of others.

The Epilogue suggests avenues for future work in a more concrete way; here I will take the opportunity to mention three limitations on the extent of the present study. Although the title refers to Britain, because so many works invoked the British Empire, and so many books were shipped to the colonies, my archival work was limited to England. Time constraints made it difficult to extend my archival research to Scottish or Welsh collections, and I was unwilling to enter into these matters without a thorough investigation. Such research is on my agenda now, and will certainly prove to be fruitful. Second, this is not by any means an example of quantitative book history. I have not systematically examined all works of history, or even all histories of England, published within the period. Indeed I have ignored some particularly well-known works, such as Charles Dickens's *A Child's History of England*. Third, the national projects of editing state papers and preparing other historical documents for publication, often by voluntary organizations such as the Camden Society, remains to be integrated into the account developed here. The stories that I told in my five Lyell Lectures, which became the five chapters of the present book were, rather, the stories that emerged from the correspondence that survives among the archives of publishers, and in the private papers of historians. They are the stories of men and women who cared deeply about books, and about history.

Acknowledgements

I was greatly honoured by the invitation of the Electors to the Lyell Readership in Bibliography to deliver the 2006 series of lectures in Oxford University. During my time at Oxford I enjoyed the hospitality of Ronald Milne, then Acting Director of the Oxford University Library Service and Bodley's Librarian; Sue Henderson, Jacqui Julier and Lucy Hodson in the Faculty of History helped with logistics and were most hospitable, and Heather Ellis provided very welcome technical support for the delivery of the lectures in the Examination Schools.

Material from the Archives of the Oxford University Press is cited by permission of the Secretary to the Delegates of Oxford University Press. I am grateful to Nicolas Barker for permission to quote from the unpublished writings of his father, Sir Ernest Barker. I am very much indebted to my good friend and great publisher, David Way of British Library Publications, for attending the first lecture in Oxford in 2006 and for engaging that most meticulous and knowledgeable copy-editor, John Trevitt, in 2009, and for everything in between. My Canadian colleagues at the University of Toronto Press, especially Suzanne Rancourt and Ryan Van Huijstee, ensured that the joint publication process went smoothly.

All the illustrations come from the collections of The British Library, with the following exceptions. Figure 2.7 (page 42) is published with the permission of the Curators of the Bodleian Library, University of Oxford and is taken from their collection; figure 3.5 (pages 66-7) is published with the permission of the Syndics of Cambridge University Library and is drawn from their collection.

This project would not have been possible without the financial support of the Social Sciences and Humanities Research Council of Canada, which provided a Standard Research Grant from 1999 to 2003 and made it possible for me to employ research assistants and to travel. Much of the archival research was carried out during a sabbatical in England in 2000 when I was a Visiting Fellow at Lucy Cavendish College, Cambridge and held a Centre for the Book Fellowship at the British Library. The Falconer Madan Prize of the Bibliographical Society, and a related visiting scholar post at Wolfson College supported my visit to Oxford in 2002. I spent the autumn of 2004 on sabbatical at the University of Toronto where I was a Visiting Fellow of the Collaborative Graduate Program in Book History and Print Culture and a Visiting Scholar at Massey College. The eventual revision of the lectures for publication was made possible by releases from teaching that were funded by the University of Windsor Humanities Research Group Fellowship in 2007.

This book owes a great deal to the help of librarians and archivists. I especially want to acknowledge the assistance of Mike Bott and Bryan Ryder, of Special Collections in the University of Reading Library; Penelope Bulloch of Balliol College Library, Oxford; Kathleen Cann and Godfrey Waller of the Cambridge University Library Manuscript Room; Rosemary Dunhill, Archivist of Jesus College Oxford; J. R. Hodgson of the John

Rylands Library of Manchester; Elizabeth James of the Manuscripts Department of The British Library; Elisabeth Leedham Green of the Cambridge University Archives; Martin Maw, Archivist of the Oxford University Press; Helen E. Roberts of the Brynmore Jones Library, University of Hull; Apollonia Steele of the University of Calgary Library and Joy McCarthy of the Royal Historical Society.

Many colleagues around the world provided advice, assistance and support of an intellectual, material or emotional kind. Special thanks to Sandra Alston, Katharine Anderson, Margaret Beetham, Bill Bell, Fiona Black, Bill Bogart, Miriam Elizabeth Burstein, Chad Carver, Gail Chester, Yuri Cowan, Melba Cuddy-Keane, Natalie Zemon Davis, Martin Deck, Simon Eliot, David Finkelstein, Aileen Fyfe, Regina Gagnier, Rosemary Halford, Ian Hesketh, Valerie Holman, Susan Houston, Kathryn Hughes, Robert Hunter, Finola Hurley, Jane Innerd, Heather Jackson, Elizabeth James, Ellen Jordan, Ludmilla Jordanova, Christopher Kent, Ken King, Marie Korey, Christine Krueger, Richard Landon, Patrick Leary, Bernie Lightman, Kate Longworth, Chris Lucki, Mary Lu MacDonald, Kate McCrone, Jason McElligott, David McKitterick, Peter Mandler, Suzanne Matheson, Elsa Meyland-Smith, Jane McLeod, Rosemary Mitchell, John North, Clarissa Campbell Orr, Robert Patten, Linda Peterson, Clare Pettitt, Yannick Portebois, Jake Redekop, Robert Ritter, James Secord, Jill Shefrin, Barbara Somerville, Paul Stortz, Jonathan Topham, Bruce Tucker, Anna Vaniskaya, David and Charlotte Vincent, Germaine and John Warkentin, Mary Williamson and Ian Willison.

The University of Windsor graduate-student research assistants who did so much to find and organize material as well as to help me think about it were (in chronological order of their appointment) Tara Beaton, Dan Milne, Scott Green, Carmen Poole, Erika Hauschild and Chris Tozer. Undergraduate student helpers funded through the University of Windsor Work Study program to undertake some tedious but essential clerical tasks were Karin Burnett, Emily Cataford, Ian Gibson, Sarah Hie, Niklas Holmberg, Johnny King, Sina Naebkhil and Jason Underhill.

The final acknowledgements go to two friends and two family members. James Raven and Jacqueline Murray (who have never met) are the historian colleagues who have taught me the most, by example and in conversation, about our discipline. And my daughter Jessica Kamphorst and my husband Neil Campbell are my irreplaceable supports.

Chapter 1

Every Schoolboy Knows: Publishing the Narrative of England's Liberty, 1850-1863

THIS BOOK is about history books – the histories that British readers encountered during the years from 1850 to 1950. Over the course of that century, history became a professionalized academic discipline while remaining a popular literary genre. The period was also a time of educational reform from the nursery to the senior common room. At the same time, print was the primary medium of public discourse, benefiting from cheap and accessible paper and manufacture, widespread literacy and leisure; there was great rivalry within the trade but little competition from other media.[1] Both the practice of history and that of publishing were unstable and, as it happens, each set of practices influenced the other.

Underpinning my approach to these parallel developments is another notable symmetry, between the historical nature of bibliographical study on the one hand, and on the other, the intrinsically bibliographical character of written narratives about the past. The study of books as physical objects is inescapably chronological, as each student of bibliography strives to order a body of manuscripts, periodical articles and monographs into the correct sequence of editions. The bibliographer's labour results in a coherent linear account, whether it delineates the works of an author, the titles comprising a genre, the imprint of a town or a region, or of a printer or a publisher.[2] Bibliographical analysis demonstrates change over time, although it may stop short of historical narrative and interpretation.

Meanwhile, an inescapable task for most historians is to write an account of written works in which the sources and problems in question have been addressed before. We call this historiography, rather than bibliography, however, and focus more on content than on the publishing process.[3] The serious historians practising during the late nineteenth and early twentieth centuries have been the subject of a rich body of historiographical – but not bibliographical –

study. With only a few exceptions, both individual and collective studies tend to leave a reader with the impression that historians are self-published: their books appear to emerge without the agency of anyone but the author.[4] The publisher and his or her editorial staff become invisible, despite their financial and intellectual capital, their stake in a commercial marketplace. Most historiography examines the texts of historians' narratives and arguments, while largely ignoring the books in which these texts first appeared and now survive.

History books have a history of their own. They are read and written, published and purchased, collected and reviewed, studied and taught. The primary sources for that history are to be found where bibliographers search for evidence – notably in the imprints of the books themselves and in the archives of publishers. These sources also remind us of the inherently bibliographical character of the discipline of history. Its practitioners depend upon the publication of their work in the material form of books and periodicals, and also upon the acknowledgement of precursors' publications. Although history, in the broader sense of the events and structures of times past, happened independently of historians and history books, another usage of the word has to do with knowledge of times past. This latter meaning is inseparable from the books in which history has been compiled and composed, conveyed and received, replicated and preserved. Like other books, historical works have been the products of complex collaborations among publishers and editors, authors and readers. The historical discipline is bookish, and historical narrative is intrinsically, if not obviously, bibliographical.

History books, in other words, are embedded within the book culture of the period when they are written and published.[5] The period from mid-nineteenth to mid-twentieth century is a particularly enlightening one, because of the transformation of the book trade during those years. Alongside changes in the economy and society that led to higher rates of popular literacy and working-class education, with changes in technology that made paper more accessible, and applied steam power to the three hundred year old technology of printing, the price of books declined sharply and their availability rose dramatically. As Simon Eliot has shown, the number of titles printed in Britain quadrupled between 1840 and 1919, and the size of impressions rose even more quickly.[6]

Past into Print pursues the publishing history of history by examining four interconnected themes: the life cycle of the reader;

the agency of the publisher; the tension between academic and popular accounts of the past; and the materiality of the history book. This chapter begins with a conceptual discussion of each theme and then returns to the life cycle of the reader, for some illustrations of history books written and published for children.

The life cycle of the history-book reader

With one of the rhetorical flourishes that were destined to infuriate his late-Victorian critics, Thomas Babington Macaulay once introduced a fragment of conventional historical knowledge with the phrase, 'Every schoolboy knows'.[7] He meant that every adult who was ever a schoolboy, or perhaps even a schoolgirl, had once learned the key events of classical and of English history. Subsequent commentators were inclined to recast the common reader as 'Macaulay's schoolboy', but paid little attention to where and how the lad might have learned his lessons, or his sister hers.[8] While the contribution of teachers cannot be overlooked, it is important to emphasize that children learned history from books, and that those books were composed and published in a commercial, as well as a pedagogical and political culture.

To organize a study around the life cycle of the reader is to open up a compelling way of thinking about the experience of reading, and behind that the histories of publishing and of authorship. Unlike a communication circuit that begins with the literary biographies of authors and moves on through the business histories of publishers, this alternative model commences with books for children and moves forward in time with the reader's life to those for adolescents and for adults, for common readers and for apprentice historians, and eventually for scholarly peers.[9] The life-cycle approach indirectly reinforces what may be an obvious point. The minds of those British people who came of age in the 1850s and 1860s, whether or not they later encountered the radically new approaches to history that became fashionable in the closing decades of the century and the opening of the next, were already furnished with historical knowledge. Macaulay had schooled them well, and so had the writers of nursery histories, and the compilers of school books.

Just as readers of evolutionary science tested their new understanding of natural philosophy against a deeply-entrenched body of biblical knowledge, so readers were coming to the new 'scientific', scholarly, revisionist history with a mental storehouse of knowledge and belief laid down at an impressionable stage in their personal development.[10] It was necessarily an uncomplicated narrative, simplified and sanitized, ordered chronologically by the reign of one monarch after the next, didactic and moralizing, and enlivened by compelling anecdotes.

The life-cycle approach helps us to recognize a tendency in historical writing to narrative replication. Writers of history often find themselves charged with retelling an account of events already well known – to themselves, to their imagined reader, as well as to their publisher. This reiteration of 'the same old story' is a side-effect of the undeniable fact that narratives about the past relate events that happened, to people who lived and are remembered. In the political and constitutional history-writing that dominated most of the period with which we are concerned, the people were rulers and other powerful individuals, and the events concerned their battles and intrigues, their wisdom and foolishness, their marriages and their campaigns. In a culture where 'nursery histories' were as much a part of childhood as Bible stories and approved fictions, this meant that most adult readers of history already knew the story, or expected to know it, when they picked up the book. They had been introduced very early to the sequence of kings and queens and to attractive anecdotes, such as what happened when King Alfred left the cakes to burn, or when Queen Elizabeth spoke at Tilbury. One writer summed up the basics in terms of 'the King's name, character, an event and a few anecdotes such as [very young children] can remember'.[11] As they became adolescent, however, some children discovered that they had been learning a history to which 'successive coats of paint' could be added, so that, for example, it was eventually deemed appropriate for them to know that Perkin Warbeck might have been a bastard.[12] Adults could be expected to take on board more explicit lessons about the constitutional underpinnings of the narrative of England's greatness than they had already absorbed as children.

But the first requirement of young men studying history at university was to un-learn this simple narrative; they did so willingly and thoroughly, replacing it with something more complex, supple and robust. It became their task as tutors and professors in the universities to help their students similarly to disdain the old lessons and the straightforward story and to be prepared for revision after revision when new material came to light or new interpretations gained credibility. What most of them failed to realize was that the great majority of readers of history books never enjoyed this opportunity. When professional academic historians cautioned their students to 'break the drowsy spell of narrative' and wake up to rigorous analysis, they were establishing a boundary between acceptable and objectionable, true and false, dependable and dodgy forms of historical knowledge.[13] The spell was not, however, in the power of historical scholars alone to break. They needed the collaboration of publishers, of educational authorities and of the writers who served the schoolbook market. This group was slow to change, and the lessons learned as impressionable boys and girls remained part of the historical consciousness of British men and women for generations.

The agency of the publisher

Over the past several decades the scholarship of 'history of the book', and of bibliography as the sociology of texts, has demonstrated the agency of publishers in the making of novels and of works of science.[14] Following on from those studies, my own research began with the assumption that publishers also exercised agency in the making of history books, and set out to discover the evidence that might confirm, deny or modify this hypothesis. Some of the evidence is mentioned in secondary sources: for example, that Robert Longman not only suggested to G. M. Trevelyan the composition of his *English Social History* (1944) but that it was the publisher who coined the controversial catch-phrase 'history with the politics left out'.[15] A. J. P. Taylor believed that others, including publishers, had dictated the subjects of most of his books.[16] Earlier, it was the Syndics of the Cambridge University Press who invited Lord Acton to embark upon a collaborative project that became the *Cambridge Modern History*.[17] Similar initiatives of intellectual entrepreneurship happened at Oxford, when the Clarendon Press decided to compete with the Cambridge histories by producing its own school History of England and later series of authoritative multi-volume, though single-authored, accounts of the past.[18] These (and other fragments I gathered from the secondary sources) were intriguing, and archival research among the records of both publishers and historians confirmed their importance. The theme of the agency of publishers in the making of history books will be traced throughout this volume.

The way in which book-trade concerns intervened in historical writing can be related to the broader question of collaboration – among historians, as well as between historians and their publishers. The practice of collaboration, when two or more – perhaps many – people work together to produce a single book, deserves more attention than it has received. On the contrary: theoretical writing about the history of the book in the modern period has emphasized the individuality, if not the individual genius, of the author – although the influence of the book trade and the experience of reading have now been admitted.[19] Robert Darnton's model of a 'communication circuit' took a book from its author, via its publisher, printer, binder and bookseller, around to its reader, simplifying the relationships for clarity but at the cost of reducing complex social structures to token individuals. Also, the rich literature about nineteenth-century books has concentrated unequally on the writers, publishers and readers of fiction and poetry, genres where the process of textual composition was, perhaps exceptionally, individualized. In the case of history, as publishers began to experiment with the series format (as a way to package and market the books on their list that concerned past times in various places), writers found themselves fitting their writing into a narrative scheme not of their own making.

Tension between professional and popular accounts of the past

During the same decades that most books were becoming cheaper, many historians were becoming scholars. Between the 1870s and the 1920s the practice of history was radically reshaped by academic professionalization. It was 'struggling' (as J. R. Green observed) 'out of that condition in which it was looked on as no special or definitive study, but as part of that general mass of things, which every gentleman should know'.[20] One aspect of the nineteenth-century reform and expansion of universities in Britain was the incorporation of history into higher education, *as* a 'special or definitive study' that served either as a training for public life or as preparation to practice the discipline itself. University-based historians, conscious of the prestige of scientific thought and practice among their contemporaries, began to argue that history was a science, a discipline for highly-trained specialists, where documentary evidence could be found in archives, systematically analyzed and the analyses replicated, in order to discover and promulgate an accurate account of the past.[21] For many of these new practitioners, the historical narratives they had grown up with – sweeping panoramas in the Macaulay or Hume tradition – were now deeply suspect. One of the new breed of historians, John Robert Seeley, called for his peers to 'break the drowsy spell of narrative' and to recognize that serious works of history were no more designed to appeal to the general reader than were specialized works of science. In an exaggerated paraphrase of Seeley's idea, by his contemporary Edward Augustus Freeman, 'To make sure of being judged by competent judges only, we ought to make history so dull and unattractive that the general public will not wish to meddle with it.'[22]

The rhetoric of history as a science, austere and authoritative, was reinforced by its association with German scholarship, and again with the historical thinking that celebrated the Teutonic roots of England's constitutional history. Although few British historians actually travelled to Germany to study with Leopold von Ranke, many of them valued the great German scholar's dictum that history must be approached from a scientific perspective, eschewing bias and recounting events 'as they actually [or essentially] happened'. In this context it is worth noting that several of Ranke's books were translated into English but never sold in significant numbers. As the Secretary of the Clarendon Press told Ranke himself in 1885, 'the reputation of your works amongst the small band of Historical scholars in England is unbounded; but it is a small number and the majority of them study your writings in the original'.[23] The Clarendon translation from the German of Ranke's *History of England*, initiated fourteen years earlier and published in 1875, had by then only just begun to cover its expenses.

Meanwhile, commercial publishers in Britain were in the business of supplying an enthusiastic general public with engaging and attractive works of history. Chapter 2 will look at the book trade's response to the austere standards now embraced by many practitioners of the historical discipline. Their reaction might be summed up in terms of professional aplomb concealing a distinct sense of dismay. Simon Eliot's statistical analysis also shows that, of recorded titles published in the period from 1870 to 1919, some twelve to fifteen per cent were in the category of history and related subjects. Although history did not equal the novel's fifty per cent in quantity, it possessed valuable attributes that fiction lacked. Historical works were steady sellers, and they were susceptible of textual revision. Like novels, their market included the general reader of any age, who sought entertainment and diversion in truth-claiming narratives as much as in fiction. And, like novels, histories could be repackaged in variant formats for different price-points in the literary marketplace. Unlike fiction, though, history's reading public also extended to what one publisher called 'the schoolmaster in all shades' and to the captive market of children requiring the provision of textbooks.[24] Macaulay's *History of England* (1855-61) had produced substantial profits for Longmans, as well as a legendary £20,000 cheque 'on account of profits' for its author, and Longmans and their book-trade competitors, on the alert for an equally compelling narrative from Macaulay's successors, were less enthusiastic about the staid products emerging from the serious new practitioners of history-as-a-science.[25]

Only a handful of the historians whose letters survive in commercial publishers' archives were academics of the scientific history school. Longmans, Macmillans and their publishing contemporaries were deeply respectful to university-based and other serious scholars, but they could not depend for their bread and butter on a small coterie of writers who might turn out a dullish book every three or four years, and who were increasingly drawn to preparing articles for specialized journals, rather than monographs. Nor did publishers, or indeed the reading public which they served, allow themselves to be convinced of the dangers inherent in narrative history, with its appeals to patriotism and its entertainment value. Despite the modernist critique of whig history, readers continued to relish a strong retelling of the old stories.[26] Both discipline and narrative mattered; publishers and readers were not prepared to embrace one at the expense of the other.

The tension between discipline and narrative often resolved itself into one between esteem and profit. Samuel Johnson famously said that no man but a blockhead ever wrote, except for money.[27] Applying that maxim to the writers of history books, we might define the first generation of academic historians, who earned little in the way of royalties, as the new blockheads. They received their compensation indirectly, of course, but their counterparts outside the academy remained deeply interested in the pecuniary rewards of their literary labours. Many of the writers whose history books were published in this period were not university-based academics, but men and women of letters. Some of the men are still well known, like J. R. Green in the 1870s and Arthur Bryant in the 1940s. Others have become obscure, but were well regarded in their time, like Sir James Ramsay. Women writers, who even as scholars were not permitted to enter the academic world until well into the period we are discussing, were energetic writers of history books, especially of histories for children. The recent recovery of serious attention to women writers has revived interest in someone like Charlotte Yonge, who wrote novels as well as 'nursery histories'. Rather more challenging is the strictly non-fiction writer Edith Thompson, a protégée of Freeman's. Although her school history of England remained in print for fifty years and about 250,000 copies, it is unlikely to find many new readers.

It would be wrong, however, to describe all the books of academic historians as dull and inaccessible. Most of these authors, in fact, prided themselves on clarity of writing and spoke of their readers in terms of 'the public', not of other scholars and students.

History books as material objects

The fourth theme that runs through this volume is that of the materiality of the history book. The substantial, perhaps multi-volume, work of history proclaimed by its format the readership its publisher expected, and so did the slender sixpenny schoolbook. History books appeared in parts as well as in volumes. History was published in periodical formats as well as in monographs, both in general literary quarterlies and in journals dedicated to historical writing. And history books were very often published in series – publishers' series of interconnected volumes, variously arranged with motives of both intellectual integrity and commercial marketing.

A great many history books remained in print for decade after decade – but with variations in text as well as material format. James Secord has characterized the variations in a single scientific text from the 1840s to the 1860s and beyond as 'literary replication'.[28] His metaphor comes from evolutionary biology, and refers to the way that a book may be reproduced in variant editions – from cheap to deluxe. A text might be distorted by abbreviation for a review, taken out of context for a debate, misquoted in conversation, or excerpted to fill up space in a newspaper. What the reader or listener experiences is the version they receive, and the concept either of authorial intention or of a bibliographically intact first edition is of no consequence to their reception and response. The idea of literary replication is useful for capturing the transmutation of historical narratives and of history books.

Subsequent chapters will develop the themes of materiality, of competing academic and popular accounts, of recognizing the significance of publishers' agency – and will argue that publishers were deeply implicated in the inculcation of the past to British children. The account below picks up the chronology in the first half of the nineteenth century, but also sets off early in the life cycle of the reader, in order to establish a sense of how, from the publisher's perspective, history books were put into the hands of boys and girls. It is only a preliminary sketch, because a great deal of research remains to be done on these works – research which is crucial to our understanding of how the young common reader, boy or girl, schooled at home or in any of a variety of institutions, got to know about history, and especially about the history of England.[29]

Nursery histories and their competition

Mrs Markham's *History of England* (1823) and *Little Arthur's History of England* by Maria, Lady Callcott (1835) were two of the best-known of the 'nursery histories' for very young children.[30] Both were written in the voice of a middle-class woman instructing children in a domestic setting. Nursery histories were expected to lay the foundations for such classroom books as *The Student's Hume* – one of many 'dilutions' on the market of David Hume's 12-volume *History of England*.[31]

'Mrs Markham' begins with an adolescent Markham grumbling about his difficulties with reading Hume, and his mother's offer to 'entertain and instruct' Richard, along with his younger brother and sister, by telling a succession of stories from the past (Fig. 1.1). This first Mrs Markham was Elizabeth Penrose (1780-1837), who wrote the book in collaboration with her clergyman husband. They sold the manuscript to John Murray on a half-profit agreement shortly after it was first published in 1823. The historian Francis Palgrave called Mrs Markham 'the strongest case of the treacherous seductions of Hume'.[32] The Penroses were anxious to introduce a moralistic note and to soften the harsher events of history for youthful ears: after recounting the wars of Henry V, the maternal narrator continued: 'History is indeed a sad catalogue of human miseries, and one is glad to turn away from the horrors of wars and bloodshed to the tranquillity of private life. Shall I tell you something about the domestic habits of the English in the fifteenth century?'

The social status of Elizabeth Penrose, hidden behind her Mrs Markham pseudonym, was modest, and her literary status obscure. Maria, Lady Callcott was a more experienced woman of letters. She wrote *Little Arthur's History of England* not for her own family but rather for one 'particular child, as an educational birthday present'

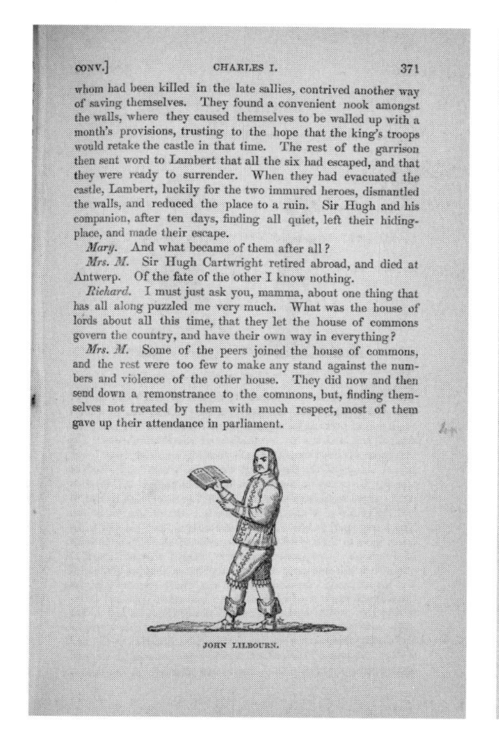

CONV.] CHARLES I. 371

whom had been killed in the late sallies, contrived another way of saving themselves. They found a convenient nook amongst the walls, where they caused themselves to be walled up with a month's provisions, trusting to the hope that the king's troops would retake the castle in that time. The rest of the garrison then sent word to Lambert that all the six had escaped, and that they were ready to surrender. When they had evacuated the castle, Lambert, luckily for the two immured heroes, dismantled the walls, and reduced the place to a ruin. Sir Hugh and his companion, after ten days, finding all quiet, left their hiding-place, and made their escape.

Mary. And what became of them after all?

Mrs. M. Sir Hugh Cartwright retired abroad, and died at Antwerp. Of the fate of the other I know nothing.

Richard. I must just ask you, mamma, about one thing that has all along puzzled me very much. What was the house of lords about all this time, that they let the house of commons govern the country, and have their own way in everything?

Mrs. M. Some of the peers joined the house of commons, and the rest were too few to make any stand against the numbers and violence of the other house. They did now and then send down a remonstrance to the commons, but, finding themselves not treated by them with much respect, most of them gave up their attendance in parliament.

JOHN LILBOURN.

1.1 Mrs Markham, *A History of England*, 1851: John Lilbourne.

22 EDUCATION OF ALFRED. CHAP. IX.

But I must tell you a great deal about King Alfred, which I am sure you will like.

When he was a very little boy, his mother wished him to learn to read, and she used to show him beautiful pictures in her prayer-book, and to tell him what the pictures were about. Little Alfred was always

Alfred learning to read.

pleased when the time came for seeing the book; and one day, when his mother was talking to him, she said that she would give him the book for his own, to keep, as soon as he could read it. Then he began to take great pains, and very soon learned to read the book, although it was in Latin, and his mother gave him the beautiful book. When he grew bigger, he loved to learn the old Saxon songs by heart, and to sing them to his mother, who loved to hear Alfred sing, and play the harp.

1.2 Lady Callcott, *Little Arthur's History of England*, 1860: Alfred learning to read.

(Figs 1.2-1.4). Callcott's preface was addressed to mothers, and she suggested to her publisher (also John Murray) that an image of King Alfred learning from his mother would 'come in very nicely'.[33] She wrote in her preface: 'Next to the study of the Sacred Scriptures, I have always held the history of our own country to be important in education, particularly in that of boys.' Callcott was persuaded that 'the well-grounded love of our own country is the best security for that enlightened philanthropy which is aimed at as the perfection of moral education'. *Little Arthur* was illustrated with rather bland reproductions of existing historical images; her proposed portrait of Alfred learning to read was perhaps unavailable, while one of a Saxon ship may have come readily to hand. Still Callcott struggled to include 'the points where children are the heroes of the stories'. Both Penrose and Callcott were anxious to repeat the narratives that would already have been familiar to parents reading their works to children. Maria Callcott told a friend 'I am going to put in the cake-tasting of Alfred, and moreover make a little niche somewhere for King Arthur'. She didn't bother to refer to authoritative

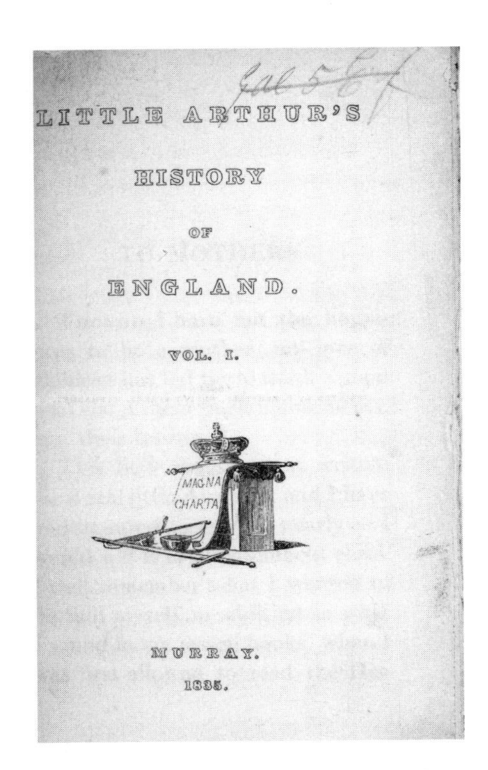

LITTLE ARTHUR'S

HISTORY

OF

ENGLAND.

VOL. I.

MAGNA CHARTA

MURRAY.

1835.

1.3 (*right*) and 1.4 (*below*) Callcott: 1835 title-page and Century edition of 1936.

Swaine

His Majesty King Edward the Eighth.

LITTLE ARTHUR'S
HISTORY OF ENGLAND

BY LADY CALLCOTT

THE CENTURY EDITION

BRINGING THE HISTORY TO THE ACCESSION OF HIS MAJESTY
KING EDWARD THE EIGHTH
REVISED AND WITH A MEMOIR ADDED

WITH ILLUSTRATIONS

LONDON
JOHN MURRAY, ALBEMARLE STREET, W.

works until after she had consulted her own memory for stories. Rosemary Mitchell describes Callcott's aim as 'consciously national and patriotic, as well as domestic and social'.[34] It was this kind of casual attitude to authorities and to historical authenticity that was to enrage the mid-century generation of historians and historical writers and inspire their counterparts in the book trade.

Alexander Macmillan, the entrepreneurial publisher who moved from Cambridge to London in 1858, was very responsive to such concerns. He saw a commercial opportunity as well as an intellectual one. Macmillan worked with Charlotte Yonge to supplant outmoded nursery histories for younger children. And where older schoolchildren were concerned, he discovered that the independent academic historian Edward A. Freeman was prepared to write little books for children as well as massive tomes on the Norman Conquest of England for their elders.[35] Macmillan identified two books that were ubiquitous at this level: 'Pinnock', first published in the 1820s and still flourishing at mid-century, and 'Ince and Gilbert', which was first published in 1834 and had sold almost 169,000 copies by 1860. Macmillan told Freeman that he wanted a one-hundred-page book on English History that would 'supersede the Pinnocks and Inces and Gilberts'. He was convinced that these books were 'doing great harm', and told Freeman, 'You can only alter the result by changing the course.'[36]

The works of Charlotte Yonge represented only a slightly more reputable class of histories for children. The evangelical novelist had compiled the 1852 *Landmarks in English History* and numerous other successful works (Fig. 1.5). She wrote in 1872 about her plans for a new 'baby history', consulting Freeman, whose *Old English History for Children* had been published by Macmillans in 1869. Yonge remarked that 'one finds children must – or mamma thinks they must – learn names and ideas about English kings before they can read your [book]s or mine, and that if one wants that intolerable "Little Arthur" to be unread, one must provide something else.' She found that 'The mistakes are so patent ... it is a wonder that no one has corrected them in so many editions.'[37]

In Chapter 2 we will see Yonge and Freeman, and their shared publisher Alexander Macmillan, struggling to replace Mrs Markham and Little Arthur in the minds of impressionable children, and we will also see how difficult those old books were to dislodge. The language used by Victorian authors and publishers about histories for children is telling: 'nursery histories' or 'a baby history'. Freeman referred to his own book as 'milk for babes'.[38] The

LANDMARKS OF HISTORY.

ANCIENT HISTORY:

FROM THE EARLIEST TIMES TO THE

MAHOMETAN CONQUEST.

BY

THE AUTHOR OF "KINGS OF ENGLAND," ETC.

LONDON:
JOHN AND CHARLES MOZLEY, PATERNOSTER ROW;
J. H. PARKER, OXFORD; AND 377, STRAND;
AND JOSEPH MASTERS, 78, NEW BOND STREET.
1852.

1.5 Charlotte Yonge, *Landmarks of History*, 1852.

moral purity of the milk was crucial. In 1877 Macmillan's assistant suggested that Yonge write a book on 'the ladies of the Crusades', presumably for schoolgirls, but she replied that 'those about whom much is known have not very edifying characters'.[39]

In 1870 an Education Act was passed, allowing school boards to be established and new schools built, and an 1880 Act was to make school compulsory for children aged five to ten.[40] So the 1870s was the crucial decade for publishers to prepare new history books for schools. It was time to render the intolerable Little Arthur unread, and to change the course with respect to the Pinnocks and Inces and Gilberts.

William Pinnock (1782-1843) was a schoolmaster who became a bookseller. Jonathan Topham has recently rescued Pinnock's career from obscurity. In the first decade of the nineteenth century he and a printer-partner, Samuel Maunder, began publishing works of popular instruction. In their heyday Pinnock and Maunder 'earned several thousand pounds a year, and one of their titles alone – an edition of Goldsmith's *History of England* – reputedly brought in more than £2000 profit in one year'. This was about 1812, the same year they began publishing 9-penny *Catechisms* of popular knowledge (Fig. 1.6). (The *Catechism of the History of England* was first published in 1822.) Their contemporary William Jerdan remembered that Pinnock's and Maunder's catechisms were adopted by 'half the schoolmasters in England'.[41] In 1819, however, Pinnock lost his money and the business of the partnership. The copyrights, including Goldsmith's *History of England*, were sold for an astonishing £30,000 to the printers G. and W.B. Whittaker. Nor did Pinnock's influence end with his death in 1843 (Fig. 1.7). The existence of numerous reprints – Whittaker's edition of Pinnock's edition of Goldsmith's History of England is illustrated in fig. 1.8 – suggests that Macmillan was quite right to recognize the Pinnock corpus as part of his competition.

Although Macmillan and others referred to 'Ince and Gilbert' as if it were an authorial collaboration, headmaster Henry Ince was the sole author of *Outlines of English History*, an 1834 book originally published by DePorquet and Cooper. Five years later the work was in the hands of another London publisher, James Gilbert, and an 1860 imprint proclaimed it the 169th thousand, with Ince's work 'corrected and very much extended by James Gilbert' (Fig. 1.9). The publisher had tacitly become a co-author.

Unlike the story-telling format of Mrs Markham and Little Arthur, both Pinnock and Ince were resolutely utilitarian, oriented

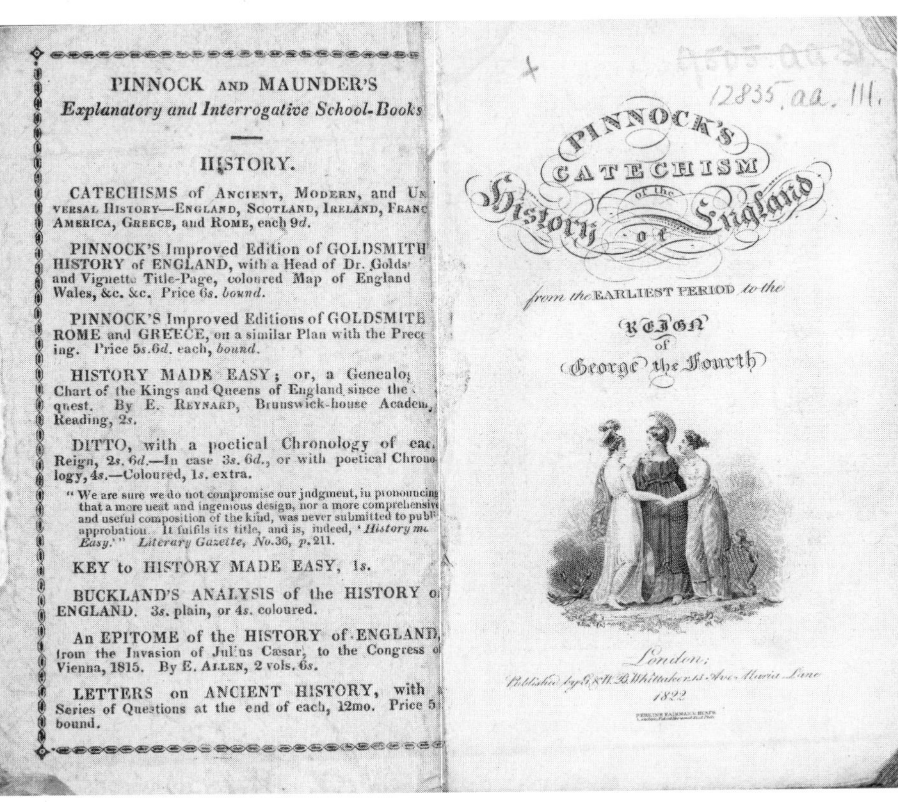
PINNOCK AND MAUNDER'S
Explanatory and Interrogative School-Books

HISTORY.

CATECHISMS of ANCIENT, MODERN, and UN VERSAL HISTORY—ENGLAND, SCOTLAND, IRELAND, FRANC AMERICA, GREECE, and ROME, each 9*d*.

PINNOCK'S Improved Edition of GOLDSMITH HISTORY of ENGLAND, with a Head of Dr. Golds and Vignette Title-Page, coloured Map of England Wales, &c. &c. Price 6*s*. *bound*.

PINNOCK'S Improved Editions of GOLDSMITE ROME and GREECE, on a similar Plan with the Prece ing. Price 5*s*.6*d*. each, *bound*.

HISTORY MADE EASY; or, a Genealo Chart of the Kings and Queens of England since the quest. By E. REYNARD, Brunswick-house Academ Reading, 2*s*.

DITTO, with a poetical Chronology of eac Reign, 2*s*. 6*d*.—In case 3*s*. 6*d*., or with poetical Chrono logy, 4*s*.—Coloured, 1*s*. extra.

"We are sure we do not compromise our judgment, in pronouncin that a more neat and ingenious design, nor a more comprehensive and useful composition of the kind, was never submitted to publ approbation. It fulfils its title, and is, indeed, '*History m Easy*.'" *Literary Gazette, No.36, p.211.*

KEY to HISTORY MADE EASY, 1*s*.

BUCKLAND'S ANALYSIS of the HISTORY o ENGLAND. 3*s*. plain, or 4*s*. coloured.

An EPITOME of the HISTORY of ENGLAND from the Invasion of Julius Cæsar, to the Congress o Vienna, 1815. By E. ALLEN, 2 vols. 6*s*.

LETTERS on ANCIENT HISTORY, with Series of Questions at the end of each, 12mo. Price 5 bound.

PINNOCK'S
CATECHISM
of the
History of England
from the EARLIEST PERIOD to the
REIGN
of
George the Fourth

London;
Published by G. & W. B. Whittaker, Ave Maria Lane
1822

1.6 William Pinnock, *Catechism of the History of England*, 1822.

to facts and dates and devoid of illustration either pictorial or literary. Ince and Gilbert, however, did not escape controversy. In 1856 a series of letters appeared in the *Morning Advertiser*, condemning 'the insidious working of Popery to make proselytes among the most infantine Seminaries even of the humblest classes of this great Protestant country'. The author, Charles Hastings Collette, was concerned that Gilbert, as a Roman Catholic publisher, had 'jesuitically and shamefully' perverted Ince's originally sound Protestant work. Gilbert responded with letters to the newspaper saying that although he was a Roman Catholic, he was not a Roman Catholic publisher. He noted that the book was now two-thirds longer than it had originally been, and that even Ince had recognized defects. 'I still believe,' he said, 'a more trustworthy and impartial manual of English history does not exist.'[42] Macmillan's problem was that too many schoolmasters and schoolmistresses agreed with Gilbert.

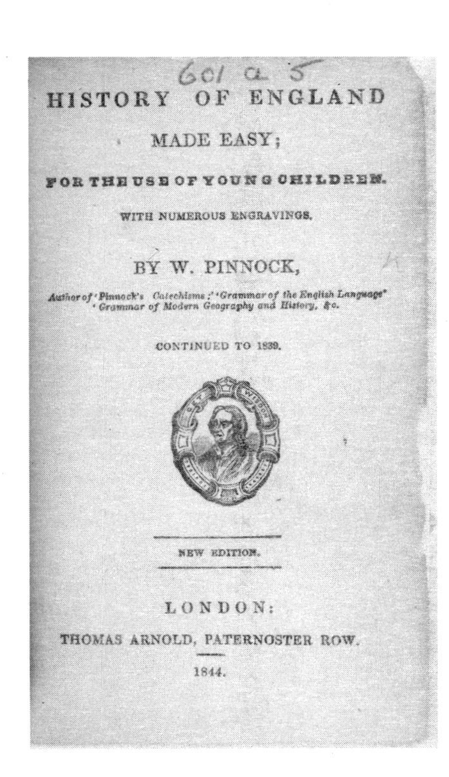

HISTORY OF ENGLAND

MADE EASY;

FOR THE USE OF YOUNG CHILDREN.

WITH NUMEROUS ENGRAVINGS.

BY W. PINNOCK,

Author of 'Pinnock's Catechisms;' 'Grammar of the English Language' 'Grammar of Modern Geography and History, &c.

CONTINUED TO 1839.

NEW EDITION.

LONDON:

THOMAS ARNOLD, PATERNOSTER ROW.

1844.

1.7 (*left*) Pinnock, *History of England Made Easy*, 1844.

1.8 (*below*) Whittaker's Pinnock's Goldsmith's *History of England*, 1876.

WHITTAKER'S

IMPROVED EDITION OF PINNOCK'S

GOLDSMITH'S

HISTORY OF ENGLAND,

FROM THE

INVASION OF JULIUS CÆSAR

TO THE CLOSE OF THE ABYSSINIAN CAMPAIGN:

ALSO,

A DICTIONARY, BIOGRAPHICAL, HISTORICAL, &c.

EXPLAINING EVERY DIFFICULTY, AND RENDERING THE WHOLE EASY TO BE UNDERSTOOD;

AND

QUESTIONS FOR EXAMINATION

AT THE END OF EACH SECTION:

BESIDES A VARIETY OF VALUABLE INFORMATION ADDED THROUGHOUT THE WORK, CONSISTING OF

Useful and correct GENEALOGICAL TABLES of the Sovereigns of England, from EGBERT to VICTORIA.
Tables of CONTEMPORARY SOVEREIGNS and EMINENT PERSONS.

An Account of the Idols worshipped by the Saxons.
Progress of Literature, Science, and Art, during the present century.
The British Constitution, &c. &c.

ILLUSTRATED BY

COPIOUS EXPLANATORY NOTES, A CLASSICAL AND MODERN MAP OF ENGLAND AND WALES, AND PORTRAITS OF THE SOVEREIGNS, AND EMINENT PERSONS.

BY W. C. TAYLOR, LL.D.

CONTINUED BY THE REV. W. H. PINNOCK, LL.D.

LATE OF CORPUS CHRISTI COLLEGE, CAMBRIDGE.

"ENGLAND! WITH ALL THY FAULTS, I LOVE THEE STILL."

NEW AND REVISED EDITION.

London:

WHITTAKER & CO., AVE MARIA LANE.

1876.

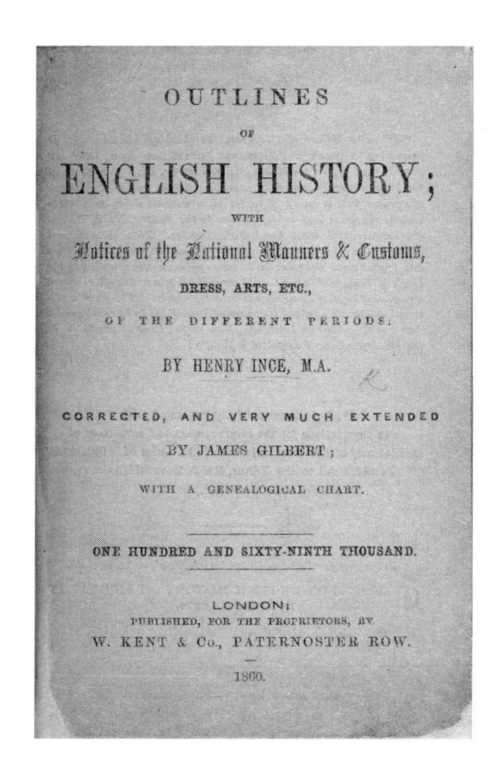

OUTLINES
OF
ENGLISH HISTORY;
WITH
Notices of the National Manners & Customs,
DRESS, ARTS, ETC.,
OF THE DIFFERENT PERIODS;
BY HENRY INCE, M.A.
CORRECTED, AND VERY MUCH EXTENDED
BY JAMES GILBERT;
WITH A GENEALOGICAL CHART.
ONE HUNDRED AND SIXTY-NINTH THOUSAND.
LONDON:
PUBLISHED, FOR THE PROPRIETORS, BY
W. KENT & Co., PATERNOSTER ROW.
1860.

1.9 Henry Ince and James Gilbert, *Outlines of English History*, 1860.

New editions of old titles

These, then, were some of the history books in use around 1850, when Macaulay's *History of England* was appearing on the dressing tables of young ladies (where Macaulay had hoped his historical narrative would replace the latest novel).[43] Moreover, all these books were still circulating twenty-five and more years later. Not only did Macaulay's work remain in the popular imagination for decades, but so also did the works that had been in print when it appeared. The latter books, however, were much more susceptible of revision and reworking.

Secord's theory of 'literary replication' points up how one scientific text could be reprinted with many variations, in reviews and abridgements, some authorized and some plagiarized, as well as in reissues many years after the initial publication. This happened with history, too, where the narrative remained the same and yet also kept changing. If Mrs Markham's conversation was suitable for the girls of the 1820s, why not recycle it for their daughters in the 1840s, and again for their great-granddaughters in the 1860s, and indeed the 1880s? Suitable revisions and updates could be added

HISTORY

OF

ENGLAND,

FROM THE

INVASION OF JULIUS CÆSAR TO THE REIGN
OF VICTORIA.

BY MRS. MARKHAM

A NEW EDITION, REVISED AND ENLARGED.

WITH QUESTIONS,

ADAPTED TO SCHOOLS IN THE UNITED STATES.

BY ELIZA ROBBINS,

AUTHOR OF "AMERICAN POPULAR LESSONS," ETC., ETC.

NEW-YORK:
D. APPLETON & COMPANY,
346 & 348 BROADWAY.
M.DCCC.LIV.

1.10 (*left*) Mrs Markham, *History of England with Questions Adapted to Schools in the United States*, 1854.

1.11 (*below*) E. C. Hadwen, *Promiscuous Questions on Mrs Markham's History of England*, 1856.

28

259. Describe the battle of Pinkie.
260. Who were appointed to draw up a Book of Offices for the use of the Church?
261. What were the contradictory commands of Henry VIII. at the time of the Reformation?
262. Describe the meeting of Henry and Francis at the Field of the Cloth of Gold.
263. In what manner did Cranmer gain the favour of Henry VIII.?
264. On what occasion did Henry VIII. distinguish himself as an author?
265. By what artifices did Charles V. dissolve the bonds of amity between France and England?
266. What caused the fall of Wolsey?
267. Describe his death.
268. What occasioned the disgrace of the Protector Somerset?
269. How did Warwick treat the bishops and clergy after the death of Somerset?
270. What was the state of commerce during the reign of Edward VI.?

29

271. Why did Henry divorce Catherine of Aragon, and where did she pass the remainder of her life?
272. Why was Anne of Cleves divorced?
273. Who was Cardinal Pole, and how did he incur the resentment of Henry VIII.?
274. Describe the insurrection of Sir Thomas Wyatt.
275. What extraordinary project was formed by Northumberland, and what means did he take to succeed?
276. What measures were used by Queen Mary to procure money for Philip?
277. Describe the death of Lady Jane Grey.
278. When was Calais lost, and in what manner?
279. What caused the death of Edward VI.?
280. How many martyrs suffered death in the reign of Mary, and who were among the first who suffered?

———

C 3

without changing the familiar title. We have seen this happening with Pinnock; and an edition of Ince and Gilbert appeared as late as 1906.

It happened with Hume, where an anonymous *Student's Hume* of 1859 was succeeded by another one, edited by J. S. Brewer in 1880.[44] It happened with Mrs Markham, even in the form of an 1854 New York edition for schools in the United States, complete with questions by Eliza Robins, who chose to dispense with the conversation format, but appropriated the authorial name (Fig. 1.10). Editions of Mrs Markham with 'Promiscuous Questions' for England in 1856 retained the conversations (Fig. 1.11). Elizabeth Penrose had died in 1837 but John Penrose continued to manage the publication of the books until the copyright ran out in 1865. The new publisher, T. J. Allman, briskly arranged for a continuation by Mary Howitt, bringing the history up to date.[45] Howitt's preface noted:

> I have, for the sake of consistency, maintained the little fiction of Authorship by supposing the wife of one of the worthy Mrs Markham's sons to continue the narrative to her own children, and I hope in so doing I have written in the spirit of the original. My endeavour has been honestly to state facts, and whilst avoiding party politics, yet to advocate the wiser, more liberal and more enlightened spirit of the age, whether in political or social life (Fig. 1.12).

Yet another editor in 1873, this time anonymously, assumed the persona of Mrs Markham more wholeheartedly. She 'took up her pen to give some account of the last two reigns' and hoped that her young readers might be willing to receive her [Mrs Markham] as an old acquaintance. In 1912 the publishers George Gill and Sons, and the editor Winifred Radcliffe, borrowed the conversational format for their *First School History of England*. Similarly a centenary edition of *Little Arthur* appeared in 1936, with a frontispiece photograph of Edward VIII quickly supplanted by one of George VI (Fig. 1.4).

Literary replication even happened with Edward Freeman, who fondly believed he and Macmillan had dealt with the inaccurate and romantic narratives of their predecessors. When Macmillan taxed him with being excessively pedantic, Freeman reassured the publisher that he had written a strong narrative ('Even a girl or a curate will go in for my portrait of Harold on the hillside and William [the Conqueror] down below,' he insisted.[46]) The portrait first captured in 1869 reappeared, abridged, as an Everyman title in

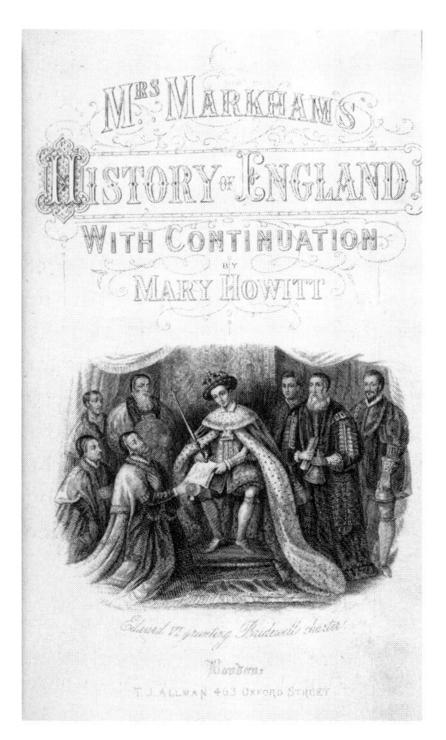
MRS MARKHAM'S
HISTORY OF ENGLAND
WITH CONTINUATION
BY
MARY HOWITT

Edward VI granting Bridewell charter

London:
T. J. ALLMAN 463 OXFORD STREET

1.12 (*left*) Mary Howitt, *Mrs Markham's History of England with Continuation*, 1865.

1.13 (*below*) Edward Freeman, *Old English History for Children*, Everyman's Library, 1911.

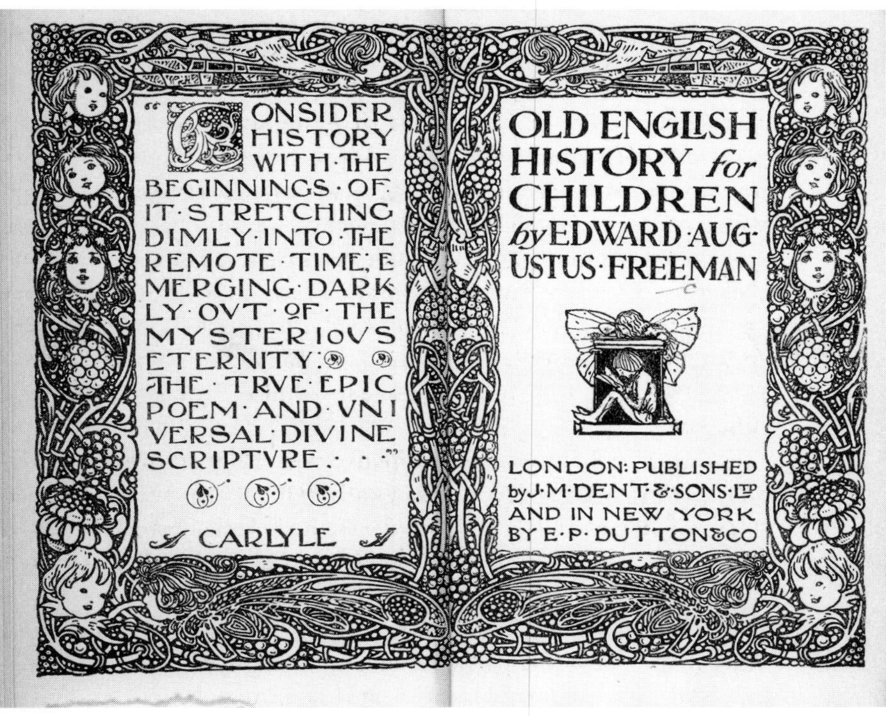
"CONSIDER HISTORY WITH THE BEGINNINGS OF IT STRETCHING DIMLY INTO THE REMOTE TIME; EMERGING DARKLY OUT OF THE MYSTERIOUS ETERNITY: THE TRUE EPIC POEM AND UNIVERSAL DIVINE SCRIPTURE . . ."

CARLYLE

OLD ENGLISH HISTORY *for* CHILDREN *by* EDWARD AUGUSTUS FREEMAN

LONDON: PUBLISHED by J·M·DENT & SONS·LTD AND IN NEW YORK BY E·P·DUTTON & CO

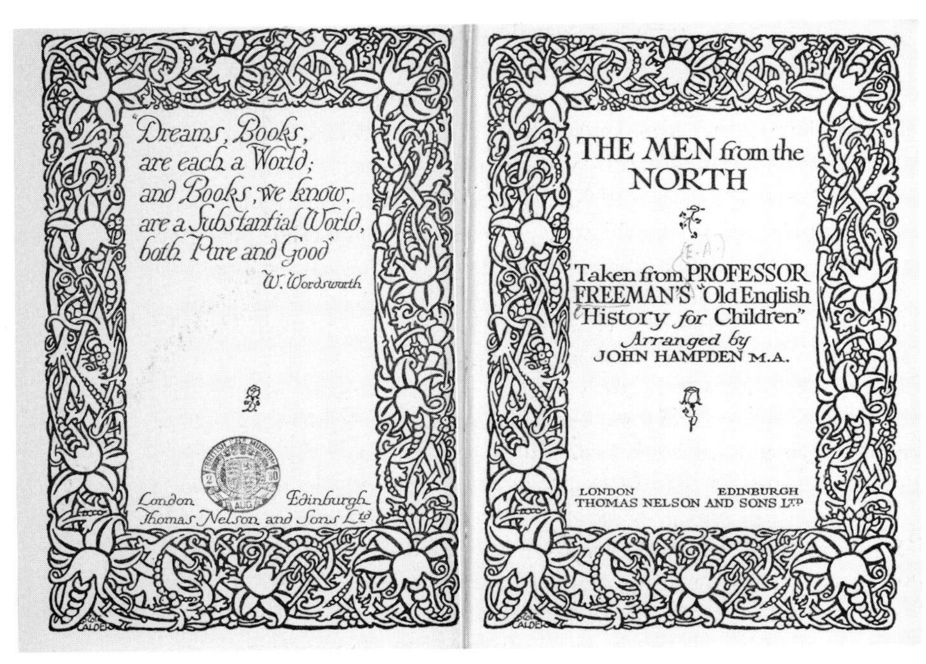
'Dreams, Books,
are each a World;
and Books, we know,
are a Substantial World,
both Pure and Good'
W. Wordsworth

London Edinburgh
Thomas Nelson and Sons Ltd

THE MEN from the
NORTH

Taken from PROFESSOR
FREEMAN'S "Old English
History for Children"
Arranged by
JOHN HAMPDEN M.A.

LONDON EDINBURGH
THOMAS NELSON AND SONS LTD

1.14 John Hampden, *The Men from the North*, 1930.

1911 (Fig. 1.13). Two years later Ella Thomson, a teacher in Lahore, in India, edited *Legends of Early England chiefly from Freeman's 'Old English History for Children'*. It was published in London by Horace Marshall and Son, oblivious to Freeman's careful distinction between legend and truth. The compelling image turned up again in 1930, in Books Within Books: A series of Episodes from English Literature, edited by Richard Wilson. The publisher was Thomas Nelson and Sons, of London and Edinburgh, who aimed 'to provide reading material as full of thrilling adventure and human interest as the most exciting "juvenile", with the added qualities of fidelity to human nature, literary craftsmanship, good English style, and high moral tone'. Each book was 'complete in itself, not a mere abridgement', and 'entirely the work of the original author' (Fig. 1.12).

By 1930, when Books Within Books were appearing, the academic discipline of history had been transformed. In 1886 Freeman's colleagues succeeded, after twenty years of noteworthy failures, in establishing a journal, the *English Historical Review*. Academic associations were established, and massive multi-volume works like the *Cambridge Modern History* and the Oxford History of England series were commissioned. But through all these years the narrative genre called history was flourishing too. And side-by-side with new works, there were fresh versions, continuations, corrections and revisions of books first written in and for the England of the post-Napoleonic war years – still in circulation when rearmament was on the turn-of-the-twentieth-century political agenda.

D. F. McKenzie spoke in his 1988 Lyell Lectures about understanding 'the book' in history. These words have a powerful resonance when the subject is the history book:

> The new forms we give to texts in the acts of adapting, printing and publishing them constitute the most basic and ubiquitous evidence we have for a history of writing and a history of meanings. Every extant artifact tells a tale which we can read historically and which, by virtue of the *edition* (multiple copies of the same forms widely dispersed, successively altered, and variously directed), supports a high level of historical generalisation.[47]

By thinking about history books in a bibliographical context, it is possible not only to bring history into *l'histoire du livre* (or 'book history'), but also to bring the history of the book into closer alignment with the historical discipline, by demonstrating the evidence of dispersion, alteration and various direction to which McKenzie refers. History books are tenacious, and they remain in the memories of readers, on the shelves of bookshops and of libraries, and in on-line databases long after their authors and publishers have moved on to other projects.

Chapter 2

Quality and Profit: New Histories of England, 1863-1880

WHEN he became Regius Professor of History at Cambridge, J. B. Bury generated much controversy by his pronouncement that history was not a branch of literature, that it belonged in the academic world (not in the London literary community), and that it deserved indirect financial support from the State, filtered through the universities, since it could not appeal to a sufficient number of readers to support its practitioners and their families through royalties. When Bury said, in 1902, that history was 'a science, no less and no more', other scholars had been saying much the same thing for twenty years or more.[1] At Cambridge his two immediate predecessors were J. R. Seeley and Lord Acton, and their counterparts at Oxford were William Stubbs and E. A. Freeman – all very different historians, but united by claims for the 'scientific' nature of history. This and the following chapter will discuss the late-Victorian argument for recognizing the difference between serious history (written for serious students), and popular history written for the general public.

Contemporary conceptions of history as a science revolved more around practice than around the positivist idea – of generating universal laws – associated with Henry Thomas Buckle. Stubbs told Freeman in a letter of 1857, 'I do not believe in the Philosophy of History so do not believe in Buckle.'[2] Those two were empiricists and practitioners – and, of course, whigs. Their terminology of 'scientific' included three aspects, of which the first was a rigorous standard – for research and for the compilation and criticism of original documentary sources. In the political atmosphere of continental Europe in the late nineteenth century, records which had been closed for centuries were now becoming available to scholars. It was possible to prepare an 'original' account, as opposed to what could now be dismissed as a mere *réchauffée* of earlier work. In England, too, old records were being uncovered, although many practitioners limited their encounter with original documents to printed chronicles. Here the model was the German historian Leopold von Ranke, who had scoured the archives for the reports of Venetian ambassadors and written their accounts into his first book, *The Histories of the Latin and Teutonic Nations from 1494 to 1514* and later works on the papacy, Reformation Germany, Prussia, France and England, and finally – incomplete at his death in 1886 – a world history. The correspondence between publishers and historians during the last three decades of the nineteenth century reveals a string of proposals to publish translations of Ranke's works – and the corresponding refusals on the grounds that what had already appeared did not sell very well.[3]

The second meaning of the 'scientific' approach concerned scholarly objectivity in the interpretation of the 'original authorities', or primary sources. Related to this was the concept of what has been called 'transpersonal replicability'.[4] The understanding was that every scholar who was trained in the same way should interpret any given document in the same objective way. There was some room for debate, but debate was constrained by strict rules for the interpretation of evidence. When these notions came to be tested during the 1890s, the laboratory was a publishing setting, that of the multi-authored *Cambridge Modern History*. In the offices of the Cambridge University Press, where recalcitrant contributors had to be persuaded and unsatisfactory texts edited while due dates were imminent, the limits of collaboration became apparent.[5] In the early days, though, when controlled observations in the natural sciences were considered to be verified if they could be replicated, the imagined laboratory for scientific history was the hierarchical and academic situation of the seminar room, and the notion that, given appropriate training, one historian's reading of the primary evidence ought to be just about the same as another's, was very compelling.

In a third and crucial interpretation of 'scientific', historians now saw themselves as writing for informed colleagues, not for the general public. The new history was intended to be an academic discipline as well as a profession. The Royal Historical Society had been founded in 1868 to meet the need for a formal organization.[6] Increasingly these professional men (the discourse excluded women almost completely) were based in the universities, a development that replaced the older occupational identity of the historian as a man or woman of letters. The 'scientific' historian eschewed narrative and popular appeal and composed instead austere accounts, exploring very precise, narrowly formulated questions and aimed at a small but appreciative readership. Such histories were documented by footnotes and bibliographies that grounded them firmly in related scholarship.

These changes in the ideas of the most prestigious writers of history books did not occur in a bibliographical vacuum. They happened simultaneously with the expanded reading public and explosion of cheap print (in book and periodical formats) that recent historians have identified as so significant. Alexis Weedon has shown that the period from 1846 to 1916 saw 'a fourfold increase in production and a halving of book prices'.[7] And as Chapter 1 demonstrated, publishers were keen to hold and increase the market, beginning in the nursery, for a readable genre. They conceptualized this in narrative, literary, perhaps even enthralling, general-reader terms, quite unlike the terms defined by the new 'scientific' history, which saw itself more as discipline than as genre. Especially for the commercial publishers, led by Macmillans and Longmans, *history* had recently, and very profitably, meant book-length narratives on the Macaulay model, and hence lengthy print-runs, multiple formats and lavish profits. But Macaulay had died in 1859, and now the people who aspired to his kind of reputation were writing histories that appealed only to a limited, specialized readership. The university presses were not, at first, prepared to subsidize most of these works, and nor were the commercial publishers. The historians who did appeal to a general reader, writers like J. R. Green or James Anthony Froude, were snubbed by the universities, and later by the new professional periodicals, as merely literary, and non-scientific, practitioners. Green was nurtured and rewarded by Macmillans, as Froude was by Longmans, but these London publishers continued to seek out new historian-authors who combined the conflicting qualities of 'respectably academic' with 'popular and readable'.

Alexander Macmillan and the historians

Alexander Macmillan was the leading entrepreneurial publisher in London in the 1860s and 1870s, the time when practitioners of the historical discipline began to think of themselves as engaging in 'science'.[8] With his brother Daniel he had migrated in the 1830s from Glasgow to Cambridge, where the partners made themselves indispensable booksellers and publishers. After Daniel's death Alexander Macmillan moved their combined families and the flourishing business to London. Literary and scholarly men gathered to dine, smoke and talk at his 'tobacco parliaments'. Macmillan was an energetic bookman with good standing in such areas as cultural criticism (he was Matthew Arnold's publisher), science (the periodical *Nature*) and literature (Tennyson, Hardy, Lewis Carroll, Christina Rossetti and Kingsley were some of the most distinguished names). Macmillan hoped to develop a similar reputation for works of history, but he needed to find reputable and readable historians who would become Macmillan authors. Longman, his competitor, handled Froude's work, which was still appearing regularly and selling well, in addition to the profitable Macaulay backlist.[9] Macmillan discovered three promising historian-authors, Edward A. Freeman, Charlotte M. Yonge and John Richard Green.

Macmillan held a peculiar position during the period 1863 to 1880. In addition to his own London business he served as publisher to the Oxford University Press. This meant acting not only as Oxford's London agent but as their confidential advisor; in Peter Sutcliffe's words, the Clarendon Press Delegates needed 'somebody to show them how to publish new books', fresh titles to supplement their strong lists of bibles and classics.[10] Oxford declared its independence of Macmillans in 1880 and, after a brief period of uncertainty, became a remarkable publisher of history in its own right. But in these earlier decades, apart from the advice they received from the University's historians, notably William Stubbs, they sought guidance from Macmillan. And to complicate matters still further, Macmillan also held sway, although informally, in Cambridge. David McKitterick observes in his history that 'The most important publisher for Cambridge during the 1870s was not the University Press, but Macmillan'.[11]

Macmillan courted the historian-authors who were anxious to renew their discipline by the practice of rigorous scholarship. Both he and Freeman participated in a circle of correspondence and conviviality that included James Bryce and J. R. Green, and that reached out to older scholars like Stubbs and younger ones like Adolphus Ward.[12] It is important to recognize, though, that Macmillan was particularly interested in their work in so far as it would reach a wide readership, including the captive and profitable one comprised of children in school. He could see the possibilities, even before the education legislation of 1870 and 1880.

In this respect Macmillan was equally supportive of the historical writing of Charlotte Yonge, whose *Cameos from English History* and

Landmarks of English History he had inherited in the 1860s from the bankrupt publisher John W. Parker (Fig. 2.1). Remarkably prolific, Yonge wrote evangelical fiction as well as history, and stories that blurred the line between the two genres. Three attractive volumes published by Marcus Ward of London identified their author as 'Aunt Charlotte' and the books as 'stories of history for the little ones'. Appearing between 1873 and 1877, these works included lavish full-colour frontispieces (Fig. 2.2). Yonge never darkened the door of an archival repository, or indeed left her Hampshire village home, and her letters to Macmillan reveal a blithe unconcern about whether the reference works she consulted for her historical texts had become outdated.[13]

Macmillans also published Charles Kingsley's books. Kingsley was Regius Professor of History at Cambridge from 1860 to 1875, but this post had more to do with the patronage of the Prince Consort than with his scholarship, and Freeman and other practitioners of the new 'scientific' history scorned his work. Macmillan did not share their disdain. He fervently admired Kingsley as a person, and benefited from the success of *Westward Ho!*, Kingsley's 1855 historical novel. In 1863 Macmillan encouraged Kingsley to contemplate writing a 'boys' History of England'. Both author and publisher had been having a look at the competition. The 'Little Arthur' books were aimed at children of perhaps six to nine years of age, Kingsley thought, whereas 'Mrs Markham's' *History of England* was intended for those of nine to fifteen. *Little Arthur* was advertised as being in its 105th thousand copy. Kingsley observed this with relish and hoped to supplant it, counting on the marketing appeal of a dedication to the children of Victoria and Albert on the strength of his having once taught the Prince of Wales. He casually alerted his publisher that the tone of his history would be 'strong Protestant'.[14]

Macmillan was fortunately not depending upon Kingsley to produce the promised non-fiction work, which eventually took the form of another historical novel. He was also negotiating with Goldwin Smith and already acquainted with Green (whose best-seller was still a decade in the future) when he entered into correspondence with Edward A. Freeman.[15] Freeman was at this stage about forty years of age and a prolific writer of journalism, especially in the *Saturday Review*. His earnings derived mostly from writing (he had a private income and did not obtain a university post until many years later). But despite this, he strongly identified himself as a historian and indeed as one of the new breed of scientific

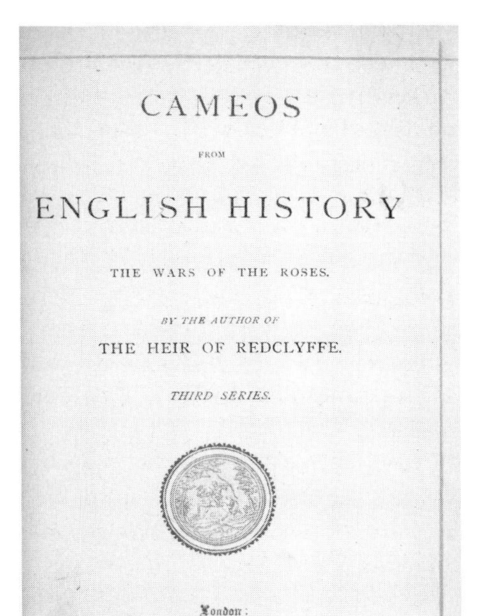
CAMEOS

FROM

ENGLISH HISTORY

THE WARS OF THE ROSES.

BY THE AUTHOR OF

THE HEIR OF REDCLYFFE.

THIRD SERIES.

London:

MACMILLAN AND CO.

1877.

2.1 (*left*) Charlotte Yonge, *Cameos from English History*, 1877.

2.2 (*below*) Yonge, *Aunt Charlotte's Stories of English History for the Little Ones*, 1873.

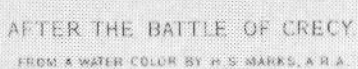
AFTER THE BATTLE OF CRECY

FROM A WATER COLOR BY H.S. MARKS, A.R.A.

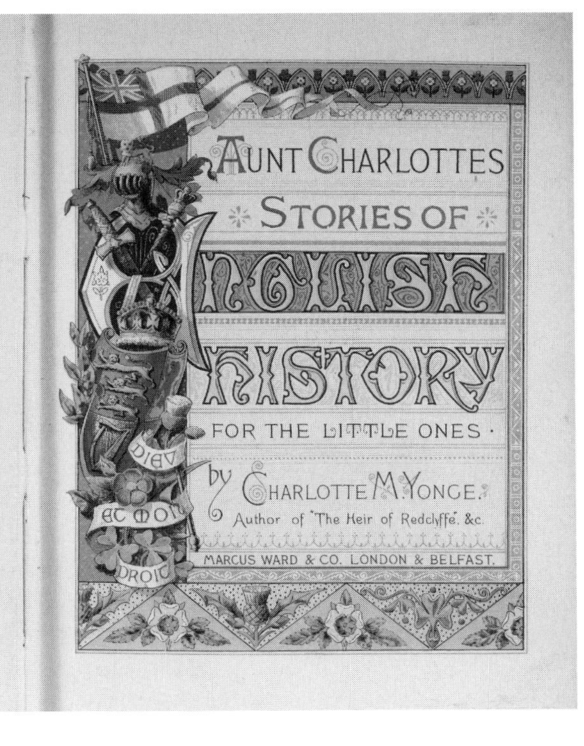
AUNT CHARLOTTES

STORIES OF

ENGLISH

HISTORY

FOR THE LITTLE ONES

by CHARLOTTE M. YONGE.

Author of "The Heir of Redclyffe" &c.

MARCUS WARD & CO. LONDON & BELFAST.

historians, friendly with Green, Smith, Bryce and Stubbs. He was vigilant about correcting past errors and determined that the original authorities be found, incorporated and criticized in all historical writing – even, as it turned out, historical writing for children and the general public. Macmillan agreed with these views, telling Freeman early in their correspondence 'I don't think that *paying* things need be done in a slovenly way. I hope some day to see you at work on a great Universal History that will pay. Why should our school books that pay best not be done by men who *know* what they are talking about? Hear the voice of the tradesman! – but shall I not claim to be a tradesman [who] also would like to see the work done honestly which passes through his hands.'[16]

Freeman replied cordially, and to the purpose: 'I see Kingsley has a History of England for *Boys*, which I am sorry for, as it may stand in the way of what I am slowly writing for my *Girls*.'[17] The eldest of Freeman's four daughters (and one son) was Margaret, then fifteen. Their home schoolroom had been enlivened by the gradual composition of what became Freeman's *Old English History for Children*, eventually published in 1869.

This work emphasized the historical period that their father was to make his own, the Norman Conquest of England. Freeman regarded Mrs Markham, Little Arthur and similar books as particularly 'rotten' in their treatment of his own period. Moreover he thought that little children should have the benefit of his opinions with respect to the new 'scientific' history, telling Macmillan

> I think you will catch the object of the book, namely to give children accurate and scientific views of history from the very first, to teach them to call things by their right names, to distinguish history from legend, to know what the sources of history are, and to distinguish the different values of different writers. I can only say that, with my own children it thoroughly succeeds. To many people I dare say it would seem hard, what they would call over-learned. The truth is that the scientific way of doing anything is puzzling to those who have learned some other way, and who are called on to *unlearn*. It is not puzzling to a child who has learned nothing; quite the contrary, because the scientific way is really the easiest because the clearest.[18]

Macmillan responded strongly to this voice of modern pedagogy, and seems to have been unconcerned about Freeman's establishing himself in both the juvenile and adult markets for history. The two men began negotiating terms for what they nicknamed 'milk for babes'.[19]

In the early 1860s, while Freeman was still market-testing the history for children on his own daughters and son, he was also approaching publishers about two massive works, a *History of Federal Government* and a multi-volume account of The Norman Conquest. Longmans declined and even Alexander Macmillan was rather daunted by the bulk of the *Federal Government* and discouraged by its 'elaborate' nature from anticipating large sales.[20] But the publisher could see that Freeman was capable, with editorial nurturing, of writing books that would sell. He was prepared to underwrite the *Federal Government* (and sponsor *The Norman Conquest* with the Clarendon Press at Oxford) in hopes of securing the lucrative school history, and perhaps future work – not only from Freeman but from his friends and protégés.

Freeman's career reached a point of crisis in the mid-1860s when Goldwin Smith began to contemplate resigning his post as Regius Professor of History at Oxford. Anxious to be considered for the succession (which occurred in 1866 when Stubbs was appointed), Freeman behaved like a twenty-first-century academic anxious to improve his or her publication record – he scrambled to get a book out quickly. Freeman seriously contemplated making this book the *Old English History for Children*. Goldwin Smith advised against the idea, and so did Bryce, who remarked that 'a history avowedly for children would, however unfairly, be laid hold of by the adversary'.[21] Freeman reluctantly gave way and returned to the idea of a monograph on the Norman Conquest. He was, after all, already deep in the period composing his book for the home classroom, and as he reflected to Macmillan, 'A certain part of the history would be told twice, in two different books, in two different ways, and for two different classes of readers.' These two classes were children and adults, not general readers and scholars. With respect to the latter dichotomy, Freeman's approach involved 'writing a text that any thoughtful person might care to read, and satisfying the most exacting scholar in the notes'.[22] Macmillan was initially enthusiastic, only later deciding to turn the magnum opus over to his Oxford colleagues at the Clarendon Press. Meanwhile, he undertook to refine Freeman's talent to make it really marketable. Upon reading the 'Norman Conquest' manuscript, he found it 'interesting and vigorous' with 'emphatic claim and vehement argumentation'. But he observed that 'the main defect as a *readable* book was the intensely 'argufying' style throughout'. As he pointed out,

> when one sits down to read a history one wants that it shall mainly be narrative ... I felt as if a great deal that was written down in your book were processes through which *your own mind* must have gone, but which necessarily can interest & be appreciated by, a very small number of readers. You are going over a vast mass of old fable, dim facts here & there glimmering through the incrustations of tradition & prejudice. *You* have to sift & *riddle* ... away all that is valueless & give your readers the result. A man does not go through the kitchens with his cook, or through the dissecting room with his physician. He wants his dinner cooked & his pill or draft in their complete form without the din of pestle or the splatter of the spit. Had Gibbon written in this style his book would have been ten times as big and not a tenth as valuable.

Macmillan continued with the observation that 'many historical students will greatly value your work, but it seems to me that histories ought to be *written* for readers, and the notes & references guide the student to the sources', and finally pleaded 'Do please *tell the story* – others than babes like such milk'.[23]

Freeman was annoyed but receptive, reassuring Macmillan that 'even a girl or a curate will go in for my picture of Harold on the hill-side and William down below'. And moreover the portrayal could be documented ('all real, none of Froude's daisies').[24] Macmillan had the last word when John Doran's review appeared in *The Athenaeum* and dwelt at length on the readable quality of the text.[25]

History attractive to girls and curates (or to grocers and cheesemongers, as Oscar Browning was later to characterize lower-middle-class readers) was exactly what Stubbs at Oxford and Seeley at Cambridge were keen to avoid. As serious students of history, these men demanded to be taken, via footnotes, through the scholar's dissecting room or his kitchen, and to be shown every scrap of the evidence as it emerged from the carcase of the archive. Academic historians insisted on watching each step of the composition of the resulting analysis, from raw data to cooked narrative, into a satisfying – but still deconstructable – whole. Other readers were prepared to take the documentation upon trust, and few contemporaries agreed with Freeman that young children could handle the elements of doubt intrinsic to a 'scientific' reading of the evidence. As Charlotte Yonge observed, children wanted to know 'which is it really?' whether the question concerned the variegated colours of a bird's plumage, or the likelihood that King Alfred actually sat by and let the cakes burn. So did the common reader.[26]

When Freeman undertook the general editing of a series of

histories of Europe and the western world for Macmillan – the Historical Course for Schools – he sought for his 'little books' authors who would be readable, but also tractable to his guidance, qualities he prized far above an academic reputation.[27] Macmillan had found it useful and profitable in other areas to group like-subject books into a series. Perhaps the best known is the English Men of Letters series, edited by John Morley and originally titled Short Books on Great Writers.[28]

The books in the historical series were initially meant for schools, although only a few found a market there. Freeman's ideal contributor was Edith Thompson (1848-1929), an intelligent friend of his intelligent favourite daughter Margaret. Thompson undertook the History of England, another young woman took 'little Scotland', and Freeman tried to recruit first his daughter Margaret, and later his colleague's daughter Kate Bryce, for Greece (Fig. 2.3). Anxious to avoid working with what he called 'a stuck-up Balliolik', he sought among his friends 'another really able woman'.[29] He broke his rule once, by asking J. R. Green to write a 'little book' on France, but in the end Green wasn't prepared to submit to his friend's editorial guidance. He said, 'You want "hacks" for your driving, and rather secretaries than authors – people who will simply write *your* little histories *for you.*'[30] The result was a somewhat reluctant request that 'Aunt Charlotte' take on the task.

Charlotte Yonge had, after all, written about France already, in her 1871 *Parallel History of France and England* (Fig. 2.4), and again in 1875, in *Aunt Charlotte's Stories of French History for the Little Ones*. Despite this experience, and even though she was manifestly docile, Yonge's work was unsatisfactory by Freeman's standards. He told Macmillan 'she never catches any of the points, never brings out the great landmarks, all oh, oh, oh & such sentences. O how long! All political matters are simply confused; she seems to understand nothing. ... I shall be thoroughly ashamed to see my name as Editor of such stuff.'[31] Charlotte Yonge, like her predecessors in the genre of 'baby history' writing, represented the unsatisfactory old regime to professional historians like Freeman.

Macmillan, however, was prepared to work with both of them. He attended with great respect to Freeman's strictures about a new scientific history, even for child readers – but at the same time he continued to encourage both Yonge and Kingsley and wrote kindly to Edith Thompson. The latter remained a profitable author for his firm until the 1920s, and her book received the doubtful accolade of an unauthorized 'analysis' published in Calcutta for Indian

Historical Course for Schools.

HISTORY

OF

ENGLAND.

BY

EDITH THOMPSON.

NEW EDITION, REVISED. WITH MAPS.

London:

MACMILLAN AND CO.

1878.

[*The Right of Translation and Reproduction is reserved.*]

2.3 (*right*) Edith Thompson, *History of England*, 1878.

2.4 (*below*) Charlotte Yonge, *Parallel History of France and England*, 1871.

REFORM IN ENGLAND AND FRANCE. 51

FRANCE.

In **1830**, Algiers was conquered and made a French province. The Polignac Ministry, thinking the liberty of the press dangerous, suppressed it violently, by royal authority alone. The whole population of Paris rose in a fury, Charles X. and his family fled, and the crown of a nation with a constitutional charter was offered to the Duke of Orleans, who reigned as LOUIS PHILIPPE I., King of the French. Polignac was sentenced to perpetual imprisonment.

In **1831**, the hereditary peerage was abolished. The Duchess of Berry made an attempt on the part of her son in La Vendée; and on the other hand the more violent republicans in Paris rose against the government on the day of the barricades, but both alike were put down.

In **1840**, *Louis Napoleon*, son of the ex-king of Holland and nephew to Napoleon I., made a descent on France, but was imprisoned at Boulogne. M. Guizot became minister of foreign affairs.

In **1841**, the great Napoleon's remains were brought home from St. Helena and buried at the Hôtel des Invalides with great enthusiasm.

In **1842**, Louis Philippe's eldest son, the Duke of Orleans, was killed by a fall from his carriage.

In **1843**, a war was carried on in Algeria with the natives. The Prince de Joinville, Louis Philippe's son, bombarded Tangier. Abdul Kader, a gallant Arab chief, waged a long war against them.

Flanders, which had been made into a kingdom, together with Holland, for the House of Orange, revolted. France and England protected it, and it became the kingdom of the Belgians, under Leopold of Saxe Coburg.

In **1832**, the cholera raged frightfully in France and England.

In **1843**, the Queen and Prince Albert visited Louis Philippe, and the next year the visit was returned by the King of the French.

ENGLAND.

In **1830**, George IV. died, and his brother, WILLIAM IV. liberally inclined, succeeded, and accepted the resignation of Wellington and Peel. Earl Grey and a Whig Ministry came in.

In **1831**, the Reform Bill, extending the borough franchise to persons renting 10*l.* houses, and regulating the system, was brought in by ministers. Parliament rejected it and was dissolved. It was carried by the next House of Commons, but rejected by the Lords. The country was in a riotous state, ricks were burnt, and there was dangerous agitation.

In **1832**, on the threat of creating Liberal Peers to out-vote the rest, the Lords passed the Reform Bill.

In **1833**, slavery was abolished in all the English colonies.

In **1834**, Lord Grey retired; and after a short ministry of Lord Melbourne, Peel and Wellington came into office.

In **1837**, William IV. died, and VICTORIA, his niece, came to the throne. Hanover passed to the male heir, her uncle, Ernest Augustus.

In **1838**, an insurrection in Canada was quelled by Sir John Colborne.

In **1840**, the Queen married Prince Albert of Saxe Coburg. Upper and Lower Canada were united. There was a short war with China to compel the authorities to permit trade in opium.

In **1841**, the English troops who had occupied Cabul were attacked by the natives, and most disastrously destroyed in the Khyber pass. The Whigs resigned. Sir R. Peel was at the head of the cabinet.

In **1842**, China was brought to a treaty; Generals Nott and Pollock avenged the losses in Cabul. Upper and Lower Canada were united.

In **1843**, Sir Charles Napier gained a brilliant course of victories in Scinde.

In **1845**, the potato crop universally failed; and Sir Robert Peel saw that the duty on foreign corn (the Corn Laws) could no longer be maintained. A great war; the Sikhs were defeated at Moodkee, Ferozeshah, and Aliwal.

students in 1880, as well as legitimate reprints elsewhere in the world (Fig. 2.3a).

Macmillan was keenly interested in periodical publishing as well as in books. He had established *Macmillan's Magazine* in 1859 and would embark upon *Nature* in 1869.[32] It was in 1867 that he intervened in the conversation between Green and Bryce, who had both, more or less simultaneously, hit upon the idea of 'a purely historical review', a periodical devoted to history.[33] Freeman quickly became involved. The four men differed, however, as to the pattern of publishing. Bryce and Freeman preferred a quarterly, while Green (the most democratic of the group) believed in a shilling monthly. Macmillan was supportive, but crucially he disagreed with the others with respect to format: he envisaged an annual volume, 'like the Oxford Essays' (Fig. 2.5).[34] The three historians wanted not only substantial, well-documented essays, but also book reviews and a summary of historical work abroad as well as at home. Blithely ignoring the lack of an established readership, Bryce believed that if the new periodical 'did not find a historic interest abroad it would create it'. Macmillan was not so sanguine, and insisted upon a compromise. An accessible narrative style (he called it 'literary excellence') must be a founding principle. The journal would have to provide the historical perspective on contemporary issues, however distasteful this might be to some purists. While catering to the public taste for biographies, it must make such life-writing 'careful and philosophical'. And the new periodical would include the histories of literature and science, not just politics.[35]

The negotiations waxed and waned over the next several years. In an 1870 letter to his publisher, Green was explicit about their mutual aspiration: 'Unless the Review is considered on business principles and business terms I think it had better not be started; and it is impossible that it could be conducted in this way unless a circulation far wider than that of the purely historical circle of students could be obtained.'[36] For his part, Macmillan made it clear that he would not undertake the financial risks unless Green undertook to be the editor. Contrary to Bryce's pious expectation that the general reader would surely value essays written by scholars for scholars, Macmillan apparently anticipated that Green, as editor, would be able to transmit his own narrative talents to other writers contributing to the journal. Green was more attuned than either of them to the interests of the reading public. In an 1876 letter finally renouncing the whole project, he realized that:

Oxford Eſſays,

contributed by

Members of the University.

1857.

London:

John W. Parker and Son,

West Strand.

2.5 *Oxford Essays*, 1857.

> Such a review [Macmillan's compromise, incorporating biography and current events] would in great part be too scientific for the general reader – not indeed to read but to take any real interest in. On the other hand it would be too popular in form to secure any warm or enthusiastic sympathy from those who desire a scientific organ of historical research. Its almost inevitable tendency would be, as the desire for 'success' pressed on editor & publisher, to become more & more popular, and less & less scientific, in tone.

The distinction between popular and academic history was being established at this very time. The proponents of a quarterly eventually prevailed, though not before several more publishers contemplated with disquiet the project of a periodical dedicated to history. Green realized that his own popularity was a hindrance to Macmillan's ambitions for him. He said, 'I do not possess that confidence of historical scholars which the Editor of such an organ must possess. I should be looked upon by the bulk of them as a person imposed on the review by the unhappy necessity of securing a publisher & a popular circulation, & as the representative not of the scientific but of the non-scientific element in it.'[37] The *English Historical Review* appeared almost twenty years after the initial conversations about a periodical dedicated to history, and ten years after Green's withdrawal from the project.

But despite his disappointment about a historical periodical based on 'business principles', Macmillan had found in Green a remarkably talented and competent historian-author. Beginning in 1869 their correspondence about a possible historical review was intermingled with Green's proposed new *Short History of England*, which was eventually published in 1874 (Fig. 2.6). Green projected 600 pages on the history of the English people, which he thought would 'supply a want in our literature – that of a book in which the past lines of our history should be fixed with precision & which might serve as an introduction to its more detailed study'. More prosaically it ought to serve both as a 'school-manual' for the higher forms and as a 'handbook' in universities. The focus was to be on England, and on political, social, religious and intellectual movements rather than on war and conquest (which Green later characterized as 'drum and trumpet history'). After a little more detail Green's letter concluded with the business arrangements.[38]

Macmillan must have been overjoyed to receive what was from the book-trade point of view a remarkably professional and innovative proposal. Whether the author was regarded as scientific or not by a body of scholars who either could not or would not send

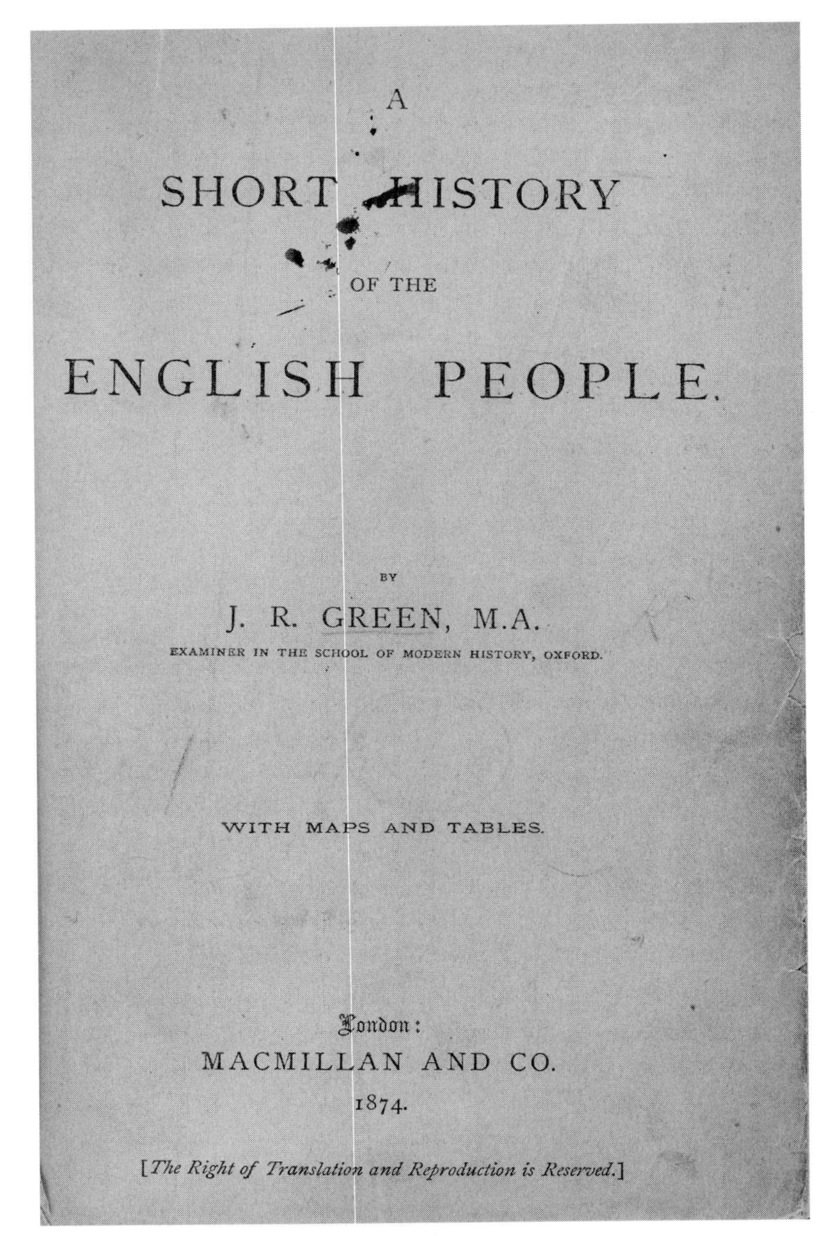

A

SHORT HISTORY

OF THE

ENGLISH PEOPLE.

BY

J. R. GREEN, M.A.

EXAMINER IN THE SCHOOL OF MODERN HISTORY, OXFORD.

WITH MAPS AND TABLES.

London:

MACMILLAN AND CO.

1874.

[*The Right of Translation and Reproduction is Reserved.*]

2.6 J. R. Green, *A Short History of the English People*, 1874.

him publishable manuscripts – or who, like Freeman, felt free to submit, unrevised, the text he had written for his children – this was someone with whom Macmillan could work. Green entered into ardent discussion of the look of his book: while anticipating sales in the educational market, he wanted a design that did not 'doom it to a purely school-boy use'. Black-letter headings were removed and discreet marginal italic notes substituted.[39]

Green's book appeared in the autumn of 1874. It enjoyed not only an immediate success but also a very long life in print and in the classroom. Scholars have attributed these achievements to its readable quality and its inclusion of cultural and social, as well as political, content. Not many observers, however, have noticed the extensive consultation that went into the text. Macmillan sought an opinion from J. R. Furnivall, who wanted 'to have the social history more brought out'.[40] He also sent the first half of the manuscript to John Morley, who acted as his professional reader and was a historian and biographer in his own right. Morley was anxious about Green's innovative arrangement:

> It is not mapped out into blocks of fact which an ordinary reader can easily carry in his mind: I mean the grouping is not definite and marked enough; is not pointed and impressed by bold lines of demarcation. The style is so even, again, so smooth as not to help us in any way towards seizing the salient parts of the matter. ... He has no doubt great merits in the even kind of writing, but does not history need a more audacious or vigorous sweep of style, unless you are writing it judicially ... or merely learnedly? You see Mr Green, tho' both judicial and learned, yet is mainly a picturesque or narrative writer, and must be measured in this style. Well then I say in this style we crave perhaps a little more boldness – not of phrase – but of conception, and of demarcation.

Furthermore, Morley continued, 'I pray for more directness. I could show you a hundred places where he refers to something as having happened, instead of looking his reader in the face, and saying "This happened". In essays, *études*, &c this oblique way of putting things is not inelegant, but in a history it is a sin against the Holy Ghost. Better be bald and yet telling the facts than elegant, and obscure or troublesome.' Morley closed with a plea for marginal dates, and a reiteration of the importance of directness. 'Look at Froude,' he insisted, 'how bad a stylist he is from the literary point of view, yet how popular, just because he has the art of direct narrative.'[41]

It is not clear to what extent Green took this advice into consideration in preparing the final manuscript. In any case, Morley's letter provides remarkably rich evidence of what a publisher was looking for, in historical writing on a large scale. And the success of the book despite (or perhaps because of) its avoidance of 'directness' betokens Macmillan's success in packaging it for school as well as general readers.

The Clarendon Press (Oxford) and the historians

Macmillan's partners at Oxford, the Delegates of the Clarendon Press, first ventured outside their established Bible-and-the-classics market and into educational book-publishing by setting up a School-book Committee in 1863. The result was the Clarendon Press Series; but editions of the classical texts were more easily secured than history books, where the lack of resources had become something of a crisis. The pedagogical resources available to the History School were not only limited, but distressfully controversial. The School recommended a *History of England* by John Lingard, but Lingard had been a Roman Catholic and students were advised to read him with caution. There was little otherwise, except a source-book of primary documents, *The Annals of England* published by Parker in 1855, until Freeman's *Norman Conquest* made its way into the Clarendon Press Series. Oxford published only seven books in 1865, one of which was a reprint and another an edited document. But despite this modest record, change was under way.[42]

Bartholomew Price was Secretary to the Delegates from 1868. 'Bat' Price was a mathematician, and a powerful figure in Oxford, especially at the Press where he had long served as a Delegate. And a student of history, the Rev. George William Kitchin, had been appointed Secretary to the School-book Committee in 1865. The process of becoming a modern publisher was slow: if an Oxford author had completed a book, he was likely to offer it to a London publisher, whereas if he had an idea for a book he would propose it to the Delegates but be slow to deliver a manuscript. As Kitchin observed, 'your Oxford Don is worked hard in Term time, and has Switzerland before him in Vacation'.[43] Nor were the Delegates very energetic: Kitchin confided to Macmillan, in a 'bit of high Treason towards my Chiefs. ... This is a brutal board! They are got together with infinite difficulty, & break up with infinite celerity. They debate questions at great length, and then refuse to do business. They want a Dictator to hit them about the head a bit!'[44] It was to be be a long time before the Oxford Delegates began to behave like a modern publisher.

The urgency of commissioning and bringing out some reliable

works of history was compounded by the parallel project, in the History School, of rehabilitating the reputation of the degree. History was widely regarded as a much less rigorous course of study than the classics – 'an easy School for rich men', as Freeman put it.[45] The history books coming out of London only compounded the problem. Readable older works like Macaulay's and Carlyle's, as well as wildly popular newer ones by Froude and especially J. R. Green, seemed to make the study of history so accessible as to be downright frivolous. Macmillan's readers were advising him to decline manuscripts that were 'not likely to attract the crowd, who like to keep to the great open road of history'.[46] There were hopes in Oxford that Goldwin Smith would write a respectably scholarly history of England, but during his eight years as Regius Professor ending in 1866, this remained a matter of discussion and never emerged as a manuscript.[47] Smith was succeeded in 1867 by William Stubbs, and it was Stubbs who rescued the Oxford History School from its lightweight reputation. He did this, not only by his learned and poorly attended lectures, but by editing for publication the primary sources on which the next generation of historians were to cut their scholarly teeth. Successive editions of his *Select Charters* and a three-volume *Constitutional History of England* were published in the Clarendon Press Series.[48]

Stubbs was not only a Delegate of the Press (from 1868 to 1884, long after he had become Bishop of Oxford), but also their most trusted advisor on historical projects. Editions and revisions of the *Select Charters* had been coming out since 1870. Stubbs's 1868 text of Magna Carta was printed for internal Oxford classroom use only, and hence without a proper binding, but had nevertheless been distributed widely, even in the United States (Fig. 2.7). A fresh edition appeared in 1879 and the Press took the opportunity to insert an advertisement of their historical works.[49]

Stubbs's advice was sought on proposals from such a diverse range of authors as Ramsay, Ranke, Freeman, Payne and Hodgkin.[50] The Secretaries also consulted him about matters of publishing format, such as whether there should be marginal notes incorporated into a new edition of Clarendon's *History of the Rebellion*.[51] A school history of Germany was proposed by A. W. Ward and one of France by Kitchin himself. The former never appeared; the latter did, and remained in print until into the twentieth century, with successive revisions undertaken by younger scholars when the original author had moved on to become Dean of Durham.[52]

MAGNA CARTA

REGIS JOHANNIS,

XV DIE JUNII, MCCXV,

ANNO REGNI XVII.

JOHANNES Dei gratia rex Anglie dominus Hybernie dux Normannie et Aquitannie comes Andegavie archiepiscopis episcopis abbatibus comitibus baronibus justiciariis forestariis vicecomitibus prepositis ministris et omnibus ballivis et fidelibus suis salutem Sciatis nos intuitu Dei et pro salute anime nostre et omnium antecessorum et heredum nostrorum ad honorem Dei et exaltationem sancte ecclesie et emendationem regni nostri per consilium venerabilium patrum nostrorum Stephani Cantuariensis archiepiscopi totius Anglie primatis et sancte Romane ecclesie cardinalis Henrici Dublinensis archiepiscopi Willelmi Londoniensis Petri Wintoniensis Joscelini Bathoniensis et Glastoniensis Hugonis Lincolniensis Walteri Wygornensis Willelmi Coventrensis et Benedicti Roffensis episcoporum magistri Pandulfi domini pape subdiaconi et familiaris fratris Eymerici magistri militie templi in Anglia et nobilium virorum Willelmi Mariscalli comitis Penbrok Willelmi comitis Saresberie Willelmi comitis Warennie Willelmi comitis Arundellie Alani de Galweya constabularii Scottie Warini filii Geroldi Petri filii Hereberti Huberti de Burgo senescalli Pictavie Hugonis de Nevilla Mathei filii Hereberti Thome Basset Alani Basset Philippi de Albiniaco Roberti de Roppelay Johannis Mariscalli Johannis filii Hugonis et aliorum fidelium nostrorum

B

2.7 William Stubbs, *Magna Carta*, privately printed, 1868.

The Press struggled with its obligations to individual Delegates and others in Oxford, obligations which sometimes competed with the commitment to enhance its scholarly reputation. Margaret Roberts had been commissioned to edit a three-part series of 'Oxford Reading Books' – compilations of literary extracts for

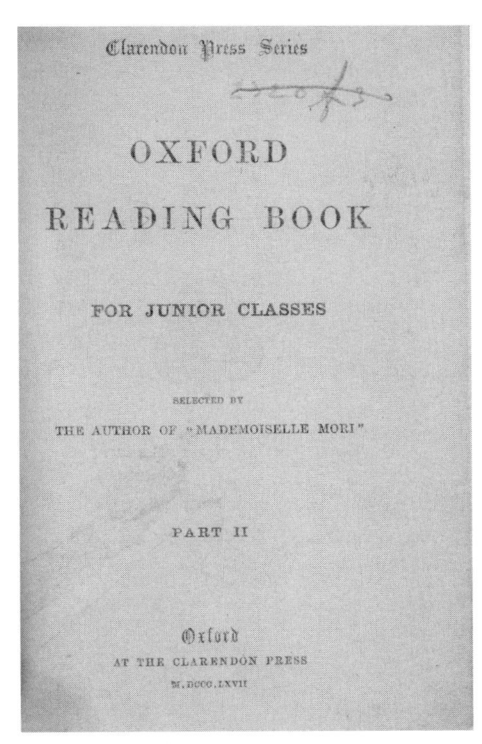
Clarendon Press Series

OXFORD
READING BOOK

FOR JUNIOR CLASSES

SELECTED BY
THE AUTHOR OF "MADEMOISELLE MORI"

PART II

Oxford
AT THE CLARENDON PRESS
M.DCCC.LXVII

16 *Long, Long Ago.*

who fed five thousand men with only five loaves, could make the little which was left to them enough and to spare. Alfred lived to subdue his enemies and be one of the best kings that ever England had. A few years ago a gold armlet was found in this part of the country with the words "Alfred caused me to be made" engraved upon it. It may possibly have been lost by this very king while hiding at Athelney, but of this we cannot of course be sure. The rest of his history, how he conquered his hasty temper, how he was persuaded to learn to read by his young step-mother, Judith, with her pretty book, and how he got scolded for burning an old woman's cakes, you must read in English History, since we have not room for it here. The last of the English kings was Harold. He fell in the great battle of Hastings, when the Normans came over from France, headed by their terrible chief, William, who then became king of England. The old verse may help you to remember in what order the different nations who ruled England followed each other :—

"The Romans in England first did sway;
The Saxons after them led the way:
They tugged with the Danes, till an overthrow
They both of them got from the Norman bow."

Before we leave these times, let us try to

2.8 'Mademoiselle Mori' (Margaret Roberts), *Oxford Reading Book*, 1867.

elementary classroom use.[53] As 'Mademoiselle Mori', Roberts had written novels and romanticized popular histories. She had the backing of one Delegate and was half-sister of another, which made it awkward for Kitchin, who found the Reading Books unsatisfactory. 'Miss R. neither writes a new book, nor gives us wholesome extracts from great authors,' he confided to Macmillan. 'I can't abide mincemeat.' And furthermore, she failed to appreciate 'History as understood *now*'. In Kitchin's view, the Oxford Press had 'no business to issue Reading books, unless they are something far above the average'.[54] Two volumes appeared, but they drew the line at Part III. Macmillan was invited either to waste it or to 'dispose of it in the Colonies or elsewhere, with a new and unimportant title page' (Fig. 2.8).

Schoolbooks remained a priority, and the Press in Oxford struggled to meet the needs of teachers and their pupils. But Oxford's incursion into the educational market created a conflict of interest for Alexander Macmillan, while from the point of view of Price and Kitchin their London agent and advisor had become a rival. Macmillan remained generous, however, even transferring books from his own imprint to that of the Clarendon Press Series. Sutcliffe describes the partnership as 'largely a triumph of good manners'.[55]

Certainly good manners were needed to mediate between the aspiring Oxford Professor, E. A. Freeman, and the Secretary of Oxford's Press, Professor Price. When in 1869 Price asked a perfectly legitimate publisher's question about the possible overlap between Freeman's short, medium and long books on the Norman Conquest, Macmillan heard from his author: 'What a deceitful Bat it is as well as a cantankerous!' And then he went on: 'Well it is not worth troubling ourselves what such a tringle without bowels thinks about anything, nor the Delegates either, stupid old Dons. ... Why we have done the very best thing that can be for their pockets, which is all that they care about.'[56] But Macmillan and Price were close, too, meeting regularly in Oxford and in London. The two publishers were the same age; Macmillan enjoyed being a bookman a good deal more than did Price, and he was a much more successful publisher.

The Pitt Press (Cambridge) and the historians

Although there was a Pitt Press Series to match the Clarendon Press series, the rivalry between the two university presses in this period was not so much over school books as about the Revised Version of the New Testament. Eventually published by the two presses in 1881, a million copies were distributed on the first day, but did not go on to sustain its publishers as had the Authorized Version for so many years.[57] Nor did it promote collaborative relationships between the two ancient university presses. When someone proposed that they work together on publishing a scholarly journal of history, J. R. Seeley replied firmly that 'the notion of the two Presses working together does not please me'. As a result of the enforced partnership over the Revised Version, he said, they were 'at daggers drawn. Our Syndics regard their Delegates as a most grasping, over-reaching, imperious body. In a large affair like the Revision ... the two bodies might consent to act together, but never, I should think, voluntarily or in a small affair.'[58] Probably even Seeley would have liked the Cambridge Press in this period to have been a little more 'pushing and ambitious.' Certainly when his own book appeared in 1878 – *The Life and Times of Stein, or, Germany and Prussia in the Napoleonic Age* – he gave the Press urgent instructions about handling the advertisements, reviews and translation rights.[59]

Cambridge published no more history books than did Oxford – perhaps even fewer – and the Syndics of the Cambridge University Press were also slow to find their publishing feet in the last three decades of the nineteenth century. Fittingly, perhaps inevitably, the prominent work of history in their list was James Bass Mullinger's 1873 *History of the University of Cambridge*. But other Cambridge historians turned to Macmillan and his London competitors, not often thinking of their own University's Press; and when they did, they were liable to be rebuffed. The Syndics declined G. W. Prothero's *Simon de Montfort* in 1876 (it went to Longmans).[60] The following year Seeley tried to urge the claims of Mackenzie Wallace's new book on Russia. Wallace had told Seeley that he had written a scholarly and lengthy version of the book but 'that none of the booksellers [i.e. the publishers] would take it until he cut it down a good deal and spiced it with insignificant personal detail much against his will. I said to myself', Seeley added in a letter to Charles Clay, then the University Printer, 'this is a case for the Pitt Press. Do you think you could do anything in the matter?' but Clay couldn't or wouldn't and the spiced-up book was published by Cassell, Petter, and Galpin.[61]

All this was to change, and from being important primarily as a printer, Cambridge became 'one of the largest publishers of educational books in the country'.[62] But in the 1860s and 1870s there was very little scope for serious works of history: Macmillans were turning down manuscripts that were worthy but dry – and neither of the university presses was picking them up.

The publishing history of history books changed a good deal in the seventeen years that Macmillan acted as Oxford's agent in London. Those changes can be illustrated by looking at the adventures both of the Oxford Delegates and of Macmillan and Company with Sir James Ramsay (1832-1925). The tenth baronet of an ancient Scottish family, Ramsay was an independent scholar whose books are remembered as being 'lucid and concise', but 'somewhat arid'.[63] His correspondence with the Oxford University Press bears all this out, but Ramsay also suffered from competition, both with the sparkling commercial success of J. R. Green, and with the new interpretation of history as a science embraced so heartily by Stubbs, Seeley and others, and warmly though ambiguously by Freeman and by Green himself.

Ramsay was about 42 years of age in 1874 when two things happened: he proposed a History of England to the Delegates of the Oxford University Press, and Green's *Short History* appeared. Fifteen years passed before one of eight planned volumes of Ramsay's history, chronologically the end of the projected series, appeared in 1892 as *Lancaster and York: A Century of English History: 1399-1485.*

In the intervening period, Ramsay's name had been considered by Macmillans to be commissioned to write a substantial one-volume history of Rome. This competed with H. G. Liddell's book, published by John Murray. Attempting in about 1882 to recruit James Bryce to build upon his reputation as the historian of the Holy Roman Empire to undertake this projected work, Green remarked 'that there has been some talk of a certain "Ramsay" to do the book, But as yet all in that quarter is hazy, and I have no doubt that if you would let me propose you for it, Ramsay would quietly drop.' Green added that a Roman history by Bryce would beat Liddell, 'out of [the field] in an hour, so that your sale would be steady year by year. And then we should really have a book which would represent an historical school instead of a miserable caricature.'[64] Freeman, who had not yet got round to writing about Rome in his own Historical Course for Schools, also got wind of this notion and howled: 'But now down swoops Ramsay & takes away my chance, like the mercenaries of William Rufus taking the bread out of the mouths of the wretched. You say he will be "on the scale of Dr Liddell's". I take for granted that he will not be like Liddell in anything but scale.'[65] Macmillan's scheme failed, and Rome, in this particular format and price-point, remained in Liddell's and John Murray's hands.

Ramsay surfaced at Oxford in 1889 with his single completed manuscript. The new Press Secretary, Philip Lyttelton Gell, sent it to Stubbs for an opinion, observing that 'So many things have happened since 1874 – Johnny Green's History for instance – and the Delegates feel they must walk very warily before issuing from here a new standard History of England.'[66] After consulting three senior historians, Gell wrote to Ramsay, trying to explain how the world of scholarship, and the market for histories of England, had changed. The Delegates now felt bound to view Ramsay's work 'in relation to the many other histories which have appeared of late years and which have done so much to promulgate sound and recent views upon English history'. The period Ramsay covered had now been thoroughly worked over. Nor had he offered any hint as to the scale of the complete work, although Gell observed that it did seem 'to have out-grown considerably the limits originally proposed'.

What was needed was coverage of the thirteenth, fourteenth and fifteenth centuries: 'It is here alone that any real need now exists,' Gell insisted, 'and it is probable that only the volume covering this portion would attract attention from the average historical reader.'[67] When Ramsay had set out in 1874, the 'average historical reader' had at his or her disposal only the broad sweep of Macaulay and other unsatisfactory or outdated works. Fifteen years later, not only Green and Freeman, but also outsiders like Edith Thompson and dozens like her had written histories of England that were published in a multitude of formats for every conceivable price-point in the marketplace.

The frank correspondence between Gell and Frederick York Powell reveals the publisher's frustration with the Delegates, who were more deferential to the nobleman historian than Gell was prepared to be. He then went on to comment on a frivolous but enormously successful recent book and observed, 'By all means let us publish [unremunerative scholarly works] but do not shackle our efforts to make money for the University in other directions also. *Your* clientele,' he told his colleague the academic historian 'is really not large enough to maintain the business.'[68]

The years from 1863 to 1880 – the seventeen years of Macmillan's term as the London publisher to the Oxford University Press – were significant because modern conventions for the writing and publication of history were being established. These conventions covered both periodical and book format; they remained in place through the twentieth century and to some extent still exist today. Macmillan's own vision was crucial, and his nurturing of Green, Freeman, Edith Thompson and other writers was of vital importance. He (and other London publishers like Rivingtons) seized the school market for histories of England, while Oxford was struggling to disentangle itself from unsatisfactory writers like Margaret Roberts and James Ramsay. In particular, the London publishers began to experiment with the series format, as a way of encompassing an ambitious historical narrative in manageable monograph-length packets.

At the same time, though, the readers' reports in the Macmillan archive show that the commercial publisher was being advised to decline works of immense and 'sterling' learning. Macmillans turned down manuscripts on even potentially popular subjects, when the 'merciless particularity' and general 'heaviness' of their style made it unlikely that many readers would chose them. Macmillan's advisor told him that 'People like to sail easily down the broad stream of history, and not to explore creeks elaborately'.[69] When the Clarendon Press liberated itself from Macmillan in 1880, and, with the Pitt Press in Cambridge, began to be bolder and more judgemental about its publishing decisions, both the university presses used variations on the series format to develop their lists in the discipline of history.

Chapter 3

Breaking the Drowsy Spell of Narrative, 1880-1914

WHEN the Oxford University Press declined to renew Macmillan's contract as its London publisher, in 1880, the ancient institution was not only declaring independence but also sharpening its own identity as an academic publisher. The years between that moment and the beginning of the First World War were punctuated by the foundation of the *Dictionary of National Biography* in 1882, of the *English Historical* Review in 1886 and of the *Cambridge Modern History* in 1896.[1] Within the practice of history, this was the time when the notion of history as a science, an austere academic discipline, became widely accepted. Unlike their predecessors, the University-based historians of this new generation now began to have a body of undergraduates to work with. The number of such men and women was small at the outset. The dons could imagine a scholarly readership more easily than their predecessors, however, now that they encountered it face to face in their studies and libraries on a regular basis and as they began to shape its tastes and values. Their rhetoric about how history should, and should not, be written, became more assured. But they still laboured in the shadow of their populist predecessors, Thomas Babington Macaulay and John Richard Green. Revised editions of the latter's compelling single-volume *Short History* continued to celebrate cultural triumphs rather than 'drum and trumpet', or constitutional history.

When the Clarendon Press Secretary wrote to Sir James Ramsay in 1896, declining to cover the losses attending the publication of Ramsay's eight-volume *History of England*, Gell said: 'I think one cannot fail to perceive the strength of the argument that the average person only reads his English History in one form, and that with Green's book before him, he will read no other in the present generation.'[2] Green's story was the narrative of England's liberty. And when the Regius Professor of History at Cambridge, Sir John

Robert Seeley, had passionately insisted (in 1883) that historians must 'break the drowsy spell of narrative' and write history in a newly analytical way, he was also calling on his colleagues to break the stranglehold of Green's work in the literary as well as the intellectual marketplace.[3] Alice Green and Kate Norgate prepared an illustrated edition of the *Short History* which circulated in parts in 1902-1903 and later appeared in volume form (Fig. 3.1).

Seeley used narrative elegance as a test to distinguish the new history from the old. History could be true, or it could be 'delightful', but seldom both. It might address other political forces, rather than retell the familiar triumphant narrative of liberty. He wanted to see a new 'aristocracy' of historical students, who could appreciate work that the 'loose democracy' of readers would find tedious.[4] When Seeley denounced Macaulay as a charlatan, and Bury insisted that history was 'a science, no less and no more', they both profoundly distressed Macaulay's great-nephew G. M. Trevelyan.[5] While others in his generation of history students were impressed and inspired by Bury's words, and by the echo of Seeley's, the young Trevelyan went on to imitate and build upon the form of books by his great-uncle book and by Green. He too was to write those sweeping narratives whose spell was so seductive with British readers at home and in the Empire, so useful to educators designing a history curriculum, and so appealing to commercially-minded publishers both in entrepreneurial firms and in the university presses. But Trevelyan was to write his books against the contemporary standards of his discipline, and outside his University of Cambridge, where others had the ear of undergraduates and research students.

J. R. Seeley and Oscar Browning were contemporaries in the Faculty of History at Cambridge; Seeley was Regius Professor while Browning was a Resident Fellow of King's and College Lecturer. Seeley had arrived in 1870 and Browning in 1875. The two men were allies in the politics of the Cambridge History Tripos, but they are brought together here to exemplify two different ways of writing about history, and two different sets of relationships with publishers.[6]

Seeley and the reading public

Seeley came to his passion for modern history relatively late in life, having taught classics at University College London.[7] He was the anonymous author of *Ecce Homo: A Survey of the Life and Work of*

3.1 J. R. Green, *Short History*, illustrated edition, 1902.

Jesus Christ, published in 1865 by his friend and admirer Alexander Macmillan. Despite the quarter-century difference in their ages, the two men had known each other since the 1830s when Macmillan worked as an apprentice to Seeley's bookseller father. In 1870 Seeley took up the invitation of the Prime Minister to become Regius Professor of History at Cambridge after Kingsley retired. Gladstone had been recommended to consider Adolphus Ward for the post, but the Prime Minister had not heard of Ward.[8] Three others declined before Seeley received his offer, but despite this inauspicious start, he set out to recast history at Cambridge as a science, and specifically in relation to political science. The History Tripos became independent from Law in 1873 but – to Seeley's regret – remained distinct from Political Science.

Seeley's first major historical work, a study of Germany and Prussia in the Napoleonic age, as seen through a life of Karl von Stein, was not well received, despite having been cast in the biographical mode – against his better judgement, but in hopes of educating the English mind.[9] It was in the early 1880s, after the publication of *Stein*, that Seeley wrote a series of *Macmillan's Magazine* articles in which he spoke about two kinds of books, for specialists and for general readers. He pointed out that 'science is essentially difficult' and that the distinction between the two reading publics is so radical that 'to the large public books written for the smaller public are as though they did not exist'. Newton's *Principia* was an important scientific work despite being difficult and uncongenial to read. Ordinary 'vulgar' readers of history didn't understand that in history 'the story is not an end, but only a means'. Seeley blamed both Scott and Macaulay for having 'spoiled the public taste' and 'corrupted' subsequent readers and writers of history. The 'final result' of this tendency was

> that to the general public no distinction remains between history and fiction. That the history is true and well-authenticated, that the proper authorities have been consulted as a matter of course, they make no doubt. All such matters they leave to the historian, whom they assume to understand his business, and they feel particularly obliged to him for not troubling them with details about them. History in short is deprived of any, even the most distant association with science, and takes up its place definitively as a department of *belles letters*.

Seeley did not regard popularization as difficult: 'All that is necessary is systematic exaggeration and occasional falsification.'[10]

Although Seeley blamed the problem of history-books on 'unintelligent popular demand', he had nothing to say in his articles about the industry of book and periodical publishing, and how it might have changed since the days when Newton's *Principia* was published. Instead he concentrated on indirectly creating a new reading public for serious works of history, by means of training it up in the Universities and in historical societies like the one he addressed in Birmingham. Despite his experience as a Syndic of the Cambridge University Press, Seeley's articles mention neither academic book-publishing nor scholarly journals as media that might serve the specialist historical writer and reader. Privately, Seeley knew a great deal about the book trade; he was the son and grandson of prominent Fleet Street booksellers, and the early knowledge derived from family was supplemented later by direct personal experience with Macmillans and other publishers. But he concealed his knowledge from the young academic historians who were aspiring to succeed as authors in the new genres.

Seeley's one really popular work of history owed its existence to its publisher, Alexander Macmillan. *The Expansion of England* (1883) was initially conceived simply as two courses of lectures delivered to Cambridge undergraduates in 1881-82.[11] The structure of the lectures, and the chapters that Macmillan cajoled from a reluctant Seeley, reflected the historian's theoretical concept of a Greater Britain, distinguishing the settler colonies from the Indian empire. Seeley told his readers that the two problematics of colonial expansion and the Indian empire would

> bring the whole modern history of England in their train. And not only is this one way of grasping English history [he continued], but it is the best way. For in history everything depends upon turning narrative into problems. So long as you think of history as a mere chronological narrative, so long you are in the old literary groove which leads to no trustworthy knowledge, but only to that pompous conventional romancing of which all serious men are tired. Break the drowsy spell of narrative; ask yourself questions; set yourself problems; your mind will at once take up a new attitude; you will become an investigator; you will cease to be solemn and begin to be serious.

The third theme, the scientific approach to historical study and the importance of paying serious attention to recent periods, reinforced Seeley's argument about turning narrative into problems. He deplored the tendency to concentrate on the conventional narrative, and thus to celebrate the achievement of England's liberty culminating at the turn of the nineteenth century. To structure the past in this way meant that the interest actually diminished towards the end, instead of increasing. If expansion were given its full importance, history would become more interesting as it approached the imperial 1880s. In fact, in the famous remark 'We seem, as it were, to have conquered and peopled half the world in a fit of absence of mind', the word 'seem' refers to historiography, not to foreign policy. Seeley explicitly named J. R. Green as one 'popular historian' who had committed the error of letting the interest diminish and overlooking empire. But Macmillan remonstrated on personal grounds, and Seeley blunted the historiographical critique by making the reference anonymous.[12]

Macmillan no doubt discerned the popular readership that developed, but neither he nor Seeley could determine how the book would be received by that amorphous collectivity, the Victorian reading public. After three years of steady sales, publisher and author began to discuss the publication of a stripped-down version of the book, omitting two of its three parts.[13] The whole section on India was cut out, as well as (to quote the preface) 'all the academic part, which deals with the method of historic study'. *Our Colonial Expansion, Extracts from the Expansion of England* appeared in 1887 in time for sale to visitors at the Colonial Exhibition (Fig. 3.2). In spite of his disdain for literary history, Seeley had written a popular book, and also consented to an abridgement that contradicted his principles.

Browning and the publishers

Although Seeley was not particularly well off, his income did not depend on historical writing. Oscar Browning's did, and Seeley's Cambridge colleague turned repeatedly and promiscuously to publishers for book contracts. The rich trove of correspondence with publishers among Browning's papers at King's College, Cambridge would form the materials for an illuminating study of the Victorian book trade, filtered through a single author uncontaminated by canonical or celebrity status.[14] Browning was a 'character' and a celebrity of sorts among the undergraduates at Cambridge, particularly the history students at King's, but there is nothing canonical about his writings. Nor is there much that is accurate, scholarly or authoritative. A bit of Cambridge gossip no less revealing because it was apocryphal had Browning confusing Siberia with Silesia.[15] What is interesting about his works, however, is the way the contracts and arrangements behind them show how

OUR COLONIAL EXPANSION

EXTRACTS FROM THE

EXPANSION OF ENGLAND

BY

J. R. SEELEY M.A.

REGIUS PROFESSOR OF MODERN HISTORY IN THE UNIVERSITY OF CAMBRIDGE

London:
MACMILLAN AND CO.
AND NEW YORK.
1887

[*The Right of Translation is reserved.*]

3.2 J. R. Seeley, *Our Colonial Expansion*, 1887.

publishers and educators were conceptualizing the problem of the history book.

Although Browning did some scholarly editing and writing, he also turned out copy for a number of school and popular histories.[16] During the 1880s he worked with two London firms, Griffith & Farran and Virtue & Company. Griffith & Farran wrote to Browning in 1882 about preparing a set of Historical Reading Books for Public Elementary Schools. After some negotiations about price and compensation in the light of fierce competition for such books, they reached an agreement and entered into correspondence with one of Her Majesty's Inspectors for Schools. The Inspector asked whether 'the series [was] to be brought out in Sections ... or, in successive coats of paint – as it were'. Sections were to follow the conventional periodization, Ancient, Medieval and Modern for standards 3, 4 and 5 respectively. Whereas the successive coats of paint would address the child reader's degree of maturity: 'stories of great deeds or about great men for Standard 3, an anecdotal history for Standard 4, a more detailed and systematic history for Standards 5 & 6'. The inspector stated his own preference for the second plan, observing that 'So many children go to work after passing Standard 4, that if the first scheme were adopted, the most interesting period of English history, viz: – The Modern, would be very seldom read!'[17] The image of successive coats of paint is reminiscent of the way that nursery histories had for so long acted as the underpainting to which later complexities and revisions might or might not adhere. In this case the result was a compromise: Book 1 was made up of 'episodes covering the whole range of English history, and expressed in simple language', while the remaining three dealt with early, middle and later periods. Browning's preface stated his aim that the books 'should be readable, and should be history'.

In 1883 when he was preparing the text of Book 4, Browning received a critical reader's report from Griffith & Farran:

> It should be a fundamental principle in the authorship, that, that which is most interesting and ennobling in English History should receive due attention and events of comparatively recent date are all-important. We cannot send our boys out of school ignorant of the life of Prince Consort, or the Repeal of the Corn Laws or of the abolition of the Slave Trade. Teachers would become laughing stocks if, pretending to teach history they omitted things like these while they devoted attention to an ignoble Treaty of Dover or the cross purposes of Whigs and Tories.

The report also insisted that Browning and his publishers omit accounts of Londonderry and the Boyne and add chapters on the Reform Bill, the Chartist Riots, the Indian Mutiny and the Electric Telegraph.[18]

Browning was chronically suspicious of his publishers, and always hoping to be paid more for books to which he had long since signed away the rights. He was particularly annoyed when Griffith & Farran used part of his text from the 1884 Reading Books, and mixed it with other work to produce a new book, *True Stories from English History*, in 1886. The preface included part of his original preface, including the aim to be readable and to be history; the text contained some of Browning's selections from the work of older writers, and some of the anecdotes he had written himself for the original historical readers, but omitted others. Here we see another example of historical material undergoing a process of replication, moving between the dull brown school readers and the shiny blue-and-gold story book. The publishers also reproduced the original Historical Readers in 1893 (Fig. 3.3). Browning asked his agent to protest against Griffith & Farran's action, but there was nothing to be done since he had sold the copyright three years earlier.[19]

Another example of Browning's popular authorship occurred while he and Seeley were struggling to revise the Historical Tripos and while he was cultivating his reputation among Cambridge history students as 'The OB'. He contracted with Messrs Virtue & Company to prepare an *Illustrated History of England*. (Virtue specialized in illustrated works.) The book came out in twenty 64-page parts from 1889 to 1891 and eventually in volume form. There was conflict between publisher and author about the preparation of copy, corrections and the rate of payments. Browning seems to have held back copy, meaning that parts were not available to booksellers who had contracted to sell them.[20]

The crowning frustration for Herbert Virtue came in November 1891 when he learned that Browning was warning Cambridge undergraduates against reading his own book. They had failed to understand that the book was addressed to lower-middle class readers, rather than to students of their calibre. Virtue's agent at Cambridge reported that two orders which a canvasser had previously taken had 'been made bad, through a statement reported to be made by you to the undergraduates that you only wrote our history for grocers and cheesemongers, and it would be no good to them'.[21] In Victorian Cambridge, Browning had to be circumspect about his homosexuality; he had to be just as careful to keep

THE NEWBERY

HISTORICAL READERS,

No. 4.

Twenty Stories and Biographies

FROM 1066 TO 1485.

BY

OSCAR BROWNING, M.A.,

SENIOR FELLOW AND HISTORICAL LECTURER OF KING'S COLLEGE, CAMBRIDGE.

REVISED EDITION.

GRIFFITH FARRAN & CO. LIMITED,

NEWBERY HOUSE,

39 CHARING CROSS ROAD, LONDON.

3.3 Oscar Browning, *The Newbery Historical Readers*, 1893.

separate his two worlds of academic and popular history-book authorship. But for Virtue and other London publishers, the names of Browning's college and university on their title-page were worth the considerable aggravation they endured from their eccentric author. Browning is a prime example for this period of the historian with a foot in both literary camps, writing one day for the university presses and the new scholarly journal, and the next for a publisher more interested in commerce than in correctness.

New formats for history: periodicals and series

Both Seeley and Browning were involved in a failed attempt during the early 1880s to bring a new periodical to Cambridge. Eleven years had passed since Green had told Macmillan of his unwillingness to try, by editing a journal for the London publisher, to bridge the gap between scholarly and popular history. The occasional effort – such as the little-known 1866 *Historical Review* – was both short-lived and unsatisfactory, and so was the publication of scholarly work in the great literary quarterlies (Fig. 3.4).[22]

Now Browning canvassed Mandell Creighton, who agreed that 'existing reviews will only publish popular and sketchy articles'.[23] The need that Bryce, Freeman and others had articulated a decade earlier was stronger than ever, for a new publication, and a new bibliographical format, to complement the archival discoveries and subsequent historiographical reconsiderations of their time. Browning suggested to the Press Syndics that 'a university would not have the temptation, to which a publisher is liable, of lowering the tone of a review to make it more popular and saleable'. Seeley put the case at a February 1884 meeting of the Press Syndicate, but his colleagues were accustomed to books, not periodicals, and essays seemed particularly 'dangerous'. Moreover they were suspicious of history. They regarded history as 'connected with politics, and the Press ought to be neutral in politics. We should have responsibility,' he reported them saying, 'and yet we could never exert any effective control, so as to prevent articles from appearing that might not be "creditable" to the University'.[24] The Syndics' caution is particularly significant in view of Seeley's insistence on identifying the interests of history as being indissoluble from those of politics. As a commercial, rather than academic publisher, Macmillan had no objection to a leavening of controversial politics, but he was terrified of the 'dullness and

The Historical Review:

A Literary Journal and Genealogical Register of the United Kingdom.

No. 1. Vol. I.] FIRST QUARTER, 1866. [Annual Subscription, 5s.

DURHAM CATHEDRAL.

PERHAPS no cathedral in Britain is more picturesquely and beautifully situated than that of Durham. It is one of our noblest edifices, and is chiefly of massive Norman architecture, containing the tomb of St Cuthbert, and the chapel of the venerable Bede; it has a fine west front, with a Galilee chapel, and two richly ornamented towers; including the western part, it is 507 feet in length, by 200 feet in its greatest breadth, having a central tower 214 feet in height. Adjoining the cloisters are the deanery, library, chapter-house, prebendal college, and exchequer.

The cathedral was founded in the year 1093, and the see, comprising the counties of Durham and Northumberland, with some other tracts, was founded towards the close of the tenth century, and for many years was the richest bishopric in England; its gross income in 1843 having been £22,416. The Ecclesiastical Commissioners have, however, materially remodelled its arrangements, the annual income of the bishop being fixed at £8000.

The city of Durham is most ancient. Its external appearance is very imposing, its cathedral and castle occupying the summit of a steep and rocky eminence, surrounded by hanging gardens and plantations, at the base of which runs the Wear, crossed in this place by several bridges. The castle, which stands slightly north of the cathedral, was founded by William the Conqueror; it contains apartments for the bishop, but is otherwise chiefly appropriated to the ecclesiastical University, which was founded in 1837.

3.4 *The Historical Review*, 1866.

overspecialisation' that almost immediately became the hallmark of the *English Historical Review*.

James Bryce had been a persistent champion of creating a periodical dedicated to history since working with Macmillan, Green and Freeman in the early 1870s. His moment finally arrived in 1885. After a meeting of historians at Oxford where Creighton agreed to be editor, they persuaded Longman to take on the journal for a year and even to pay the contributors.[25] Longman's neutrality as a London commercial publisher permitted both Oxford and Cambridge scholars to participate on level ground, but Creighton soon acknowledged the editorial burden, telling Seeley: 'I am not over sanguine about the Historical Review. Its besetting danger is dullness & overspecialisation. I can only use such material as I get & the best writers are busy on their books. But my hope is that they find the Review useful for their own purposes.'[26] Creighton's correspondence reveals his continuing efforts to include essays attractive to the general reader, a compromise that was necessary given that he was working with a commercial publisher and still undertaking to pay contributors.[27] Such payments didn't last long. The kind of authorship the *EHR* published was remunerated indirectly; it did not really need a financial subvention. On the other hand, the kinds of authors who depended on a financial return for their writing were now shut out of the long-awaited 'purely historical review'.

The dedicated historical journal was one answer to the problem of how to disseminate the work of the newly scientific historians with their inconvenient commitment to 'dullness and over-specialization'. The other was the publication of books in series – what one book-trade journal called 'sustained literary ventures'.[28]

The series format was not altogether novel in the 1880s and 1890s. Well-established entrepreneurial publishers, like Longmans, Macmillans and Rivingtons and newer ones like Griffith & Farran, Cassells and Bells were doing well in those decades. In 1891 a long-standing problem was solved when the United States government passed the International Copyright (Chace) Act, thereby ending their tacit sanction of unauthorized transatlantic editions.[29] Now British publishers and authors could make co-publishing arrangements for the lucrative American market without establishing expensive New York offices, as Macmillans had in 1869. In 1894 the pattern of novel-publishing was revolutionized by the decision to abandon the three-volume format, and the Net Book Agreement of 1900 created fixed prices for books and ended a damaging level of competition among retail booksellers.[30] Both novels and works of non-fiction appeared in important reprint series, such as George Routledge's *Railway Library* and Macmillan's *English Men of Letters*. The latest books in science as well as in history also appeared in series format, bound uniformly and marketed collectively.[31] The series seemed to be an ideal way to publish, package and present works of non-fiction to the huge audience of English-speaking readers, whether they were in school or had graduated into the general reader category.

The series had particular advantages for the publishers of history books, in that the development of a set of connected works on a single theme, with one volume succeeding the next in both chronological and thematic sequence, allowed them to conceptualize projects on a grand scale. They could imagine a work of history larger than the one-volume form that Macmillan and Green had established as a norm, but more tightly focused than the leisurely multi-volume works of Hume – or indeed Ramsay. They could begin to aspire to comprehensiveness, and hope to be able to claim that the product they offered was not only 'definitive' but 'complete'. Ludmilla Jordanova has characterized this unattainable ideal as 'the chimera of comprehensiveness'.[32] Scholars as well as publishers became caught up in the ideal of a comprehensive series, especially those academics who worked closely with their publisher colleagues. But the demands of the series format could be relentless, and arguably had a dampening effect on the historical imagination.

It was in this period, and partly because of the way the university presses began to feel their way with the series format, that Macmillan's leadership in history-book publishing was supplanted by the two presses at Oxford and at Cambridge that he had dominated in the 1870s.

Acton and the Cambridge Modern History

The *Cambridge Modern History* was published between 1902 and 1912: twelve fat volumes of text and one of indexes, taking up the story of a 'modern world' at the Renaissance and carrying it through to its own present day, two years before the First World War gave a new meaning to the word 'modern'. The *History* was to prove a publishing success, but its comments on late-nineteenth century diplomacy and politics became demonstrably and embarrassingly inaccurate by 1918. It was superseded – after two false starts and a Second World War – by the *New Cambridge Modern History*, most volumes of which are still in print.

The *Cambridge Modern* was planned by Lord Acton, at the invitation of the Syndics of the Cambridge University Press. The inspiration, however, came from their Secretary, Richard Wright. Like the Oxford Delegates, the Syndics were cautiously entering the world of scholarly publishing, and this venture was to put them in the lead for a few years. They too had left most such work to London firms like Macmillans, concentrating instead on printing bibles and the classics. Once Acton was appointed in 1895 to succeed Seeley as Regius Professor of Modern History, the Syndics asked him to be General Editor of a major work of historical scholarship.[33]

Acton had written virtually nothing, at least not for publication, but he read a great deal, and he lectured inspiringly about history, as well as about liberty. He was a big, charismatic personality, and the Syndics hoped to take advantage of that to publish a big, consequential work of historical scholarship under his direction. Acton agreed readily, plunging almost immediately into the drafting of chapter headings and lists of contributors. Although he again wrote nothing, Acton developed the structure of the work, and its premise and organization remain influential. When he died in 1902, just as the first volumes were appearing, the *CMH* was carried on by his successor A. W. Ward and subeditors G. W. Prothero and Stanley Leathes.[34]

The plan was for a book that would be as liberal, as scholarly and as ambitious as Lord Acton himself. In his first detailed proposal to the Syndics of the Press, and again in his initial directions to contributors, the General Editor called for a work that would use the principle of a division of intellectual labour. The book he imagined would have to be as colourless as possible ('We shall avoid the needless utterance of opinion and the service of a cause'). The discovery and printing of archival material meant that government secrets could now be revealed ('at last the Vatican discloses the guarded treasures of Galileo's tower'). And the completed work was intended to 'be aloof from speculation and system', bearing evidence of 'impartial reserve'.[35]

The narrative of liberty that Seeley had found so unsatisfactory in Green's work was Lord Acton's story, too. Beginning with the Reformation and Scientific Revolution, it carried on through the contrast between absolutism in France and constitutional government in England, to the French Revolution and Napoleon, and on to liberalism, industrialism and urbanization, ending with a curiously unsatisfactory coda in the later nineteenth and very early twentieth centuries.

The text of this story had to be extracted piecemeal, with varying degrees of success, from a team of contributors. The process set the pattern for a whole series of multi-volume Cambridge Histories. The Press had first wanted a History of the World, and it was Acton who insisted on lopping off the Ancient and Medieval periods and leaving a thick (and now much-contested) scar through the premodern centuries.[36] Later on, both the Ancient and Medieval periods were accorded Cambridge Histories of their own, as were the British Empire and several other historiographical constructs.

The story of Lord Acton and the founding of the *Cambridge Modern* has been told many times, but it features here as strong evidence for of the agency of publishers in the making of history books. Despite its massive scale, the *Modern History* resembles other studies where the relationships of more literary and popular historians (like Charlotte Yonge or Edward Freeman, or J. R. Green or Oscar Browning) with their literary and commercial publishers (like Macmillans or Longmans or Griffith & Farran) reveal the publisher's influence.

This time the influential person was the Press Secretary, the formidably competent lawyer and scholar Richard T. Wright. The *Cambridge Modern History* (*CMH*) was Wright's idea; he sold it not only to his colleagues on the Press Syndicate but also to the general editor, Lord Acton. Wright's agency is not, however, apparent in an illustrated pamphlet of which he was the anonymous author, and which has formed the basis for some of the earlier studies describing the inception and history of the *CMH*. The 1907 pamphlet, *The Cambridge Modern History, an Account of its Origin, Authorship and Production*, begins with lengthy quotations from Acton's initial report to the Press, in a section on the planning of the History, followed by accounts of the editors and writers and of its scholarly value, and then by extracts from some of the set-piece chapters on turning-point events (Fig. 3.5).

Moving from history to publishing history, there follows a section on the printing, binding and shipping of the *History* itself, where a description of the various binding materials available makes a coy reference to the order form which appears at the end of the book. It becomes clear that the pamphlet was produced to advertise the series, and hence should be treated with caution as a source of evidence for the events of 1896 to 1902. The 'chapter' about the 'Terms on Which the History May Now be Obtained' makes it clear that this publication is a special-offer marketing-piece. The Syndics, it said, were of opinion that 'a large number of readers and students would be glad of the opportunity of acquiring so important a work by small periodical payments'.[37] The pamphlet ends with a tear-out order form, offering not only four variant bindings with related prices, but also a specially-designed fumed-oak book-case.

As it happens, sales were slumping in 1907, four volumes from the finish, and the Press was motivated to go in for direct marketing on the instalment plan. While the pamphlet is a useful source for

Acton's conception of the History, its unique value – as an insight into how the Press and the book trade thought about the work – has been overlooked.

Marketing materials, like all documents, have their own obvious built-in limitations and the scholar wants to know the shadowy dealings behind the scenes. Fortunately, we also have access to manuscript documents created by Acton's two chief lieutenants. The better-known and more historiographically respectable was A. W. Ward, whose retirement at age 60 from his appointment at Manchester freed him up to work on the Modern History.[38] The other was a younger man, W. A. Archbold, a Fellow of Peterhouse, who acted as a research assistant and secretary to Acton.[39] Archbold's letters give an unparalleled view of the negotiations with contributors. Wright, the Press Secretary, agreed to pay Archbold's salary, and to supply an honorarium to Ward.[40]

Archbold was not only well-qualified (he could stand up to the master when necessary, albeit in a very respectful way) but also well-connected. 'I have found holes for nearly all the pegs but I want to write to you about them,' he reported on one occasion, and went on to warn that Acton's ideas about a potential contributor were ill-founded, and suggest who might do what. 'There are plenty of clever men, but I don't like merely to write down the name of a man who would read up the subject if asked to, or at all events not too many of such.'[41] Archbold was not aware of many clever women. Only two 'lady contributors' were regarded as 'suitable' because they were 'thoroughly teachable' – Acton's friend Charlotte, Lady Blennerhassett and Frederick William Maitland's protégée, the Newnham College scholar Mary Bateson.[42] Archbold thought Roger Fry would do very well to write about the history of art, primarily because 'he is young & not obstinately set up in business so to speak with a set of artistic notions'. Acton might have found it difficult to influence more established critics of art, but he could 'take Fry & breathe into him & he will work away in the lines that you wish'.[43] On the other hand Archbold looked askance at Acton's wish to involve Flora Shaw, whose journalism had been published in *The Times*, in writing for the *CMH* about colonial matters.[44]

Project management, the prestige of contributors, collaboration: we can pursue these elements by looking more closely at Wright. He was the first to be appointed to a senior staff post at the University Press, that of Secretary. It was Wright who persuaded Acton to contemplate the general editorship of a modern history; he also convinced the Syndics to sponsor it. Certainly Frederick William

3.5 (*pages 66 and 67*) *The Cambridge Modern History: an Account of its Origin, Authorship and Production*, 1907.

MAKERS OF CAMBRIDGE HISTORIES

9. *Professor C. W. Previté-Orton*
10. *Dr Z. N. Brooke*
11. *J. B. Bury*
12. *Professor S. A. Cook*
13. *Professor F. E. Adcock*
14. *Mr M. P. Charlesworth*
15. *Professor N. H. Baynes*
16. *Mr C. T. Seltman*

Maitland, the historian on the Press Syndicate, was an important academic voice in the process; but on the business side, Wright was the person with the bright idea at the right moment. He was a former Lecturer in Law, who had only recently become Secretary, with a self-defined mandate to make the University Press behave like a modern publisher at last, after decades of hesitancy about what it should be doing apart from bibles, the University's printing jobs, and a few editions of the classics.[45] Acton unburdened and unbuttoned himself to Wright, referring to

> the importance of your proposal, that we should have an Introductory chapter, describing the ideas, the motives, the problems, the conditions of European life that the middle ages made over to those that were to follow. ... The Introduction will, as you say, be a means of pitching our note and setting up our standard, and it will strengthen our hold over contributors. It might even do more if you thought it practicable to entertain the idea I am going to submit to you, in the freedom of private correspondence.

And Acton went on to suggest that this crucial transition chapter be pre-printed, fully documented, both in English and in translation to 'show the world on what foundation of unseen research we intend our smooth structure to be erected, and would tell our writers what we expect of them. Perhaps it would increase my authority with them, and would dissipate the suspicion that our work is done by beginners.'[46] Wright was Acton's sounding-board, and his paymaster.

The idea for the introductory chapter, which was central to the plan (although never properly written), was not Acton's, it was Wright's, and it came from his publisher's knowledge, that readers would need a clear starting point from which to orient their experience of the *History*, and possibly he also anticipated the need to keep contributor/collaborators, especially non-English ones, under control.

Ward's participation in the editorship, masterminded by Wright, was more troublesome than Archbold's, because Ward had a formidable scholarly reputation of his own to maintain. As the volumes began to appear and problems with contributors multiplied, Ward asked to have his name added to Acton's as a joint editor. This was acceptable to the historian, but not to his publisher. Wright and the Syndics refused to dilute the power of Acton's famous name on their expensive book – or rather, they refused until Acton's death made the change a necessity.[47]

The principle of collaboration among historians, which is

implicit in the design of the *Cambridge Modern History*, is worth exploring.[48] Acton's general editorship and that of his successors was a model chosen and developed by the Cambridge University Press. It was not adopted at Oxford, where monograph series became the rule. Later on, in the 1920s, the *Cambridge Modern* and other multi-volume collaborative histories were to be described at Oxford as the Cambridge 'sausages' and 'regarded as a confession of failure: [in Oxford's view] the soundest principle was one man one book'. Peter Sutcliffe reports this in his *Informal History* of the Oxford University Press and continues: 'The prevailing opinion in Cambridge was that this was sour grapes, and it is true that one of the objections to the Cambridge "sausages" in Oxford was that they used up too many authors at once, authors who might have been better employed writing books of their own for Oxford.'[49] From an academic publisher's point of view, one large collaborative work made a lot of sense: the massive investment could be focused, and to some extent controlled, by the management of contributors through the professional authority of the editors.

From the perspective of most academic historians, the Oxford view – that monographs are best, one author/one book – was to become a matter of consensus for most of the twentieth century. But this was not so in the 1890s, when Wright's and Acton's ambitious design for a new format was still in the planning stage. As bibliographical scholars have demonstrated in other contexts, we take publishing formats for granted at our peril. Publishing format means more than just the width of margin and leading of type and style of binding, although all these are crucial. The distinction between scholarly and popular history was a distinction not between genres, but between diverse literary forms and bibliographical formats. A similar contest over textual and material form took place in the realm of the novel, where late-Victorian literary naturalism seemed out of place in the old three-decker format. In history, too, there was experimentation about how the genre was to be written, for whom, and why. The multi-volume collaborative history, aspiring to be comprehensive, was an innovation, as fresh and risky in its own way as Gissing or George Moore seeking to introduce gritty reality into their fictional works.[50]

For contemporary historians, publisher-enforced collaboration might even, in a curious way, have reinforced the Rankean doctrine of objectivity. Acton told his contributors that 'our Waterloo must be one that satisfies French and English, Germans and Dutch alike', and that no one reading the *Cambridge Modern History* should be able to tell where one historian laid down the pen and another took it up.[51] That doctrine contained an implication about narrative: every properly trained historian, who entered the archives and read what the documents actually said, ought to be able to report to his or her readers 'what actually happened'. Not that Ranke or Acton, or anyone, anticipated that properly trained historians would report these events in identical words, or in parallel volumes, ordered in similar chapters, with the corresponding narrative flow from one paragraph to the next. But the concept of a planned collaborative history, controlled by an authoritative scholarly editor with a Press behind him, does seem to reinforce this related concept, of unity, even homogeneity.[52]

Perhaps the historians did not even anticipate that the search for objective historical truth, carried out in Europe's archives newly opened to the investigations of appropriately professional scholars, would result in a multiplicity of books. Debate is intrinsic to historical scholarship, but these men (and their handful of women protégées) were in debate with the old narratives of their youth, still annoyingly in print. They did not always agree among themselves – but the terms of that disagreement had to do with convincing their opponent of an error, and persuading them to correct their analysis of the evidence, not necessarily in rewriting their narrative.

How many words can be found, to tell the truth about the Stuarts, or about Napoleon? Revised editions would be needed, when new documents were found and analyzed. But would there really be a need for new phrases in which to tell the acknowledged true story? Perhaps not. Acton spoke about how his generation would be able to 'dispose of conventional history ... now that all information is within reach, and every problem has become capable of solution'.[53] At a more mundane level, however, publishers, even university publishers, had to solve the recurring problem of finding new books to bring out every publishing season.

Another difficulty over collaboration immediately became apparent. Some aspects of the very recent past eluded this coolly professional narrative deployment of fact and judgment. Wright and Acton anticipated trouble over Italy – historical justifications for Italian independence were not long off the *contemporary* agenda.[54] Similarly, satisfactory answers to questions of Britain's colonial expansion were unlikely to be found in the Public Record Office. The politically-fraught nature of such problems may answer Seeley's question about why few people who pursued the historical discipline as a profession in the nineteenth century had addressed them, or undertaken the necessary research and authored the eventual monographs. A project like the *Cambridge Modern History* forced the issue. Once entered into the plan, each chapter had to be written, which meant that a contributor had to be found, if not a scholar of experience, fluency and authority, then someone into whom Lord Acton and his associates could 'breathe', inspiring them to work away within the model that the project dictated. This was an ideal impossible to reach, but the attempt to reach it is worth reconstructing.

The publishers' and editors' and contributors' (the list could go on) collective experience of making such a book is left behind at the moment of publication, rather as labour pains are forgotten when a child is born. Sometimes fragments of that experience have been preserved in the archival or printed record, but the impulse to uncover it is not very compelling when the book seems to have taken on a life of its own, breathing independently in the atmosphere of the book trade and the library, and nourished by the reader's imagination. However, a project like the *Cambridge Modern History* does not have a life independent of the contemporary factors that shaped both the text and the material form. These factors were not only ideological; they were also the commercial interests of publishers, and the cultural *mentalités* of readers – who differed as to what they wanted out of history, but agreed that their times needed it badly, and that it had to be true.

New blood at Oxford

The opposite number to Richard Wright at the Clarendon Press in Oxford was Philip Lyttelton Gell, who presided over the first dozen or so post-Macmillan years. He was appointed in 1884 to replace Bartholomew Price as Secretary to the Delegates of the Clarendon Press (and left under a cloud in 1897). He had an Oxford history degree and experience in the London publishing house of Cassell & Gilpin. Sutcliffe reports that Gell was remembered for years as 'idle, quarrelsome, and incompetent' – and mythology reported him arriving every morning at ten in a coach and pair, complete with a luncheon hamper furnished with champagne, and leaving at four.[55] Contrary to this impression is the fact that Gell, only thirty-three years of age when he arrived, suffered from ill-health due to overwork. He found the Delegates to be slow and unbusinesslike; they thought of him as impertinent and an iconoclast.

Although the Cambridge Syndics regarded the Oxford Delegates as 'a most grasping, over-reaching, imperious body' (at least so J. R. Seeley said in 1883), history-publishing at Oxford during this period may be characterized as rather cautious and conservative, plagued by the necessity, for the staff, of exercising excessive deference to senior members of the University, particularly to those who were Delegates of the Press. This often entangled Gell, like Price before him, in serious financial losses, and sometimes in unpleasant squabbles with authors.

William Stubbs continued as Oxford's most dependable historian-author, but they had to look elsewhere for scholarly editions after he became a bishop. When it became impossible for Stubbs to undertake projects himself, the Press encouraged him to keep the books coming out by working with 'one of our younger students under your supervision'. The first of these were Arthur Lionel Smith, of Balliol College, Oxford and George Walter Prothero, then University Lecturer in History at Cambridge. When Smith prepared for his own pupils an 'analysis' of Stubbs's *Documents & Charters* the Delegates overcame their 'uneasiness' over the perceived violation of copyright and urged Stubbs to agree to regularize the situation and authorize Smith's publication. After all, as Gell noted, Smith was 'the great champion of a systematic study of "Documents & Charters" here [at Oxford], & there is a general impression that such an index would increase the sale & the popularity of the book'.[56]

Beginning in 1885, Frederick York Powell became a Delegate and began to take over Stubbs's role as chief advisor for history. Powell was not trained in history but rather in Icelandic language and literature. Sutcliffe describes him as a 'maverick intellectual and dabbler in all things quaint and arcane ... [with an] incomparable gift for procrastination', but also notes Powell's 'special intuition about books', his encouragement of authors and assistance with the production process.[57] This side of Powell at work was apparent as he helped Gell to manage Sir James Ramsay, and he became even more useful when it came to dealing with the now-elderly and acerbic E. A. Freeman. Although Gell was critical of Powell, we see in their partnership over history books a lower-key version of Richard Wright's with Lord Acton at Cambridge.

Powell and Gell were increasingly busy with history projects in the mid 1880s, dealing with Hastings Rashdall on a study of medieval universities, with G. W. Kitchin on finding a modest junior scholar to update his *History of France* now that the author was Dean of Durham, and with W. H. P. Greswell on a failed 'History of

Canada'.[58] In addition to all this they began to share Macmillan's load in handling Freeman. In his late sixties, a year before his death, Freeman was finally Regius Professor of History, and still unwilling to accept the ruling of his publisher in the matter of revisions. He made extensive corrections, at the expensive proof stage, of his new *History of Sicily*, and refused to pay the cost as provided for in his standard author's contract. Freeman had long since begun to refer disparagingly to Gell as a 'shopkeeper' and now he grandly observed that 'the Press exists to print learned works'; but, as Gell told a correspondent, 'it does not necessarily exist to supplement Professors' salaries!'[59] Gell knew that the Delegates might well be intimidated, but he dug in his heels. 'Why,' he asked Powell, 'should public money be spent for Freeman on terms on which it would not be spent for Stubbs?'[60] In the end, two individual Delegates broke the impasse by guaranteeing the Press against any excess charges that might occur as a result of going ahead with setting Freeman's book up in type, and a vaguely-worded resolution made it possible for Freeman to continue taking advantage of his publisher. The Professor of History took the high ground, commenting that 'I know not how it may be in the writing of novels or in the editing of small school-books; but every one who has ever written a great work of learning must know that new knowledge is constantly coming in, that improvements are constantly suggesting themselves, up to the very last moment. In a wide field of research this must be so.'[61]

Gell was in a difficult position, placed between the Press Delegates and the Professor of History, and himself out of touch with the academic politics of the University. He wrote: 'It is always easy for anyone in charge of other people's money – like myself – to buy popularity and avoid unpleasantness by a lax administration of it – and the temptation is particularly great in a close society like that of Oxford.'[62]

It was to be a further forty years before the Oxford History of England began to appear, challenging the collaborative Cambridge 'sausages' with a linked progression of discrete historical works. But about the same time as his conflict with Freeman, Gell tried to mastermind a four-volume 'Oxford School History' of England, with Powell as general editor and intended primarily for the use of candidates at the Oxford Local Examinations. The project began in the spring of 1888; two years later Gell sought to 'stir up' the 'delinquents in the matter of the English history'.[63] These delinquent authors were Owen M. Edwards of Balliol, G. Noel

CONTENTS

PART I.—Owen M. Edwards.

ENGLAND BEFORE THE CONQUEST.

PAGE

Chap. I. The British Isles and the British People . 1
II. The Early Conquests of England . . . 3
III. Christianity and the Tribal Kingdoms . . 8
IV. The Danes and King Alfred 13
V. The Greatness of Wessex 17
VI. The Great Earls and the Danish Kings . 21
VII. The House of Godwin and the Norman Conquest 26

PART II.—R. S. Rait.

THE NORMAN KINGS OF ENGLAND.

William I (1066–1087) 31
William II (1087–1100) 35
Henry I (1100–1135) 38
Stephen (1135–1154) 41

PART III.—H. W. C. Davis.

THE HOUSE OF PLANTAGENET.

Chap. I. The Reign of Henry II (1154–1189) . . . 45
II. The Sons of Henry II (1189–1216) . . . 56
III. The Reign of Henry III (1216–1272) . . . 68
IV. Edward I (1272–1307) and Edward II (1307–1327) 80
V. Edward III (1327–1377) and Richard II (1377–1399) 96

Contents vii

PART IV.—G. N. Richardson.

LANCASTER AND YORK.

PAGE

Chap. I. Henry IV (1399–1413) and Henry V (1413–1422) 126
II. Henry VI (1422–1461) 131
III. Edward IV (1461–1483), Edward V (April–June, 1483), and Richard III (1483–1485) . . 135

PART V.—A. J. Carlyle.

THE TUDORS.

Chap. I. Henry VII (1485–1509) and Henry VIII (1509–1547) 142
II. Edward VI (1547–1553) and Mary (1553–1558) . 159
III. Elizabeth (1558–1603) 166

PART VI.—G. N. Richardson.

THE HOUSE OF STUART.

Chap. I. James I (1603–1625) 183
II. Charles I to the Outbreak of the Civil War (1625–1642) 194
III. The Civil War (1642–1649) 204
IV. The Commonwealth and the Protectorate (1649–1660) 213
V. Charles II (1660–1685) 223
VI. James II (1685–1688) 230
VII. William III and Mary (1689–1702) . . . 233
VIII. Anne (1702–1714) 240

PART VII.—W. G. Pogson Smith.

THE HOUSE OF HANOVER.

Chap. I. George I (1714–1727) and George II (1727–1760) 248
II. George III (1760–1820) 268
III. George IV (1820–1830) and William IV (1830–1837) 316
IV. Queen Victoria (1837–1901) 326
GENEALOGICAL TABLES 359
INDEX 367

3.6 (*above*) Owen M. Edwards et al., *A School History of England*, 1901.

3.7 (*right*) C. R. L. Fletcher and Rudyard Kipling, *A School History of England*, 1911.

A SCHOOL HISTORY OF ENGLAND

BY

C. R. L. FLETCHER

AND

RUDYARD KIPLING

PICTURES BY HENRY FORD

OXFORD
AT THE CLARENDON PRESS
1911

Richardson of Oriel, W. G. Pogson Smith of St John's and three others. After a further two years, only Richardson and Smith had produced manuscripts, and Edwards remained 'delinquent'. In 1893 the Assistant Secretary C. E. Doble said of Edwards: 'While he is making promises, the market for the book is passing away from us. In any case we should not be ready with our History for the candidates at the examinations of 1894.'[64] This was optimistic. Copy was finally extracted from a reluctant Owen Edwards; H. W. C. Davis was roped in during 1898; and the book was published in 1901, more than a decade after the initial idea (Fig. 3.6). The death of Queen Victoria meant one final revision, 'as it would look too ludicrous to bring the book out at such a time without some reference to it'.[65] Edwards went on to a distinguished career in Welsh education and literature, and the book which had taken so long to appear also remained in print and in use for many years. In fact Herbert Butterfield was embarrassed, when he sat his scholarship examination in 1919, to admit that the first history book he ever read was none other than the Oxford School History of England.[66]

The Fletcher-Kipling English history project took less time but was more controversial than the Oxford School History. Published in 1911, it had been written by C. L. R. Fletcher, a tutor and fellow of Magdalen College, Oxford who was known for his conservative, imperialistic and anti-catholic ideas (Fig. 3.7). Fletcher was also a Delegate of the Oxford University Press, and he disarmed the concerns of Charles Cannan and his colleagues there when he offered the services of a collaborator, Rudyard Kipling. The resulting work included twenty-three Kipling poems to embellish Fletcher's prose; it was reviewed by the *Manchester Guardian* as a deeply pernicious work even while the *Church Family Newspaper* called it a great literary event.[67] The Marxist author of a 1929 book on bias in textbooks, *Lies and Hate in Education*, characterized it as 'the worst of a disappearing type', and an example of 'deliberate incitement to preparation for war'.[68] Like other histories of England, the Fletcher-Kipling work had not lived up to the scholarly ideals of Acton and Stubbs, but it had done its propaganda work, to furnish the minds of the schoolboys who became soldiers in 1914.

Chapter 4

Historians and Publishers in an Age of War and Revolution, 1914-1929

THE COMBINATION of muddle, horror and disillusionment that characterized the First World War was particularly painful for historians.[1] Germany had been their discipline's intellectual touchstone in the project of writing a new political and military history for Britain and the world; now Germany was Britain's military and political enemy, and the intellectual superiority of German scholarship came into question. In particular, to associate Britain's constitutional history with Teutonic models now sounded unpatriotic. On the other hand, readers wanted to know what had happened, in recent German history, to instigate the militarism of 1914, and both publishers and historian-authors were ready to respond. As young men in the colleges and universities, and in the publishing houses, prepared to leave for the trenches, their seniors were faced with unanticipated problems. How would new history books in progress, and standard works ready for reprinting, need to be revised to respond to the realities of war and revolution in the new twentieth century?

A few examples will illustrate some of these problems and responses. At the age of 68, Edith Thompson was still revising and updating new editions of the 'little' *History of England* that Macmillans had first published forty-one years earlier as part of the Historical Course for Schools. She told her publisher 'I am troubled with the question, how far I am at liberty to modify the Teutonic views of my dear master E. A. Freeman. I do not think that it is *merely* their present unpopularity that weighs with me. Events have proved that, if we are Teutonic, our Teutonism is very different from that of the Germans.' Rather than every few years simply adding to her school history a paragraph on recent events, Thompson now felt impelled to go back and revise its initial chapters on what she called 'the early peopling of Europe by "Aryans" or others'.[2]

At Cambridge in 1914, the *Cambridge Medieval History* had been underway for ten years, designed as it was to replicate the successful model of the *Cambridge Modern*.[3] But progress was slow, and as the war began only one volume had been published, though authors had signed contracts for the other seven. Now the Germans among those contributors had become enemy aliens, out of reach even had their contributions still been acceptable. The stalled *Medieval History* was to take twenty-five years to complete, while its modern counterpart became increasingly unsatisfactory as it continued to sell steadily.

The publishers at Oxford spent much of this period seeking a formula and a format with which to counter Cambridge's ingenious approach to packaging historical narratives. They responded to the hostilities with a quickly-put-together but influential book by a group of historians entitled *Why We are at War*.[4] Another possibility, which seemed lucrative as well as useful, was a suggested series of 'Histories of the Belligerents' suggested by Ernest Barker. It was intended to capitalize on popular curiosity about political affairs, as well as to take advantage of Oxford expertise and publishing capacity.

One casualty of the war was a new magazine, *History*, which had been aimed at teachers and general readers, or as the masthead put it, 'the student and the expert'. The editor was Harold F. B. Wheeler, a Fellow of the Royal Historical Society and author of popular books on historical subjects (Fig. 4.1). For the four years of his editorship, Wheeler worked closely with the Historical Association, listing meetings and giving members a discount on subscriptions. But the wider audience he sought seems to have been distracted by the onset of the war. Volume 3, Number 4 included not only an editorial entitled 'The World War', but a personal plea for readers' support, and only two more issues appeared. The Historical Association, led by A. F. Pollard, took over the title and the subscription list, and began to issue *History* in a new series and a new, much plainer, format (Fig. 4.2).[5] Pollard wanted his journal to look as much like the *American Historical Review* as possible, and did not expect it to circulate outside the membership of the Association.[6] The publishers were Macmillans – the descendants of Alexander Macmillan, who had been so anxious that any historical periodical be accessible to the general public. The younger generation, however, were not committed financially; this journal was published on commission.

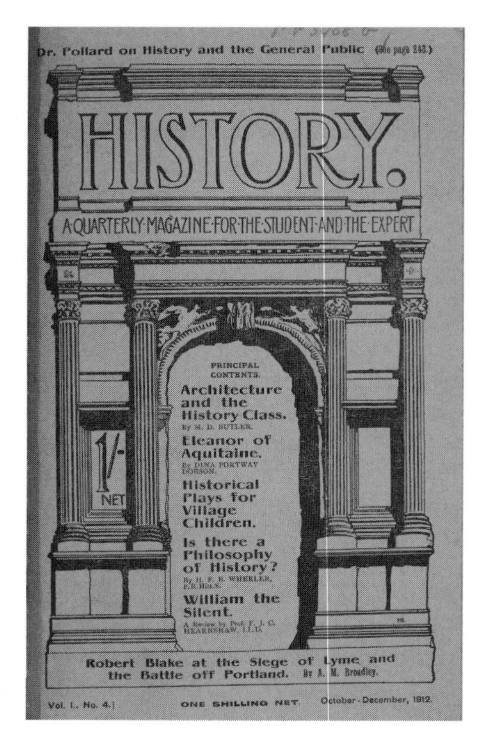

Dr. Pollard on History and the General Public (See page 243.)

HISTORY.

A QUARTERLY MAGAZINE FOR THE STUDENT AND THE EXPERT

1/- NET

PRINCIPAL CONTENTS.

Architecture and the History Class.
By M. D. BUTLER.

Eleanor of Aquitaine.
By DINA PORTWAY DOBSON.

Historical Plays for Village Children.

Is there a Philosophy of History?
By H. F. B. WHEELER, F.R.Hist.S.

William the Silent.
A Review by Prof. F. J. C. HEARNSHAW, LL.D.

Robert Blake at the Siege of Lyme and the Battle off Portland. By A. M. Broadley.

Vol. I., No. 4.] ONE SHILLING NET. October-December, 1912.

4.1 *History*, 1912.

HISTORY

THE QUARTERLY JOURNAL OF

The Historical Association

Edited by

A. F. POLLARD, M.A., Litt.D.

Fellow of All Souls' and Professor of English History in the University of London

NEW SERIES

VOL. I.

APRIL, 1916—JANUARY, 1917

MACMILLAN AND CO., LIMITED
ST. MARTIN'S STREET, LONDON
1917

4.2 *History* (new series), 1917.

Revisions and reiterations

Historic events, in the shape of war and revolution, caught up with the British historians whose intellects and imaginations had been formed in the late-Victorian decades of liberal optimism and imperial power. Men like Adolphus Ward, James Bryce and George Trevelyan responded as scholars, and again as citizens, while their younger counterparts responded also as soldiers. At the same time, readers who experienced the events of 1914-18 and their aftermath – as citizens and as soldiers – found themselves asking very different historical questions than their schoolbooks had ever asked or answered. The complacent narrative of England's liberty was now broken, not as Seeley had anticipated by a freshly optimistic narrative of empire and a British world, but by devastating losses and diplomatic bungling. In Oxford, Cambridge and London, publishers mediated as always between readers and scholar-authors, and began to imagine a new market for historical works. The chimera of comprehensiveness remained as a vision, but a new awareness of complexity threatened to overwhelm attempts to write bold new narratives for a new century.

Caught in the midst of all this was Adolphus William Ward, historian of Germany, protégé and colleague of Freeman in his younger days (when Ward was overlooked in the 1870 selection of a Regius Professor) and later Acton's trusted assistant. Ward was a student of German history and of English literature.[7] He spent over thirty years at Manchester University, where he founded the History School. He left Manchester in 1897 at the age of sixty, intending to settle in London and concentrate on historical writing; he was already involved in the editorship of the *Cambridge Modern History* and the Syndics were paying for his services. Ward was understandably touchy about being upstaged by Acton, but the situation was resolved after three years when he became Master of Peterhouse, moved to Cambridge and became indispensable to the University Press both before and after Acton's death.[8] The war was particularly distressing to Ward, who loved German culture and regarded contemporary militarism as an aberration.

The war and its aftermath created a public demand for different histories, different types of historical author, and even a different way of thinking about history itself. Macmillans had a contract with H. G. Wells for what became the *Outline of History*. And in 1918 the Clarendon Press at Oxford commissioned a book for schools, on *Movements in European History*, from D. H. Lawrence; the author was short of money and the Press was still chronically in need of suitable and competitive works for the various educational markets. The book began by declaring 'The old bad history is abolished', and claimed to seek a balance between the 'graphic' and the 'scientific'. The Press was nervous about Lawrence's reputation in light of the suppression of his novel *The Rainbow*; they published the book under the pseudonym Lawrence H. Davison in 1921.[9] It was not a failure; in fact an illustrated edition appeared in 1924, but the Epilogue Lawrence wrote at that point was judged unsuitable. In 1925 he reported having to 'maul' his text once again, to prepare it for an edition for use in the Roman Catholic schools of Ireland, removing 'every word in praise of Luther and any suggestion that the Pope had erred'.[10]

If the idea of D. H. Lawrence writing European history for school children in England (not to mention Ireland) sounds rather absurd, then it points up a desperate quest on the part of the Clarendon Press and other publishers to find something suitable for schools and general readers. In a similar vein, A. B. McKillop has made a persuasive case for Wells having leant heavily, for the structure of his 1920 *Outline of History*, upon a manuscript unethically secured via Macmillans from an obscure Canadian woman writer.[11] J. R. Green's work was still ubiquitous, as were various Epochs and other narratives; but publishers were asking who was going to re-write those books for the twentieth century.

Arthur Bryant's popularity did not really begin to flourish until the 1940s, but in 1931 the thirty-two year-old school teacher had his first history-book success with Longmans.[12] Bryant's biography of King Charles II became a Book Society selection and may have influenced the decision of the Cambridge University Press to invite Bryant to write the biography of Samuel Pepys. The Press and its Secretary S. C. Roberts had originally planned a single volume, but Bryant pressed for two. Already conscious of his literary talents and readership, Bryant told Roberts 'I believe such a volume might prove to have a far wider appeal than one could normally hope for a work of close scholarship'.[13] As both Bryant's reputation and the depth of the Pepys material became apparent, Bryant pressured Roberts to authorize a third volume.

The writer who best answered the call for a serious popular history, however, was G. M. Trevelyan, the great-nephew of Thomas Babington Macaulay. Trevelyan had taken umbrage at both Seeley's and Bury's dismissals of Macaulay as a charlatan. Trevelyan left Cambridge in 1903 for literary London, and achieved a commercial success and critical acclaim with his *England under the Stuarts* and his Garibaldi trilogy. In 1926 Longman published Trevelyan's *History of England*, the first one-volume survey since Green's in 1876.[14] Because the correspondence has not survived in Longmans' archives, the present account can throw no fresh light on that publisher's intervention in Trevelyan's writings.[15] The records that do survive, however, reveal a recurring theme of Trevelyan-envy on the part of other publishers. In 1905, again in 1922 and yet again in 1927 he refused invitations to contribute to the Cambridge Modern, Medieval and British Empire Histories respectively, and in March 1914 he declined a 'suggestion' from Cambridge that he write a history of England in the nineteenth century.[16] Two years later, Adolphus Ward was judging an unsatisfactory manuscript of a handbook of modern European history ('from Waterloo to Armageddon') in terms of how much better it might have been done by Trevelyan.[17] Ward, as a Cambridge Syndic, commented again in August 1918 on the need for a new popular work on Britain's 'national history': the sort of writer he had in mind, he said, was Trevelyan, 'in whose style there is life'. In 1929 publishers at Oxford were observing ruefully that there were 'no bestsellers among the historians', except Trevelyan, and possibly Halevy.[18] And when the same publishers were beginning, in 1929, to plan their Oxford History of England, they agreed that they were not prepared 'to offer the same outright payment for the work of a comparatively unproved man as for a book by, say G. M. Trevelyan'.[19] Clearly the compelling attraction of narrative that Seeley had dismissed thirty-five years earlier remained powerful.

Ernest Barker at Oxford

The austere and colourless history that Acton had evoked twenty years earlier was also powerful. Publishers of history books were aware of changes in historical practice and of debates over interpretation and methodology; some of them were keenly interested in such questions. Their professional interest, however, remained with producing a product that not only fitted the material and cultural conventions of the book trade but also achieved critical and commercial success within those conventions. For publishers, as for historians, there was an unspoken tension – between the established and conventional form of the history book and the new ways of thinking about the past.

The most accomplished and prolific publishers of historical

works seem to have addressed the problem by making a practice of allying themselves with certain dependable historian-authors – with individuals who could be trusted to have the publisher's interests at heart and to keep those interests in mind as they moved in academic and literary circles. Earlier examples of this practice include Macmillan's relationships with Bryce, Freeman and Green, that of the University Press at Cambridge with Acton and later Prothero, and of Oxford with Stubbs and later Frederick York Powell at the turn of the twentieth century. Beginning in 1914 and continuing well past the end of the Second World War, for the Oxford University Press, that scholar was Ernest Barker.

Born in Manchester, educated on a scholarship at Oxford, and holding appointments in history and political science at Oxford, at King's College London, finally at Cambridge, Barker was a force in political thought for half a century.[20] He was intensely loyal to the Clarendon Press, once writing that 'There is no press like the Oxford Press, even in Heaven. ... It treats an author as a scholar and a gentleman.'[21] The Press archives during the First World War and the interwar period bulge with letters to and about Barker, especially with reference to two ambitious series which he conceived. Barker wrote most of his own books as single monographs, but he imagined the Clarendon Press's books in terms of series. One was a series of 'Epochs' which never really materialized, although arguably the discussion of these non-existent books played an important part in the thinking that eventuated in an Oxford History of England. A second series was a direct response to the war.

As far back as the 1870s, publishers of histories for the school and popular markets had developed series they designated as 'Epochs'.[22] Louise and Mandell Creighton, Oscar Browning and many others had written Epochs for Longman.[23] Alexander Macmillan's Historical Course for Schools was that publisher's somewhat more high-minded version. By the late nineteenth century the most aggressive publisher in the field was Rivingtons, and in the early twentieth Methuen was also inviting historians to prepare volumes of Epochs. It was a crowded and competitive arena. In 1915, at the instigation of their new Assistant Secretary John de Monins Johnson, the Oxford University Press decided they could do better. They aimed 'to have a cheap series covering ancient and modern history, European and English, for the upper forms of schools'. The historian Henry (H.W.C.) Davis advised Johnson that the Rivington and Methuen series were out of date for university purposes; he said some volumes 'resembled articles in the

Encyclopedia Britannica or the inferior parts of the *Cambridge Modern History*'. However, it would be difficult, now, for the Press to 'get together such a team as Longmans enlisted ... the new Series [would] have to be done by comparatively junior historians', he observed, noting that 'the seniors are tired of small series'. The proposed series 'had better be planned strictly for schools'.[24] It was envisaged as eight books, of about two hundred pages each, costing a modest two shillings and sixpence. They decided to include volumes on North and South America, as well as Africa and Asia; a planned volume on Britain's colonies would overlap with these, of course, but 'there is no reason against having both'. Davis suggested a number of names but he noted that 'the men whose names naturally occur appear to be engaged in military or other service'. Indeed one promising young scholar, Llewellyn Woodward, became available to write a medieval Epoch only because he had been wounded in France.[25]

Not only had the war intervened, but Barker now took an interest in Johnson's still unrealized Epochs scheme and in 1916 'was roped in to be general editor'. Although Johnson admitted to a colleague that 'the scheme has gradually grown more ambitious & has drifted rather towards the university & away from the schoolboy', he hoped the series would nevertheless 'remain sufficiently a hybrid to attract the two markets'.[26] Now they were planned to cost four shillings and sixpence for some 200,000 words each and be documented with footnotes. Despite the labour shortage among male historians, the Oxford Publisher in London, Humphrey Milford, warned that the newly ambitious standards meant that it was risky to engage 'ladies' as contributors 'except faute de mieux'.[27]

For four years, however, nothing was written, and in 1920 in the face of rising costs Johnson returned to the scheme of small books, now rationing them to only 96 pages, 350 words to the page with maps but still no pictures – 'broad and lively sketches such as [one] might like to read to get an idea of the main developments of a period'.[28] Johnson complained to a colleague that 'Bookshop windows are simply brown in Oxford with the jackets of the Methuen six shilling series & I walk about feeling rather small – they must have hit a pretty big University market in the man who wants something sketchy & modern & cheap'.[29] In 1924 Barker 'abdicated' and the Oxford Press, faced with fresh competition, 'decided to drop the idea of a cheap Epoch series', in favour of a new series of large books. But as Johnson ruefully observed to Davis, 'to improve on an existing idea for series is not much of a stimulus which will drive on a gang of authors'.[30] By 1926, as a fresh manifestation of the old idea gathered strength, he admitted that any such series required 'a strong hand'.[31] The latter proto-series also evaporated. A. L. P. Norrington, reporting to his Press colleagues, observed that 'it is impossible to get anyone actually to write a book it seems!' Meanwhile Longmans', Rivingtons' and Methuen's well-worn Epochs remained in print and continued to flow out of the bookshops and through the classrooms.

Belligerents and ex-belligerents, a series

While he was neglecting their projected Epochs, however, Ernest Barker was hard at work for the Oxford University Press on a scheme for a different and very timely series of books aimed at general readers, the series of Histories of the Belligerents, of the nations involved in the war that was consuming the popular imagination. As Johnson described the plan to Harold Temperley, 'The volumes are frankly popular designed to give a rapid historical survey with due emphasis on tendencies'.[32] Rapidity meant that narratives began in the past, but devoted most of their space to the modern period. Two volumes appeared early, one on Prussia and one on the Balkan nations (Fig. 4.3).[33] It was more difficult, however, to find authors to contribute 'rapid surveys' of the other nations at war. Temperley never responded to a persistent invitation to write about Austria.[34] Barker and the Press worried about the political soundness of someone who wished to write about Poland. She (Miss M. A. Czaplica) had taught in London and 'had a following'. Indeed 'Mills & Boon paid something outrageous for the popular sketch of her last travels'. No wonder Johnson was 'suspicious'. So was Barker, whose remark 'this is a touchy volume', was surely an understatement in July 1916. He warned Johnson 'against attempting anything unless you are pretty sure of your author's sanity', and added that 'the colour that a writer gives to his views of past history will show his views about the present and future; and unless one is careful, one might get into trouble with e.g. the Russian papers'.[35] They asked the American historian R. B. Merriman to write two books, one on Spain and one on Spanish South America, informing him that the Belligerents series had 'been a great success' with 'a big and rapidly growing public'. Moreover it was 'important to get a large body of intelligent public opinion beforehand with regard to the world-situation as it [would] have to be settled at the making of peace'.[36] A similar invitation, couched in terms of public service, went to G. L. Beer, to write on the United States.[37]

THE EVOLUTION
OF
PRUSSIA

THE MAKING OF AN EMPIRE

BY

J. A. R. MARRIOTT, M.A.
FELLOW AND MODERN HISTORY TUTOR OF WORCESTER COLLEGE

AND

C. GRANT ROBERTSON, M.A., C.V.O.
FELLOW OF ALL SOULS
AND MODERN HISTORY TUTOR OF MAGDALEN COLLEGE

OXFORD
AT THE CLARENDON PRESS
1915

4.3 J. A. R. Marriott and C. Grant Robertson, *The Evolution of Prussia*, 1915.

By the time the Press got back to thinking about South America, however, the war was over and Charles Cannan told J. S. Mann 'Our Belligerent Series is turning into Histories of the Nations'.[38] Austria and Poland were still in the works, and by 1922 it was being described in-house as the 'Ex-Belligerent Series'.[39]

Barker had abandoned the putative Epochs series in 1924, and the History of Nations (formerly Belligerent) Series was tailing off about the same time. It was a further five years before the first discussions of an Oxford History of England. Despite his academic appointments in London and later in Cambridge, Barker's work for the Oxford Press continued, and he became involved in yet another history scheme during the 1939-45 war, that was to echo the enthusiasm of this younger self during 1917-18 (see chapter 5). He had many other preoccupations, however, and despite the trust placed in him for consultation on histories by the staff of the Press, it is worthwhile to emphasize that Barker was primarily a political thinker, rather than a historical researcher. He was not directly involved in the great interwar project of the Clarendon Press, the Oxford History of England. Barker's energetic advocacy of both conventional and contemporary history contributed significantly, however, to the shaping of what became the Press's flagship historical enterprise.

Imagining an Oxford History of England

The Oxford History of England eventually became the Clarendon Press's answer to Cambridge's multi-volume, multi-author histories which had begun in 1896 when Richard Wright and the Syndics persuaded Lord Acton to undertake the Cambridge Modern History. The term used to describe this format in Cambridge was 'syndicated', and later 'collaborative' histories. In Oxford, as we have seen, they were referred to disparagingly as 'sausages' or 'sausage-machines'. The alternative principle of 'one-man-one-book', preferred in Oxford, was reiterated frequently. Each discrete volume should evidence a distinct authorial voice and a recognizable scholarly authority – but such books would nevertheless exist in series, connected by format, price and title, as well as by the guiding hand of a general editor, and marching in chronological sequence from the beginning to the end of history.[40] More ambitious than any series of Epochs, more scholarly than any schoolbook or History of Nations, the Oxford History of England aimed both at the general reader and at educators. The school and university markets in Britain and the English-speaking world now included not only the British Empire but also the United States.

When the new series was first contemplated in January of 1929, Assistant Secretary A. L. P. Norrington and his Junior Assistant, Kenneth Sisam, were working closely with G. N. (George Norman) Clark. Leisurely conversations turned urgent when they discovered that another publisher – not the Cambridge 'Tabs', as they called the Syndics and their staff, but George Bell and Sons – were already talking to Oxford authors about a similar series.

For both Oxford and Bell the time was ripe. The Longman and Methuen series were now twenty years old; not very much history had been written in those two decades, because of the war, but now in the late 1920s research was more active and output was growing. Every historian who was over thirty years of age and under sixty had had their work interrupted by the war. Most of them were in a hurry: the scholarly and literary work schedules of Victorian historians, habitually taking five years to write a book as did Green, must now have seemed impossibly leisured. Although Clark recognized that historical writers should be steeped in both recent and earlier knowledge, he also knew that there were 'several periods for which the men best qualified in this way [were] not good writers, [not] sufficiently learned, who adhere[d] to an old-fashioned point of view'. In his opinion 'the best results in some of these difficult periods would be got by choosing young men and telling them not to be in too great a hurry'.[41] Although Clark knew this was a risky policy he probably did not anticipate that it was to take twenty years to complete the series, not to mention another world war.

In January 1929, Clark and Norrington were guardedly optimistic. They contemplated an English History in twelve volumes, 'by experts, saleable separately ... but designed to form a series which, by its weight, could impose itself upon libraries etc.'. Norrington told one of the Delegates, 'It seems a great opportunity for forestalling the Syndics, who seem to be getting to the end of their sausages and are likely to turn to monographs next.'[42] They wanted an increased emphasis on economic and social history, and more attention to geography. Conscious of their reading public, however, they left the medieval and early modern periods to one side, and focused on finding a 'really potent star' to write the volume planned to cover the period from 1870 to their present day, the 1920s. Clark admitted to having 'envious thoughts of Winston', but knew that the Clarendon Press couldn't afford him, even though they would have paid Winston Churchill more than a less potent star such as H. A. L. Fisher.[43] Nor did they believe Churchill would consent to write on the Press's terms, within the constraints of an orderly and connected series.

At the same time Oxford politics had to be considered, especially where the History Faculty intersected with the Press Delegacy. The 'danger point' was the irascible Charles Cruttwell, who was writing his own history of the Great War and who had to be handled with care.[44] But when the scheme came before the Delegates in June, the difficulty was overcome. So was the confusion when the Oxford University Press publisher in London, Humphrey Milford, as well as the New York office, complained of not being informed. Both were told that the initial stages had been handled in secrecy because of the threat from Bell's planned series.[45] William Hogarth, the OUP's staff person in New York, thought there should be an advisory committee of leading American historians of Britain, at least if it were 'to be an undertaking anything like on the scale of the Cambridge Modern History'. He drew the Oxford men's attention to 'a strong feeling here that English history prior to the eighteenth century is the common property of English and American historians', and remarked that 'some move of this kind might be politic and might gain an authoritative position for the History in this country'. The suggestion was politely dismissed, in terms of the format of the series. A collaborative work like the *Cambridge Modern* would have been able to use American contributors, but in this case the very capable general editor of a projected series of monographs was being left to 'pick his own team', from Englishmen and primarily from Oxonians.[46]

'The view taken in the office,' stated an internal memorandum, 'is that this is not a gold-mine, but would probably do quite well; that we have tended, in recent years, to produce books rather on the fringe than at the centre of historical studies, and that it is better worth while, from every point of view, to go for an ambitious venture than to content ourselves with monographs of a highly special kind.' Not only had they forestalled a London publisher from poaching on their authors, but now Oxford had a historical project more modern than Cambridge's vaunted *Modern History.* When the question arose of giving the series a name, some feared that 'Oxford History of England' might sound an echo of *Cambridge Modern History* but G. N. Clark regarded the title as 'equivalent to giving the book its blue'.[47]

More histories at Cambridge

At Cambridge, meanwhile, the University Press had been through what David McKitterick has characterized as 'a difficult period', and the collaborative histories were using up all the academic resources that could be fed into them, contributions from Cambridge, London, Oxford, Manchester, Scotland, Ireland, the Empire, the USA and continental Europe.[48] Adolphus Ward was now a Syndic of the Press as well as Master of Peterhouse. He reported at length in August 1918 on a variety of proposals for new or revised works of history. Four of these are of particular interest.

There had been talk of preparing an abridgement of the *Cambridge Modern History*, a project Ward opposed. Speaking as a senior editor, he reasoned that neither the multiplicity of authorial viewpoints nor the work's structure lent itself to abridgement; nor could a single-volume version include the bibliographies which were in many ways its *raison d'être*. He was more supportive of the idea of preparing a new national history: 'a large (though not necessarily a very large) History of England'. It should be 'a history of the people and of ideas in a wider sense even than Green's. It should ... include the outlines of the history of our colonies and of British India,' but not of the United States.

There was a third possibility. Ward hoped that the early discussions of preparing a *Cambridge Ancient History* would reach fruition in 'a tripartite Cambridge History' – Ancient, Medieval and Modern. And finally, he made the initial suggestion for 'yet another historical work of a wider scope, for which I think there is, or ought to be, a growing demand'. This eventually became the *Cambridge History of British Foreign Policy*. Ward's proposals were ambitious.

Despite his editorship of the multi-authored *Cambridge Modern History* and his support for extending the model in new areas, Ward had severe criticisms of the collaborative form when it came to the narrative of England's own history. He wanted the new national narrative to emphasize social and intellectual trends, and to underplay military and political matters. He also aimed for 'unity of authorship, or at all events a very limited joint authorship, which implies constant discussion and final agreement between the authors'. Ward recognized the limitations of the enforced collaboration produced by Press-instigated editorial projects. This imagined work 'should be of metal thoroughly fused, and written throughout in an effective and sympathetic style'. Like J. R. Green, the author should devote years to the task, 'and make it part of his life'. Ward's ideal writer was Trevelyan, whose writing was lively 'and who I should think has much of the necessary learning ... In any case, I would not start the book, till I were sure of the man.'[49]

Ward's 1918 memorandum did not discuss at any length the Cambridge Historical Series, edited by George Walter Prothero, his *Modern History* co-editor. Prothero had been Professor of History at Edinburgh but then moved to London to edit the *Quarterly Review*.[50] The series had been in progress since 1896 and now amounted to some seventeen titles, devoted to the histories of nations over the past four centuries. It was solid, but neither flashy nor profitable. Prothero blamed the unprepossessing format, and criticized the reading public for being unprepared to swallow serious history. In May 1913 he had told A. R. Waller, the new Secretary: 'I am sorry to hear that so few books in the series pay their way. I don't know how that is, for most of the volumes have run into two or three editions; but I believe you are right about the format. I suppose it would have been better if they had looked more important.' But format and price were, of course, in the hands of Waller and the Syndics. As with Oxford's History of the (formerly Belligerent) Nations, the difficulty with a historical series was that it imposed a certain geographical imperative. When E. J. Payne was replaced by A. F. Kirkpatrick as potential author for a book on South America, Prothero noted that not only was a good short book on that subject needed, but that the series would be incomplete without it.[51]

Literary style was as much of a problem in the series as public interest and historical accuracy: Prothero observed that A. J. Grant's book on the French monarchy did not appear 'to have got the ear of the public, and his style, tho' quite decent, is not brilliant or attractive. There is likely to be more enhanced interest in French History owing to the war,' he went on, 'but this would probably only affect the history of quite modern times.' Meanwhile, there was nothing better in print in the English language on this particular period than Grant's book. Waller proposed a larger format and Prothero agreed that the series should be gradually transformed to 'ordinary 8vo'. A few years later, he remarked that 'The books are, I hope, important enough to appear in the more dignified and imposing shape'. But in 1921 Prothero wanted a revised and updated edition of William Miller's *The Ottoman Empire* although the first had not yet sold out. 'The public,' in his opinion, was 'strangely averse from sound information, while ready to swallow any amount of ginger-beer gossip.' In March of 1922 Prothero was 'horrified by the balance-sheet', on his series, though still uncomprehending that a book that had gone through several editions could register a loss.[52] The books appeared on some university reading lists, and revised editions were still being published in the mid-1930s, but they were not suitable for the much more lucrative school market (Fig. 4.4).

CAMBRIDGE HISTORICAL SERIES

Edited by G. W. PROTHERO, Litt.D., LL.D , Honorary Fellow of King's College, Cambridge, Editor of the "Quarterly Review," and formerly Professor of History in the University of Edinburgh.

The Volumes already published are indicated by an asterisk, those not so marked are in hand, for which the orders are registered, and others will be added from time to time.

***1. The French Monarchy, 1483—1789.** By A. J. GRANT, M.A., Professor of History in the Yorkshire College, Leeds. With 4 Maps. In 2 vols.

2. Germany and the Empire, 1493—1792. By A. F. POLLARD, M.A., late sub-editor of the "Dictionary of National Biography," and author of "England under Protector Somerset."

3. Italy in disunion, 1494—1792. By Mrs H. M. VERNON (K. Dorothea Ewart), late scholar of Somerville College, and author of "Cosimo de' Medici."

***4. Spain; its greatness and decay, 1479—1788.** By MARTIN A. S. HUME, author of "Philip II," "The Courtships of Elizabeth," &c. With an Introduction by EDWARD ARMSTRONG, M.A., Fellow of Queen's College, Oxford, author of "Elizabeth Farnese," "Lorenzo de' Medici," &c. With 2 Maps. Second Edition, revised and corrected.

5. Eastern Europe, 1453—1792.

***6. The Revolutionary and Napoleonic Era, 1789—1815.** By J. HOLLAND ROSE, Litt.D., author of "Life of Napoleon I." With 6 Maps and Plans. Fourth Impression. Rs. 2–14.

7. Modern France, 1815—1900. By W. A. J. ARCHBOLD, M.A., author of "The Somerset Religious Houses"; and late sub-editor of the "Dictionary of National Biography."

8. Modern Germany, 1815—1889. By J. W. HEADLAM, M.A., author of "Bismarck and the Foundation of the German Empire," &c. In 2 vols.

***9. The Union of Italy, 1815—1895.** By W. J. STILLMAN, L.H.D., formerly "Times" correspondent in Rome, and author of "The Life of Crispi," &c. With 4 Maps. Second Edition.

10. Modern Spain, 1815—1898. By H. BUTLER CLARKE, M.A., author of "The Cid Campeador," "Spanish Literature," &c.

4.4 Cambridge Historical Series, 1904.

The Cambridge collaborative histories

There were five collaborative history projects underway at Cambridge during this period. All four of the *Medieval History*, the *History of India*, the *Ancient History* and the History of *British Foreign Policy* were published, but a fifth, the projected new edition of the *Cambridge Modern History*, was overtaken by events. A cheap reprint had been issued in 1934, but historians and publishers alike realized that too much had changed to allow of any but the most minor of revisions to the very unsatisfactory Volume 12 on the late nineteenth and early twentieth centuries. But despite the pervasive problem of revision, the model of collaborative histories, branded with the Cambridge name and imprint, had become institutionalized.

The German and Austrian contributors to the *Medieval History* were suddenly unreachable at the outbreak of war in 1914. At first the editors and publishers decided to delay, but eventually they realized it was necessary to replace the 'enemy aliens' with contributing historians who were citizens of allied countries. Only two or three of the seven German-authored chapters were by 'first-rate authorities', but the authorities' intellectual status was irrelevant in view of the state of British public opinion; and nor did opinion in Germany permit their scholarly work to appear in an English-language publication.[53] P. A. Linehan has shown how, as late as 1920, some of these contributors had still not been replaced and as communications between Britain and Germany re-opened, it became necessary to enter again into discussion.[54]

By 1921 the book trade had begun to assume that the Press had abandoned its *Medieval History*.[55] The effects of the First World War, on the scholarship of the Middle Ages, reverberated long after the armistice. J. R. Tanner was joined by Zachary Brooke and Charles Previté-Orton as co-editors in 1922. They discovered that few male researchers were available since the war. Nor did the women of their own generation seem as dependably conventional and deferential as Edith Thompson and Mary Bateson had been in the past. Against his colleagues' better judgement, Previté-Orton commissioned a chapter on medieval literature from the Arthurian scholar Jessie Weston, only to receive a script that was almost, but not quite 'a rhapsody on phallic worship'. Brooke joked that Tanner, as well as Previté-Orton who should have known better, had been 'misled by [Weston's] handwriting into believing her to be a worthy associate of our most revered maiden aunts'.[56] The academic filters through which male scholars could be evaluated did not work well for the now-ubiquitous women writers of history. For most of them, training and experience had been gained outside of the academic network where dons recommended their protégées to publishers.

The history of India presented very different problems than did medieval Europe. E. J. Rapson, Professor of Sanskrit, was asked to draw up a plan for a large-scale history of India after he had submitted a one-volume 'little book' on Ancient India, and after Richard Wright had visited India in 1911 to sell Cambridge bibles and the *Encyclopedia Britannica*.[57] In Rapson's view there was a 'boom in history just now' in India. But he warned that the problems of research and composition were immense – perhaps greater than those encountered by Acton and his team of experienced scholars of the modern history of Europe. Just as Freeman had needed his own *General Sketch* of European history as a model for contributors to Macmillan's Historical Course for Schools, Rapson asked the Cambridge Press to rush the printing of his small book as a guide to his own contributors, who had started work in 1913.[58] As he explained in 1919, 'The plan of this work differs from that of the other large Histories undertaken by the Press. It covers a very large period — from about 1200 BC to the present day. That is to say it attempts to do for the sub-continent of India what we are projecting to do for the continent of Europe & Western Asia in three distinct publications — the Ancient, Medieval & Modern Histories.'[59] This explained the necessity of having three editors, Rapson himself, Sir Wolseley Haig and Henry Herbert Dodwell, given that no single scholar could or would have undertaken the whole project. The modern sections (the so-called Muhammedan and British periods) were relatively straightforward, because all the primary materials for volume three were already in print and several potential contributors at hand. But the first two volumes required original research, not only in manuscript sources but in the archaeological record.

Rapson thought it would be unwise to publish the volumes in chronological order. The ancient one would not only take longer than others but was of reference and scholarly interest, rather than appealing to the general reader. By 1923 the plan had expanded to six volumes, and in 1926 an unusual bibliographical and commercial arrangement was made. Volumes five and six covering India in the *Cambridge History of the British Empire* were to be identical to the two volumes on British India in the *Cambridge*

History of India.[60] There were, of course, complex negotiations about editorial responsibility and format. As with the *Cambridge Modern History*, the editors and publishers also discussed the possibility of a profitable abridgement: Dodwell mooted 'the desirability of producing an alternative to [Vincent] Smith's *Oxford History of India* which is definitely bad (& unpopular) as a text-book'.[61] He suggested that the three editors of the Cambridge history might prepare a book with two hundred pages on Hindu India, two hundred on Muslim India, and four hundred on the European period. 'This (if done) could then form the basis for a school abridgement.' This project foundered, however, because Rapson was unable to produce a manuscript and no alternative contributor could be found.[62]

Where the *Cambridge History of India* was prepared with an eye to the market, that of *British Foreign Policy* sprang from patriotic and pacifist motives. Conceptualized in 1918, it was to be a co-operative work like the *Modern* and *Medieval Histories*. Ward's memorandum had stressed 'the real national usefulness' of such a book, stating that if it were not part of university curricula then it ought to be. The impetus was diplomatic and political rather than historiographical: he envisaged two or three volumes on the period 1815-1914 (later amended to 1783-1919) 'not too long or too much encumbered with documents ... of which the last [volume] would naturally not appear for a few years'. This long view was reflected in his advice that the chosen editors should be young men. George P. Gooch was forty-six: he first had to finish a confidential appointment in the Foreign Office in connection with the peace negotiations. However, neither H. A. L. Fisher nor Prothero was prepared to join Gooch in the editorship; instead his collaborator was the elderly Ward himself.[63] (The Press Secretary S. C. Roberts later remembered Ward, still actively editing in his eighties, complaining that one chapter was troublesome: it was 'a bit lively'.[64]) Gooch and Ward were unfazed by writing history before all the archival materials were available. But world events again outstripped the cautious practices of the historical discipline. In 1943 Gooch – himself now seventy – had to admit that the twenty-year-old Volume 3 ought not to be reprinted, 'as we wrote before the opening of the archives of the Great Powers'.[65]

The *Ancient History* was the earliest chronologically but the last in terms of publication of the tripartite set of Cambridge Histories. *India* and *British Foreign Policy* were conceived of separately, as was the *Cambridge History of English Literature* (with which the indefatigable Adolphus Ward was also involved). Waller had begun planning the *Ancient History* project, first with Leonard Whibley and then with J. B. Bury around 1918, but Bury died and from 1925 the senior editor was Frank Ezra Adcock. Like other editors, he discussed with the Press the possibility of publishing an abridgement of his multi-volume collaborative work: but Adcock warned in 1925 that 'a cheaper form might have the air of a text book and might, to some people, injure the standing of the whole work and be a grievance to some contributors who expected their work to appear only in the full dignity of the main History'.[66] Like his predecessors, Adcock had to worry about contributors, balancing distinguished (but over-committed) 'names' against dependable writers of straightforward prose, and younger scholars (who might be available for revisions two or three decades hence) against their better-known seniors. However he observed that a competent but unknown contributor did not present a problem: 'The only "name" needed is the word "Cambridge" and by now the reputation of the Ancient History, whatever it is, is well established,' he said in 1927.[67]

Not until the auspicious year of 1939 did the Press celebrate the completion of the whole three-part series, thirty-three volumes in all.

The Power sisters and Cambridge histories for children

At the same time as Cambridge wrestled with the complexities of multi-volume, multi-authored (and sometimes multi-editored) histories, they were also publishing small and attractive books for children. Eileen Power, the medievalist, was 33 years of age in 1922 when the Press published her scholarly *Medieval English Nunneries*.[68] Soon after that Power wrote what she called 'a rather "popular" little book' for Methuen, called *Medieval People*.[69] Her sister Rhoda Power was also a writer, though not a scholar. Roberts, the Press Secretary, encountered Eileen Power in the University Library and suggested that the two sisters collaborate on children's books of history. Power had assumed that the Press only published 'tombstones' and would not be interested in 'a little book', but Roberts retorted, 'How do you think we can provide the money for your tombstones if we don't have the chance of making it on something more popular.'[70] She told him she and Rhoda were both 'much attracted' by his idea of 'an introduction to social history by means of scenes from the life of the past, as they would have appeared to a child of the period'.[71] The collaboration – of Roberts,

Rhoda and Eileen Power – resulted in *Boys and Girls of History* (Fig. 4.5).

Like Macmillan four decades earlier, Roberts and his staff were wary of having the word 'Children' in the title.[72] Eileen Power wrote to Roberts of her enthusiasm, she 'tingled in the fingers' to get started on the boy king's working day, or that of the boy actor in the Middle Ages. Other lives were 'more ordinary, but must go in if the book is to be a social history reader. We can do them all from original sources; & if you will let us have some nice pictures,' she concluded, 'it ought to make a jolly little book'.[73] The arrangement between the two sisters was that Rhoda did the writing while Eileen supervised the research and the historical accuracy. By 1926 Eileen Power was rather chagrined to find that 'All my historical colleagues keep rushing up to tell me how much they like Boys & Girls; indeed I have an uneasy conviction that they think it the best thing I have done, which, seeing that my sister did it, is rather chastening.'[74] The books and their sequels were picked up in the United States by Macmillans and remained in print through the twenties and thirties, and the BBC later broadcast stories for children by Rhoda Power and lectures on history by Eileen Power.

At this stage the Oxford Press was thinking about children as readers of history only in their classroom aspect, still selling the unsatisfactory 1901 School History of England and indeed 'Lawrence H. Davison's' 1921 *Movements in European History* while the Cambridge Syndics and Secretary were combining the authority of Eileen Power with the sprightliness of her sister Rhoda to publish books that children read at home.

London publishers 1914-29

The university presses were not, of course, the only publishers of history books during the First World War and its aftermath. But both the nineteenth-century dominance of Macmillans and Longmans, and the diffidence of Oxford and Cambridge University Presses about becoming academic publishers, were now, emphatically, themselves things of the past. Now the London houses were associated with popular histories, and particularly with illustrated books – with works that reached a wider market. They sought authors with the 'brilliance' of A. G. Bradley, author of *The Fight with France for North America*. Harold Temperley said of Bradley, 'He is not in any sense an original historian – but he makes good

4.5 (*above and below*) Eileen and Rhoda Power, *Boys and Girls of History*, 1926, and *More Boys and Girls of History*, 1928.

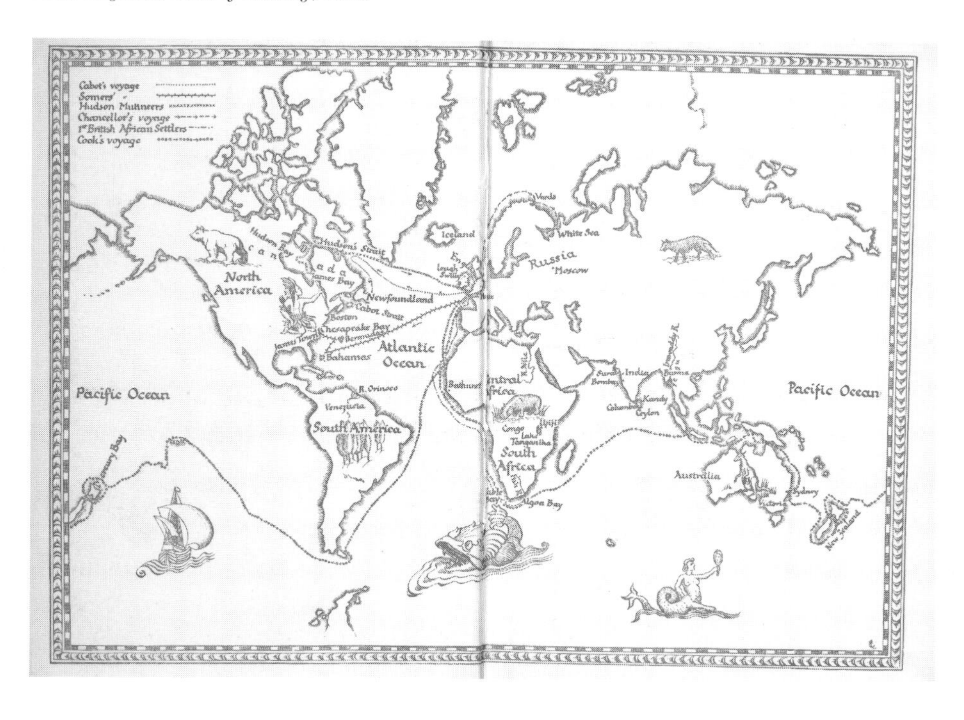

pictures for the public – and throws in a dash of scholarship to varnish them.'[75] His publisher was Constable.

Macmillans had become a global operation and were publishing schoolbooks for the whole of the British Empire, and particularly for India. From 1916, as we have seen, the firm published the journal *History* on commission for the Historical Association. Macmillans were still working with Alice Green on reprints and updates of J. R. Green's *Short History* and other works, and they remained intensely loyal to the memory of the man who had given them the gold-mine that was Green. In 1923 Alice Green wrote to Sir Frederick Macmillan asking him arrange for repair of a watch that the firm had given her late husband as a wedding-present almost half a century earlier.[76]

One promising Macmillans project was interrupted by the outbreak of the war. Charles Harding Firth, the historian of early modern England, had in 1904 become Regius Professor of History at Oxford and in 1906 President of the Historical Association. He was highly qualified, though regarded as rather a dull writer, which was perhaps why Macmillans had encouraged him to take charge of an illustrated edition of Macaulay's *History of England*. For his part, Firth allied himself with Macmillans because he disliked the efforts of the Clarendon Press; he regarded them as unsatisfactory publishers, and wished that Macmillans, rather than the Press, had taken charge of the *Dictionary of National Biography*.[77] In 1913 Frederick Macmillan sent Firth a 'very liberal advance' (of £300) and the first two volumes were published and reviewed early in 1914. Firth was particularly excited about the release of Volume 12, which dealt with Londonderry and the Battle of the Boyne. 'In view of the present political crisis,' he told Macmillan, 'this volume & chapter will be exceptionally interesting to the public.' But the index had been entrusted to an Edinburgh man, B. Gray, who became a lieutenant in a Scottish regiment. 'So the war,' Firth noted, 'has stopped his work' (Fig. 4.6).[78] The 1914-18 war stopped, or interrupted, the work of many men; it also presented a few women with the opportunity to work at historical research and writing. Edith Thompson again revised her *History of England* in 1918, excusing delays in meeting due dates because of her war work in the local Food Controller's office.[79]

In the postwar years, and in the 1920s, history-book-publishing was largely a matter of names. Macaulay's still loomed large enough for Macmillans to invest in a splendid illustrated edition. Trevelyan's was in demand by publishers in London, Oxford and

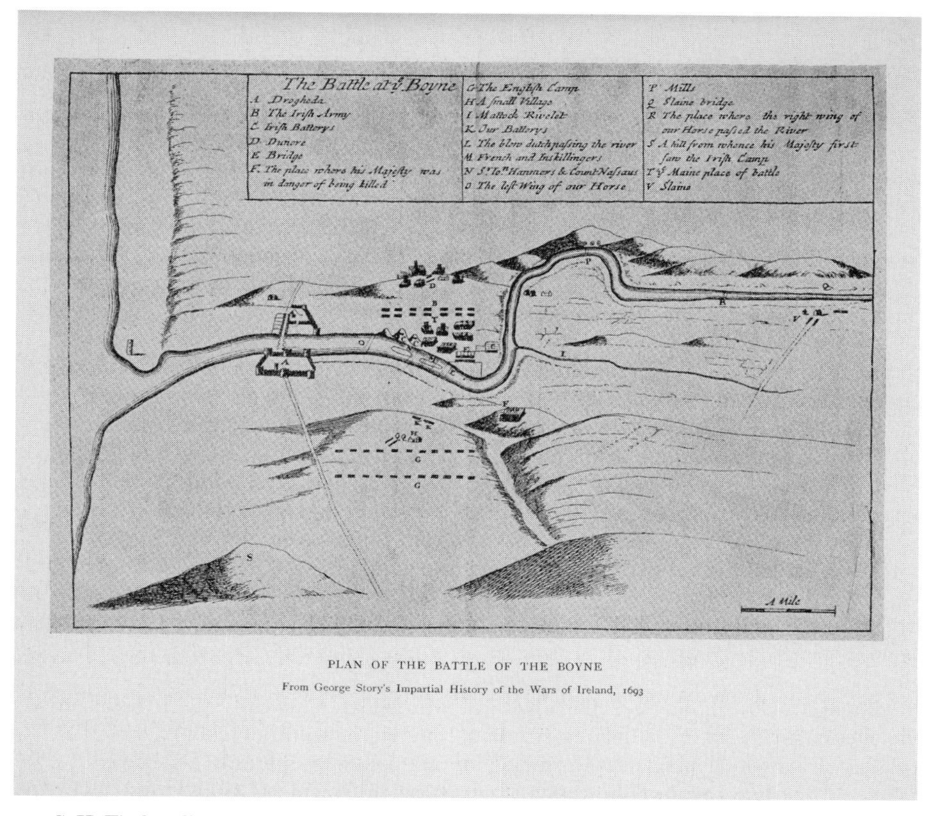

PLAN OF THE BATTLE OF THE BOYNE

From George Story's Impartial History of the Wars of Ireland, 1693

4.6 C. H. Firth (editor), illustrated edition of Macaulay's *History of England*, 1914.

Cambridge, and Churchill's was a matter of envy. But the two names that meant the most were those of Cambridge and of Oxford themselves. The new generation of nursery histories written by the Power sisters were also Cambridge books, appearing under the same imprint as the multi-volume collaborative histories. And to call a new series 'the Oxford History of England' was to 'give the book its blue'. The competition between the two university presses, as one grumbled about the other's sausage-machine, while modifying the model for its own purposes, echoed the competition among historians, who built upon their colleagues' work while politely denigrating each other's scholarship.

Chapter 5

Knowledge in the Marketplace, 1930-1950

WHEN Jonathan Cape published John Ernest Neale's biography of *Queen Elizabeth* in 1934, it was a commercial success. But the regard in which the book was held by Neale's fellow academics was tempered by its publication without any footnotes or bibliography. Neale was charged with having betrayed a cardinal principle of the historical discipline: readers who wished to trace and replicate his encounter with the sources of knowledge would be unable to do so. Eileen Power heard it said that Neale had 'sold the pass', and she replied 'He has also sold 10,000 copies'.[1] Neale was a serious scholar whose footnotes, had they existed, would have documented his extensive work in archival manuscript sources but – in deference to the general reader – he agreed with Cape not to do so in this case. The book remained in print and popular for over two decades. In John Kenyon's words, 'It owed its success not only to its style and scholarship, but also to its glorification of England's past greatness, its mood of nationalist euphoria, which the public found comforting in a decade of disillusion, depression and fear. They continued to draw comfort from it during the Second World War and on into the austerity-ridden era of the Welfare State.' Despite this perceptive statement about the reading public's appreciation of a work of history written by an authoritative scholar, Kenyon nevertheless calls the 'controversial' decision to manage without scholarly apparatus 'unwise', if only because it encouraged less scholarly writers to do likewise.[2]

Kenyon's useful monograph, *The History Men*, a collective study of the historical profession in England, shares with many biographies of individual historians the convention of referring to a historian as having 'published' his or her own book or article. But in Neale's time as in Macaulay's, it was publishers who did the publishing and in the process they often brought a good deal of influence to bear upon the text that appeared over an author's name.

The intertwining lives and works of historians and publishers in the 1930s and 1940s were marked by the Depression and the War to which Kenyon alludes, and also by changes in the practices of the book trades and of historical scholarship that took place during those years. The combination of dreariness and anxiety, of heroism and frustration, so well documented by so many writers, was also the experience of publishers and of historians. It was the time of John Lane and the paperback revolution, which began with the first Penguins in 1935.[3] It was the time of R. H. Tawney and T. S. Ashton, as well as M. M. Postan, Eileen Power, John Clapham and others who were building the economic-history foundations for the social-history revolution that was to come. The influence of their work did not often reach the wider reading public. Such cautious scholarship – and it had to be cautious in order to secure their reputations within the discipline – did nothing to meet the needs of the kind of general reader who had enjoyed reading Neale's *Queen Elizabeth*, or the work of other literary historians – or indeed of Power herself in her collaboration with Rhoda Power on histories for children. And nor did the austere scholarship of the multi-authored comprehensive histories, or the careful precision of multi-volume histories of England relentlessly covering every era from prehistory to the modern world.

Now it was the modern world that demanded attention: readers wanted to know how they had got into this mess. Might Hitler be compared to Frederick the Great, or to other tyrants of the past?[4] What could be said, in the brusque twentieth-century idiom of modern readers, to evoke the kinds of patriotic feelings that Green and Macaulay had engendered in their parents and grandparents?

The attempts to meet these needs served to widen the gap between popular and academic (or professional) history. Trevelyan remained the bestseller, and after 1939 Arthur Bryant abandoned the fourth volume of Pepys into which he had persuaded the Cambridge Press, in order to embark upon the much more popular (and lucrative) *English Saga* and other books. The Oxford University Press was fortunate that Arnold Toynbee had offered them his massive *Study of History*, in 1931.[5] And Winston Churchill would speak stirringly of how knowledge of Britain's history could help Britons win the present war.[6] Publishers struggled with paper shortages, and with rationing, in the face of a gratifying public demand for wartime reading material.[7] But through it all, the great multi-volume series in which so much had been invested continued to absorb their share of both historiographical and publishing attention. When such works were massive exercises aiming at both comprehensiveness and reliability, this could become a demoralizing enterprise.

The Cambridge collaborative histories

On 20 April 1939 Cambridge University Press held a party to celebrate the completion of the *Ancient History* volumes and hence of the whole tripartite history of Europe and the Middle East: twelve volumes on the Ancient world (1923-39), eight volumes of the *Medieval History* (1911-36) and thirteen of the *Modern History* (1902-12). It was an occasion for marketing as well as for celebration: Sydney Roberts had tried to inveigle Trevelyan into writing an article for *The Times* to be published on the day, on the grounds that this was 'something of an event in Cambridge publishing'. Trevelyan declined, professing an ignorance of the Cambridge histories of which the Press Secretary was all too well aware.[8] Instead it was Ernest Barker who wrote of how the *Modern History* 'sprang from the ingenious mind of the Secretary to the Syndics of the Press, R. T. Wright', and enumerated the strengths of two great university presses: 'From Oxford, dictionaries; from Cambridge, collective histories.'[9]

But while the public was asked to regard the several Cambridge histories as complete, fixed, authoritative and permanent, historians and publishers in the University had for some years been quietly undertaking revisions. In 1931, George Coulton had been engaged to correct minor factual errors for part of the *History of English Literature*, but his work came up against the structure and format of the book, which was as usual based on signed chapters by distinguished authorities. First Coulton proposed to 'revise' an essay in terms that directly contradicted the original author's judgements. Rebuffed, he went public in a 1932 lecture to the British Academy, making a very lightly veiled criticism of the Press, for 're-issuing a bulky work of reference' without correcting statements which were now 'recognised as untenable; here and there, even diametrically opposed to the facts'. These passages were being recirculated without 'even the least warning to the public that particles of poison may be found in the good wholesome food'. Coulton had a point, of course, but it would have been unrealistic to issue a completely revised Cambridge collaborative history every time a flourishing and increasingly controversial discipline changed its collective mind.[10]

Similar problems of textual revision and historiographical revisionism beset the *Modern History*. Harold Temperley had suggested a revision in 1927; the Press agreed, but there were differences and a delay.[11]

In the autumn of 1935, publisher and editor began to negotiate yet again for a 'New Series' of the *Cambridge Modern History*. Temperley was prepared this time to oversee and plan the work, as Acton had. He was beginning to make his reputation as a student of recent diplomatic history, and was in fact co-editing the official documents on the origin of the First World War – with G. P. Gooch and assisted by Lillian M. Penson. Gooch was an independent scholar based in London but with strong ties to Cambridge; Penson was appointed to the chair of modern history at Bedford College for Women. The plan for updating the *Cambridge Modern History* was to graft two new volumes onto the 1911 work, leaving intact the unsatisfactory, error-riddled Volume 12. Its authors, editors and publishers had tried to be authoritative about their own time, which now looked very different, but their successors of 1935 were optimistic that the Press could 'keep the whole History alive for another generation'.[12]

It was to be edited by collaboration. This time Penson, a trusted Englishwoman, was put together with a well-connected American, Bernadotte Schmitt. The latter was Professor of History at Chicago and editor of the *Journal of Modern History*. Temperley assured the Press that Penson had 'a very good knowledge indeed approaching uniqueness' of the sources, and had proved herself as a writer. Perhaps more important to these experienced makers of large complex histories, she was 'very good at the executive and editorial side of things'. Because Penson had yet to make her wider reputation, there was concern that her collaborator be an 'editor of distinguished reputation and achievement, sufficient to attract attention in the world and to justify, by his name, this co-operative venture'. Schmitt's name had 'commercial value' in the United States, where he had won the 1931 Pulitzer Prize.[13]

The collaborators settled down amicably to work but by mid-1936 were concerned about the relationship of their own project to the great Actonian enterprise. As Roberts said, 'we should naturally like to convey the impression that anyone who possesses the *Cambridge Modern History* will bring his library up to date by securing the two new volumes'.[14]

The origins of another war, however, interfered with the editors' priorities. In September 1939 we find Penson rushing to take up war-work in London and depositing the contributions collected so far in a country cottage, for the duration of the War. Schmitt was out of touch for some time.[15] It was not until January 1944 that the editors faced up both to the intrinsic weaknesses and to the new vulnerability of their project. Now some parts of Volume 12 would absolutely have to be abandoned, and the revised work somehow 'fused into a continuous whole'.[16] Finally in April 1945 Schmitt withdrew from the venture, in favour of a whole new *Cambridge Modern History* which he hoped would replace, not supplement, the old. Perspectives on many issues had changed, as he noted, not just the origins of the First World War, but also on the French Revolution and on United States history in general. Economic, social and intellectual history were now much more important. In Schmitt's view the original *Cambridge Modern* was comparable to the *Encyclopedia Britannica* before the revisions that had created its eleventh edition. He begged the Cambridge Press editors not to be content with redrafting only Volume 12: 'If the CMH cannot be revised *in extenso*, he told Roberts, it should be allowed to stand as a proud monument to the historical scholarship of 1900-1910.'[17]

John Clapham, G. N. Clark and Herbert Butterfield were appointed as co-editors of the brave new enterprise, but their plan was equally unsuccessful. Butterfield expressed some doubts about the whole project of collaborative histories as undertaken at Cambridge, but by this time they had become, as he put it, 'something of an institution'.[18] Clark, in correspondence with Butterfield, admitted that 'editing has an attraction for me'. This was an understatement, since he had been editing the Oxford History of England since 1929, not to mention the *English Historical Review* between 1920 and 1939.[19] Clark eventually carried on as editor of the *New Cambridge Modern History* but with much less control than his predecessors had exerted, since the decision was taken in 1946 to edit each volume separately.

History from the Oxford University Press

At Oxford, meanwhile, the Clarendon Press was finding that its vaunted 'one-man-one-book' strategy did not prevent problems similar to those Cambridge experienced with their complex multi-author 'syndicated volumes'. By 1934 Oxford still only had only one man, the series editor G. N. Clark himself, and one book, on the later Stuarts. Several of the historians who had contracted to produce further volumes for the Oxford History of England, begun in 1929, had not written a word five years later. Clark struggled with how to title individual volumes in a way that each would not only stand alone but also make sense as part of a series.[20]

Schoolmasters meanwhile clamoured for the new series to supplant those dull and excessively political series published (by Methuen) some three decades earlier, and still in print.[21] As the 1930s went on, the complaints from readers and teachers grew more pressing: in December 1937 a Press officer, Kenneth Sisam, pointed out to a reader that: 'unfortunately the scholars competent to write works of this extent and character are not very many, and they are busy men, so that though we share your wish to get the series finished early, we do not think it would be brought to fulfilment by harassing the authors'.[22] Although Sisam and his colleagues did hold off the harassment during the war, by 1945 Clark was wondering if he should threaten to resign as general editor in order to frighten tardy authors into completion. One of the non-performers, Austin Lane-Poole, was a Press Delegate, which made it awkward to treat all the delinquents in the same way. And loyal Oxonians were embarrassed when they 'had to endure kind enquiries as to the fate of the missing volumes' from history dons at Cambridge; as one man noted, 'indeed the Oxford History is becoming rather like the Boat Race'.[23]

The Clarendon Press was a great deal more sophisticated in 1945 than it had been in the 1890s, and the scholars whose names appeared beside the titles of works in the Oxford History of England were more distinguished than those of Owen Edwards and his colleagues who had been so dilatory in submitting copy for the Oxford School History of England. The problem at the level of publishing remained exactly the same – no copy meant no books – but at the level of historical scholarship and of the reputation of both University and Press, it was different. The discipline of history was implicated in the publication of history books, and the scholars' commitments had become publicly known.

The most sensitive volume from the point of view of contemporary politics, if not from that of historical research and practice, was again the last in a series, projected as a history of England from 1870 to 1914. Various names were bandied about, including, inevitably, Trevelyan's. Clark sounded the Press Assistant Secretary, A. L. P. Norrington, on the subject of inviting the political journalist Robert [R.C.K.] Ensor, who was not only out of a job in 1930 but had all the qualifications 'except that of being a historian. It is a long shot,' Clark added, 'and I think it might be a bull's eye, but don't like to pull the trigger until someone else has had a look along the sights.' Norrington asked around the office and reported a general 'vague feeling that [Ensor was] a literary man', who had written a book on Belgium in the Press's new Home University Library series as well as what Clark called 'some rather jolly poems'.[24] The long shot reached its bull's eye in 1936 and when other volumes in the series were still floundering, Sisam reported that Ensor's was 'generally reckoned to be the most brilliantly written historical book of recent times'.[25]

If the two large competing series of books emerging from Cambridge and from Oxford were difficult to complete and impossible to keep up to date, contracts with individual historians for single, or 'independent' volumes were both livelier and more risky.

At Oxford from the 1930s to the early 1960s the Press staff was absorbed by Arnold Toynbee's *Study of History*. Toynbee was Research Professor in International History at the University of London and Director of Studies at the Royal Institute of International Affairs.[26] He wrote to Humphrey Milford on 31 December 1931, announcing 'a large work of mine which I have on the stocks ... an attempt at a kind of morphology of History in general'. He compared the scale of his own work to that of Frazer's great anthropological synthesis, *The Golden Bough* (1889), and mentioned that another publisher was already expressing interest. Milford 'couldn't resist' the project, 'vast work though it be'.[27] Toynbee was disarmingly modest, and sensitive to the publisher's anxieties. He told Milford that he had 'tried it on the dog in the shape of half-a-dozen serious scholars and they do seem to take it quite seriously, but of course,' he added, 'one really never knows how a book will be received till it is before the public – by which time the publisher has, I am afraid, committed himself'.[28]

Two and a half years later, the question rose of managing the massive and growing manuscript, which Toynbee had joked would be delivered in a pantechnicon. A one-volume abridgement seemed to be in order. Clark was convinced that this would become 'a formative epoch-making work, like the *Golden Bough*', so that many people would want to read its central ideas without undertaking the commitment of money and time that six volumes demanded. He imagined the process of abridgement as more a 'skimming of the cream' than a 'boiling down', and urged Norrington not to wait for the larger work to be completed and reviewed. Better, he thought, 'to strike while the iron is hot. In ten years time Toynbee [might] have followed Spengler into comparative obscurity.'[29] As the war continued to complicate and delay his commitments, Toynbee reluctantly came to realize that he should not make the abridgement himself; perhaps his assistant Veronica Boulter might undertake the task, since she had a profound understanding of the structure of the work.[30]

On the other hand, an abridgement already existed, prepared for classroom use by a schoolmaster, David Somervell, and sent to Toynbee for his approval. Somervell later described himself in deprecatory terms: 'Though he has written many small books on great historical subjects Mr Somervell has always disclaimed the honourable title of historian: he is a schoolmaster who has schooled himself to be brief without being dull and simple without being superficial.'[31] Toynbee's initial reservations were overcome. Even if, after completing the whole project, he himself undertook a one-volume edition, which would be 'more than just an abridgement', the two versions would likely appeal to different markets. Somervell was agreeable (indeed, delighted) and deferential about revisions and royalties. It was the abridgement that was later considered in the United States for a Book of the Month Club selection, and that was remembered by thousands of readers as their experience of Toynbee's *Study of History* (Fig. 5.1).[32]

There have been strong criticisms of Toynbee's work, on the part of academic historians who observe that he assumes the existence of patterns and laws in history which the discipline has been at great pains to deny. While this critique is altogether valid on the grounds of historical study, it is important at the same time to give weight to the reality of Toynbee's impact (via Somervell) on a reading public for whom a narrative stressing patterns and laws made sense of an inchoate past. Whether respected or not by his disciplinary peers, Toynbee was an ambitious historian, and the Press at Oxford worked tirelessly to meet their commitment to stay with him through twenty-seven years and ten volumes, not to mention an abridgement and various other paraphernalia.

A very different historian, Ernest Barker, remained a confidante of the managers of the Oxford University Press as well as influential in academic and political circles during the 1940s as in the 1920s. He chaired a Books Commission set up by the Conference of Allied Ministers of Education that met in July 1943 to plan a remarkable project. In that time of preparation for peace while the War was still going on, the Ministers of Education of the Allied countries set in motion plans for an 'objective' and collaborative history of the War.

A STUDY OF HISTORY

BY

ARNOLD J. TOYNBEE

HON. D.LITT. OXON. AND BIRMINGHAM, F.B.A.

Director of Studies in the Royal Institute of International Affairs
Research Professor of International History in the University of London
(both on the Sir Daniel Stevenson Foundation)

Doloris
Sopitam recreant volnera viva animam.
Anon.

ABRIDGEMENT
OF VOLUMES I–VI
BY
D. C. SOMERVELL

Issued under the auspices of the Royal Institute of International Affairs

GEOFFREY CUMBERLEGE
OXFORD UNIVERSITY PRESS
LONDON NEW YORK TORONTO
1946

5.1 Arnold J. Toynbee, abridged by D. C. Somervell, *A Study of History*, 1946.

Sisam at the Press got wind of the confidential project and wrote 'that if a first-rate objective account can be produced in English, the Press would be interested'. Barker forecast that 'the difficulty may be the official and governmental character of the plan' and Sisam replied with caution: 'We ourselves should hardly want to be connected with an ostensibly official history, for we must all reckon that the propaganda weapon has been overused in war-time, and is losing its edge. I should guess that an official history of controversial matters published by HM Stationery Office after the War would be regarded with the deepest suspicion at home and in the occupied countries.' The problem seemed to Sisam's 'uninformed mind' to be one of 'producing a responsible and authoritative book or books without obvious marks that it is promoted by a government or governments for the purpose of government'.[33]

Only three months later Barker was ready to propose a History of European Civilization in two volumes, by an international body of writers, for use in European secondary schools after the War. Oxford's qualms about producing collaborative works had apparently been set aside in favour of a conviction that the postwar world needed such a book to counterbalance Nazi propaganda. A French historian, Paul Vaucher, was already involved, and a Czech was in view.[34]

At the same time as the idealized 'objective history' of Europe was in the planning stages, so was an even more urgent project for a history of the War itself. The Conference of Allied Ministers of Education also wanted a 'brief documented narrative of events ... avoiding discussion of causes and attempts at interpretation, having the general public in view, and designed to counter the spread of false legend'. About 80,000 words in length, it was to 'be based on the idea of a common European civilisation ... so that it would show not only how the war had disturbed that idea, but also how that idea had reasserted itself during the war.' But the Education Ministers wanted it immediately, in time to drop from aircraft over occupied Holland, and another million copies for the Dutch post-armistice military Government. 'They don't want anything learned,' Norrington reported to his colleagues, 'but simply a straight-forward factual account for people who have had no free news since June 1940.'[35]

As it happened, Robert Ensor had written a 32-page pamphlet along those lines, addressed to both soldiers and general readers and entitled *The Uphill War* (Fig. 5.2).[36] Since the publication of his volume in the Oxford History of England, Ensor had secured a

No. 66 Price 6d. net

THE
UPHILL WAR
Sept. 1939—Nov. 1942

By R. C. K. ENSOR

OXFORD PAMPHLETS
ON WORLD AFFAIRS

5.2 R. C. K. Ensor, *The Uphill War*, 1944.

fellowship in Oxford, but he continued to produce newspaper commentary as well as pamphlets of this sort. He would have to write a much longer book to meet the needs of the Allied Ministers of Education. They also envisaged special editions tailored for each country, since a place like Norway could not be 'fully enough dealt with in a general history of 80,000 words', while at the same time each country's own national story needed to be told in full. Ensor was intrigued, regarding it as 'a difficult but very attractive job. Incidentally, of course,' he added, it would be 'a scientific history, fully documented and aiming at infallibility.'[37] Altogether, three books were under discussion: Ensor's existing Oxford pamphlet addressed to the English-speaking world, the lengthy 'factual account', and something in between, 'a shortish propaganda story' for the Allies to distribute when they returned to occupied countries. Into 1944 Ensor was struggling between his scholarly values as a historian and his mandate from the Allied Ministers: 'they naturally want something early, whereas I want something permanent'. He never finished this ambitious project, pleading in 1947 'the increasing daily demands of washing up and weeding'.[38]

These various proposals for an 'objective' or a 'scientific' history – of events that were still incomplete, for which the documentary record was unavailable to scholars, and over which political emotion and national pride ran very high – are of great interest. When Ensor spoke of 'a scientific history, fully documented and aiming at infallibility', he was affirming values inherited through Stubbs and Seeley from Leopold von Ranke, values which had been reinforced both by historians and by the university presses with whom they worked, that were still part of the language of the wartime academic world.

Much to Barker's annoyance, word about the Europe-wide 'objective history' project was leaked to the press, and a cartoon appeared in the *Daily Sketch* (Fig. 5.3). He suspected that the American observer at the meeting had been the culprit, and remained deadly serious about co-ordinating and editing an 'inter-allied history of European civilisation'.[39]

Contributions were flowing in during 1947 and 1948, but some were unsatisfactory. The difficulties of cross-channel, not to say transnational, collaboration had not become easier since the initiation of the *Modern History* at Cambridge. Professor Daniel Mornet of the Sorbonne had undertaken and prepared a manuscript on France, but to Barker's chagrin, it would not do.[40] It was 'entirely literary ... *not history*'; and it was 'written on the assumption of the literary "hegemony" of France', rather than on the 'general basis ... of the Common European inheritance'.[41] Mornet was in fact an early proponent of *l'histoire du livre* as eventually articulated by the *Annales* school of historians: he employed what Barker described as 'mathematical technique, which [became] a wearisome reiteration, of the number of editions of books ... published in the 18th century, and of the number of times they are mentioned in catalogues'.[42]

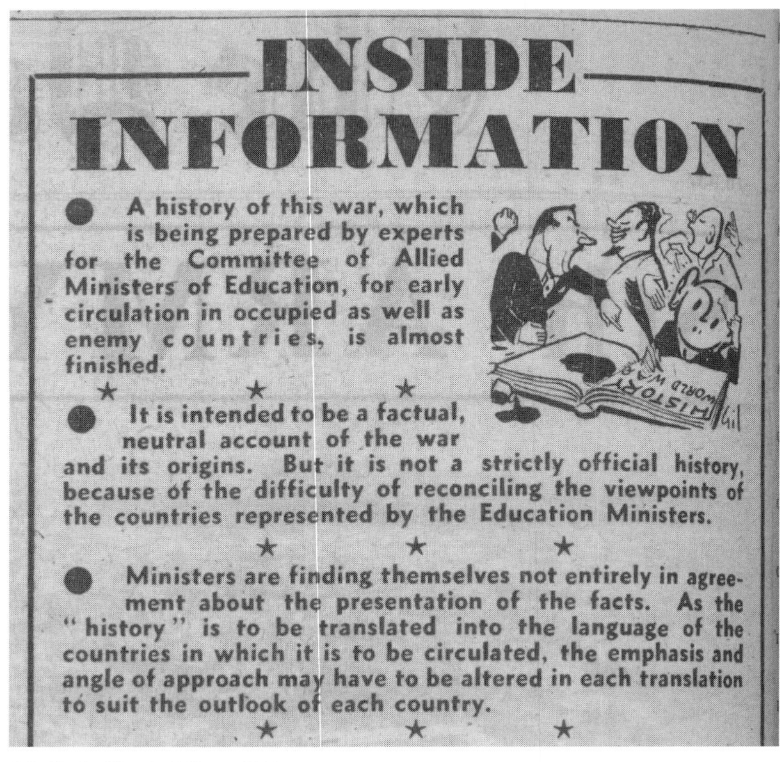

INSIDE INFORMATION

● A history of this war, which is being prepared by experts for the Committee of Allied Ministers of Education, for early circulation in occupied as well as enemy countries, is almost finished.

★ ★ ★

● It is intended to be a factual, neutral account of the war and its origins. But it is not a strictly official history, because of the difficulty of reconciling the viewpoints of the countries represented by the Education Ministers.

★ ★ ★

● Ministers are finding themselves not entirely in agreement about the presentation of the facts. As the "history" is to be translated into the language of the countries in which it is to be circulated, the emphasis and angle of approach may have to be altered in each translation to suit the outlook of each country.

★ ★ ★

5.3 *Daily Sketch*, 5 June 1944.

Sisam responded blandly that if all else failed, Barker could blame the Press for Mornet's contribution being scrapped: 'our shoulders are not inexperienced in bearing blame'.[43] It may have been at this point that the volume on the eighteenth century was divided into two sections, between Paul Vaucher, one of the co-editors of the work, and Mornet.

With Barker and Vaucher, G. N. Clark had his name on the title-page of *The European Inheritance* as an editor and had written a section of the 'objective history' in 1944. But in the cold light of 1950 Clark wanted the right to publish its text elsewhere. Norrington referred to 'this wild project', and described it in unflattering terms to his colleague, D. M. Davin: 'The Council of Allied Ministers came to the Delegates and asked them to undertake in advance to publish a collection – a Tower of Babel of pigs in a poke – and to pay the authors in advance. ... In any case the risk of our getting left with a torso on our hands was immense.' He remembered the patriotic terms under which the project had been undertaken, but now the Press's obligations seemed heavy, certainly too heavy to allow Clark or anyone to benefit from their generosity.[44] Meanwhile the project inched towards completion; Barker was seeking translations into English of those chapters that had been written in French.

Finally, in 1954, *The European Inheritance* by eight authors in three volumes (and eventually three editions) saw the light of day. The political and cultural mood was very different from the optimism of 1944. Barker's 'persistent faith' and energy were acknowledged by the Press, although he himself spoke slightingly of having merely 'done the hack work'.[45] Even in 1950 the then-Minister of Education, W. R. Richardson, had commented: 'It is almost too painful to contrast the high hopes of those days with the realities of today.'[46] There was talk of an abridgement, if sales went well, by none other than D. C. Somervell.[47] And 'a solemn ceremony in London ... in the presence of the Allied ambassadors', was planned, at which Barker and the Oxford University Press was to 'present the work to the Council of Europe as our gift to the cause for which it stands'.

As Julia Stapleton writes, this book is evidence of Barker's commitment, even into retirement, to both teaching and learning.[48] But it also stands as a commentary on how the idea for a book, conceived in the enthusiasm of a moment, can become something quite different when the resulting work is reconsidered by later scholarship and a fresh generation of readers.

History books: text, object, context

During the 1930s and 1940s there was a strong public interest in history – books as different as Toynbee's, the Cambridge collaborative histories and the Oxford series attest to this. It would be rewarding to look at other historical writers: at H. G. Wells, or more extensively at Trevelyan, or at a figure like George Coulton, whose contribution to the Cambridge History of English Literature was so disastrously unsatisfactory but whose accessible monographs, especially *The Medieval Panorama,* supported his family and profited the Cambridge University Press. Or at Arthur Bryant, who was invited by the same press to take over the project for a Pepys biography from J. R. Tanner in 1931, the year that his unexpectedly successful life of *King Charles II* was published by Longmans. By 1935 Bryant had come to enjoy what he called 'a curious little public of my own' and was chafing at the restrictions of working with a cautious scholarly publisher. He ended a long letter to Charles Carrington at CUP about terms, format and promotion of his book with a self-deprecatory postscript: 'I suppose you all hate me. And I'm afraid this is a very Pepysian document. Perhaps some poor devil doing a thesis on the relations of publisher and author will stumble on it 200 years hence.'[49]

The present book, following the lectures on which it is based, addresses the relations of publishers and their historian authors. It has outlined a chronology and some of the themes for framing the practice and representation of history in terms of its bibliographical materiality – for a study of history books *as* books. Such thinking does not come easily to people trained in the discipline; we are more accustomed to thinking in terms of research and teaching, argument and interpretation, than of authorship, publishing and reading. A bibliographical historiography – which is also a historiographical bibliography – implies a focus upon historians as writers of books and articles. It entails the recognition that historians wrote both big and little books, popular as well as scholarly articles, and that some of their work brought substantial material returns. It identifies publishers and editors as facilitators and mediators of historical knowledge, as keepers of the gateway between those who write and those who read. It also opens up questions about readers – about the individual reader who makes use of historical knowledge, and about communities of readers who pool their knowledge and use it together.

Scholars trained in different disciplinary traditions understand the history of books differently: literary scholars are most interested in the text, bibliographers in the material object, and historians in the cultural transaction that is mediated by the abstract book-as-a-means-of-communication. In this sense the three core disciplines orient themselves respectively to writers and authors, to publishers and libraries, and to readers and users of the book. Each of the three disciplines also reveals the mutability of the book form in print culture. The conventional codex looks, and is designed to look, fixed and permanent, reliable and efficient, replicating as it does numerous identical copies of an agreed-upon text. But a text can be changed, by the intellect and imagination of its writer, by the material intervention of its publisher, and by the interpretive power of its reader.[50] History books are both texts and material objects; each one exemplifies a cultural transaction as it is conceptualized and contracted; written, edited, put into print and sold; purchased, read and collected; revised, printed and circulated anew. The experience of reading a history book is limited by both object and text, but each reader will still make his or her own interpretation.

These concluding comments are organized in three sections, addressing first the work of history as literary text, then the history book as material object, and finally the cultural transaction it encapsulates, by way of the processes of authorship, of publishing and of reading.

History as text

In some ways, history does not lend itself particularly well to being written down. (Or, as we say in the case of research results, written up.) Either way, the imposition of a coherent narrative on the inchoate past is inherently problematic. Much of the difficulty is chronological, and every writer struggles with where to start, when to finish and how to structure the narrative. Not every historical text is sequential, or even narrative. Some postmodern projects have experimented with alternatives to the linear before-and-after, but narrative has been central to the discipline's sense of itself. Historiography struggled in the 1970s with debates over 'the return of narrative', and recent attempts to surmount the colonial/postcolonial divide have brought us back to similar conversations.[51] My argument has been that publishers – and the editors who work for them – have a strong commercial interest in narrative, and they have been instrumental in shaping and revising the texts that historians write. Alexander Macmillan begged Edward Freeman to 'tell the story' to adult and child readers, and his successors half a century later cajoled a narrative from H. G. Wells. Trevelyan was in constant demand; Bryant was encouraged by Longman and later by William Collins to entertain and inspire his 'curious little public'.

The editors and compilers of collaborative histories had a different problem with text. They developed editorial strategies to smooth out the 'liveliness' A. W. Ward detested in his contributors' prose. Monograph series like the Cambridge Historical Series and the Oxford History of England were less inhibiting but still imposed a disciplinary constraint. Here the influence of publishers has been more in the matter of material format than of the literary text.

History books as material objects

The material form of a history book changed considerably between 1850 and 1950. At first glance, the alterations might seem minimal:

at the beginning and the end of the period books started out as sheets of machine-made paper, folded after printing into signatures that appeared as discrete pages, the letterpress upon them composed and printed by mechanized equipment, the bindings made of cloth constructed in prefabricated cases: sometimes there were dust-jackets and latterly there were paperback covers. Quite straightforward and unremarkable. But it is nevertheless possible to identify roughly the decade at which a volume appeared, by reading its binding design, typography and page layout. The dates on the title-page apparently document the exact moment of production, but these too have to be read, and interpreted, carefully to distinguish between first and subsequent editions, and among the numerous reissues which may or may not have concealed substantial further revisions.

Two aspects of the material history book have become apparent – relative size and the series format. Edward Freeman spoke, in correspondence with his publisher and his colleagues, of both 'big books' and 'little books'. When he undertook to edit the Historical Course for Schools series, he called the volumes 'little England', 'little France' and so forth. He diminuated his *Old English History for Children* even further by calling it a 'wee-wee-wee-bit bookikie'.[52] The reality behind this self-indulgent formulation continued to resonate in the publishing history of history books by Freeman's contemporaries and successors. Scholars managed their working lives – balancing the demands of researching and composing the big books that were to take decades, against those of dashing off the little ones, for which a publisher had dangled a lucrative or flattering contract. Little books seemed relatively insignificant to most of their authors, and from a strictly historiographical point of view, so they were. But if we consider the impact, in terms of print-runs and edition sequences, of some of the more successful 'little books', the judgement of significance might have to be reversed. It was the smaller works in one manageable volume – affordable in the classroom or for recreational reading – that formed the history-reading experience of most people. Freeman told Edith Thompson that boys at City of London School habitually referred to their copy of her *England* as 'my Edith' as in 'where's my Edith? I have lost her'.[53] It is striking to read in C. T. McIntire's biography how the young Herbert Butterfield realized that as an aspiring scholar he would be well advised to suppress his actual experience of having first read the history of England in that ill-fated, long-in-the-making schoolbook that the Clarendon Press had had such difficulty in extracting from its authors. The substantial octavo monographs he was supposed to remember were not necessarily equally massive in their popular influence.[54]

My argument – that history books were often conceptualized and commissioned by publishers – is subject to qualification, in that some historians have planned and executed their works quite independent of book-trade influence. Where the agency of publishers was paramount, however, was in the series format. Series took many forms: the Clarendon Press at Oxford disparaged the Cambridge Modern, Medieval and Ancient histories as 'sausages', produced on a 'sausage-machine' which chopped up the past into texts by many authors, and bound them together in arbitrary and uniform packages. Oxford adopted the principle of 'one-man-one-book' – to adapt the food metaphor we might call the Oxford History of England a mixed grill, or perhaps a menu of successive courses leading from Collingwood and Myres' starter of Roman Britain to Ensor's dessert course of current events. Their single-authored, multi-volume Histories of England (and Europe and other constructs) were series too, with an established limit on length and format, as well as price. These series followed on from earlier ones, such as Macmillan's Historical Course for Schools, Putnam's Heroes of the Nations and George Allen's British Empire Series. It is in the series format that the materiality of the history book in the late-nineteenth and the twentieth century is most evident.[55]

Although series are valuable in many ways, the strict demands of format nevertheless impose limitations of periodization and emphasis that constrain the historical imagination. Publishers enjoyed working with dependable historians who could turn out successive editions of a steady-selling volume in a prestigious series; and they often looked askance at anomalous projects.

The social and cultural processes of book-making

The history of the book is sometimes described in terms of a circuit of communication wherein the processes of publishing and printing, binding and bookselling, intervene between the mind of a writer and that of a reader. The connected cultural transactions of authorship, of publishing and of reading are emphasized, rather than the literary text or the material object.[56] These terms of process are particularly useful for historians seeking to understand the cultural work that a book, or books, might accomplish. However, all three categories work better for creative works than for those of scholarship or of ideology. They are also problematic in that they imply a single heroic and creative author, and a reader who may be equally solitary or who may combine with others to form an interpretative community. To apply the categories to history books, in the spirit of experiment, is to return to some of the key themes with which this book has been concerned.

When authorship is the focus, it is the tension between popular histories and academic writing that manifests itself as a hallmark of the period. J. R. Seeley argued that it was essential to differentiate, that a serious work of history was no more meant for the general public than was Newton's *Principia*, although the general public of the 1880s had failed to accept the distinction. Twenty years of practice made it a reality. G. M. Trevelyan, in *Clio: A Muse* (1903), spoke harshly of what he called 'publishers' books', arguing that 'The public understands that this type of prurient journalism is history lightly served up for the general appetite; whereas serious history is a sacred thing pinnacled afar on frozen heights of science, not to be approached save after a long novitiate'.[57] But just what was the public meant to understand?

Popular writers of history (of 'publishers' books) were charged, by their publishers, with writing afresh stories that had been written many times before, merely adding new twists to narratives with which readers had been familiar since the nursery, or since their school days. Research was a matter of consulting books or articles that could provide some raw material, sometimes gossiping and even prurient and sometimes merely novel and engaging. There was no need to insert oneself into a scholarly debate or to make a unique contribution to knowledge. The concern was with writing something that would be a literary success and earn its initial financial reward, perhaps even continue to provide royalties into the future.

For most academic authors, royalties did not amount to enough to supply the necessities of life, and other considerations were more pressing. One of these was to support the acceptance and flourishing of a newly serious academic discipline. Historians were dissatisfied with the structure of contemporary publishing, and sought to set up a new separate model, a 'purely historical review'. The more compact structure and recurrently-appearing format of the scholarly article were eminently suitable for reporting the results of research and for carrying out scholarly debate in a collegial spirit. But what worked for articles did not apply to longer texts. Few scholarly books were published outside the mainstream system, where both academic and commercial publishers held the purse-strings and insisted on retaining control. Some historian-authors were drawn to the newly-important series format, which as we have seen was inspired from outside the discipline. The quarterly academic periodical, on the other hand, developed from within the practice of history. The journal was a medium well suited for promoting the ideology of objectivity and transpersonal replicability, the notion that professionalization meant that one trained scholar's interpretation was essentially the same as another's. The series was not. Indeed, it might be argued that by embracing the series format, publishers actually distorted the ideal of transpersonal replicability, by slotting in one writer after another to cover one period after another, in a sequential but not really collaborative history.

Academic historians continued to write books, both in and out of series, sometimes at the behest of publishers and sometimes on their own initiative. Almost all of them, though, implicitly addressed these works to their scholarly peers and to their student protégés. Some, like Oscar Browning and his scorn for 'grocers and cheesemongers', were openly contemptuous of the general public and its banal taste for an outdated and frivolous history; others were merely oblivious. On a deeper level, the disdain that Trevelyan mocked may have cloaked a certain anxiety. Because of the tensions between the practices of their discipline and the problems associated with narrative texts, academic historians as a set of authors may have realized how difficult it was to capture in book form their new way of conceptualizing history. But the book was the only medium they had – at least for many years – and it remained the most prestigious one.[58]

The general public was well acquainted with history books and unwilling to entertain much in the way of experimentation. As early as the 1870s, Freeman wanted to teach even his child readers, and certainly the adult ones, to 'distinguish history from legend, to know what the sources of history are, and to distinguish the different values of different writers'. But Charlotte Yonge knew that readers wanted to know 'which is it really', whether the matter in dispute was the colour of a bird's plumage or the question of whether or not King Alfred had truly left the cakes to burn. With the striking exception of Eileen Power, Freeman's successors were less optimistic than he about conveying the nuances of source criticism to non-historians. From about the 1890s, many of them gave up the effort of reaching the great majority of people, despite those people's continuing captivation with their subject-matter.

All kinds of history books were published, but when Trevelyan referred scathingly to 'publishers' books' he was addressing a phenomenon still quite new in 1903. The men and women of the book trade knew that there was a market for works of history, both a captive market in the schools, and one that needed to be courted in the person of the ordinary general reader.[59] Commercial publishers sought out the generalists, although some of the most prominent of these were quasi-academics, beginning with Green, later Trevelyan himself, and later still Bryant. The university publishers were also attracted to these great stylists, but they could not often afford to compete with the London book trade. In any case their mission was primarily to serve the academic world, without losing track of commercial realities. Their response to this dilemma was to aim for comprehensiveness, to brand their books, or rather their series, with the name shared by both University and Press; Oxford and Cambridge were displayed more prominently than the names of the authors. Of course there were exceptions, high-profile ones like Toynbee at Oxford, and lower-keyed ones like the Power sisters' children's books at Cambridge. But the archives of the two great university presses reveal a great deal of energy and commitment being put into the collaborative histories and the multi-volume packages. (And tellingly, the archives also show the two Presses collaborating to seek legal protection for their names, when they were borrowed without authorization by George Gill & Sons for an *Oxford and Cambridge History of England*).[60]

However comprehensive they might be, standard histories that remained in print and continued to be consulted had to be updated as new events unfolded and new interpretations came into use. Although it was expensive and time-consuming to manage such revisions, 'new and thoroughly updated' editions and versions of standard works would also be newly marketable and saleable, and later generations of scholars could be pressed into service to write them, as well as to read them. Fresh scholarly interpretations, and innovative approaches to the past – such as economic and social history – eventually made their way into print, even into series, but the scholars had to negotiate their scholarship with the publishers who controlled the gate.

The generalist publishers made different demands on their historian-authors: they could insist upon limited or expanded texts, they could try to enforce firm delivery dates, they could budget for substantial royalties because of their lengthy print-runs. But there were also similarities: both academic and generalist publishers were essentially commercial. Although the latter liked to point out the vast resources in the infrastructure behind the academic presses, the subsidies did not preclude the need of university presses to cover costs and earn income from publishing projects. Both mediated between producer and consumer; both had to work with authors and texts on one side, and with the readers and teachers who used the resulting books on the other. Correspondence and readers' reports surviving in their archives give tantalizing evidence of a few of the events in a largely submerged experience.

If little is known about historical authorship and publishing, even less is known of the reading experience. What did readers remember or communicate about their experience of reading history? How did readings differ according to class, ethnicity or gender, and over time? Historians of reading are hampered by the lack of evidence; few people normally leave any trace of even the most profound reading experience. When records do survive, they are fragmentary and incommensurate, though often susceptible of illuminating interpretation.[61] The present study has side-stepped these difficulties by focusing on the process of publishing, taking for granted that publishers knew something, however flawed their knowledge, about the needs of readers. And although the indirect approach has its limitations, it does allow the posing of a new question: what has been the public understanding of history in the past?

Comments on the public understanding of history in our own time have focused extensively on the presentation of the past in the broadcast media of film, television and the internet. During the period from mid-nineteenth to mid-twentieth century, the dominant medium was print; for more than half of the period, the book and periodical were the only media available outside the classroom. What did people make of the dichotomy between popular and academic history, with its implication that the only fully authoritative version of history was deemed to be beyond their grasp? What was the effect of learning at the parental knee, and again in primary school, and further in secondary school, maybe again at university, successively detailed accounts of the same basic story – and then being told that scholars were hard at work undermining these powerful truths? The constant stream of revision, in the shape of new books of history every year, in series and in other formats large and small, must have unsettled British people's sense of their own history, and of their own national identity.

Epilogue: History, out of print

WHEN I presented the Lyell Lectures in the spring of 2006, and throughout the present book, I identified four themes that had emerged from my research: thinking about historical knowledge as it develops over the life-cycle of the reader; the crucial role of the publisher in the making of history books; the tension between academic and popular approaches to the past; and the materiality of the history book. Each of these calls for further consideration and will, I hope, be taken up and addressed by other scholars in future research. The experience of revising the lectures has made me aware of four further themes that cut across the original four – attitudes towards women historians, projects of collaboration including the editing of series, the importance of periodical publication and the use of history books to make transatlantic and indeed transnational communities.

It was two or three decades after my period, the century from 1850 to 1950, ended before women historians were finally made welcome, and women's history became a fixture in the academic world. Feminist scholarship has begun to redress the earlier indifference both to practitioners and to subject-matter,[1] and my study makes a modest contribution by observing the attitudes of some publishers to certain women writers of history. Publishers, almost exclusively male in the 1850-1950 period, often worked together with the historian mentors and patrons of women scholars. Alexander Macmillan valued Charlotte Yonge; he and his successors fostered the work of Edith Thompson from the 1870s to the 1920s. Freeman sponsored Thompson with Macmillan and also provided opportunities to his own daughter Margaret. James Bryce, Sir James Stephen, J. R. Green, Mandell Creighton and other Victorian and Edwardian male historians did the same for their sisters, wives and daughters.[2] In the 1890s Lord Acton worked closely with his friend Lady Charlotte Blennerhassett; his colleagues vouched for the work of Mary Bateson, so that the latter was regarded as 'thoroughly teachable' and hence 'the most suitable second lady' to be permitted to join the *Cambridge Modern History* list of contributors.[3] The Oxford University Press made good use of Lillian Penson's talents during the 1930s. She worked in the shadow of a distinguished male American, but at the same time she was well placed to monitor any excesses in which he might indulge. The men involved in these situations were condescending about women's work, and others were downright scornful. Examples of the latter include W. A. J. Archbold and his denigration of the reputation of Flora Shaw, the suspicions of A. J. de Monins Johnson with respect to Marya Antonina Czaplicka, and the sniggering of Z. N. Brooke about the anthropological research of Jessie Weston. Perhaps even more damaging was the attitude of someone like Humphrey Milford who disparaged wholesale the work of 'ladies' as writers of serious history books.[4] These attitudes did not prevent the publishers in question from using educated women to prepare the infrastructure of scholarly works; the names of women appear quite often in publishers' records as translators, indexers and others kinds of research assistants and anonymous collaborators. But the century-old identification of women like 'Mrs Markham' and the author of 'Little Arthur' with popular, widely-read and pervasively influential histories for children worked against the academic careers of their successors.

The *Cambridge Modern History* and the partnership of Richard Wright and Lord Acton provides the best, but not the earliest, example of an experiment in collaboration. In 1896 the ambitious publisher and his distinguished historian-editor partner set out to harness together the knowledge of a team of scholars. In 1872, Macmillan's Historical Course for Schools had similarly been planned to take advantage of Freeman's formidable reputation and bring together a number of lesser-known writers to cover the histories of a large part of the world. The later Cambridge histories followed on the Wright-Acton model, with varying degrees of success; other publishers developed relationships with editors and inaugurated series of their own. The career of G. N. Clark, working as an editor for both Cambridge and Oxford University Presses, is a strong testimony to how the ideal of a comprehensive history, in a series of connected volumes, could appeal to scholars as well as to their publishers. The foundation and management of publishers' series needs further study. In the cases of Freeman and Acton, clear demarcations of power are obvious: the publisher has made use of a senior scholar's authority to harness and control the work of lesser writers. Freeman used agricultural language when he referred to Yonge's fellow-contributors as being 'thoroughly ashamed of their yokefellow', while Acton employed the industrial metaphor of a division of labour. In each case, collaboration in the publication of a historical series was not the collaboration of equal minds or an open sharing of research results. (Ward characterized the ideal collaborative work as 'metal thoroughly fused'.) Rather, it was a way in which substantial books could be put together with a relatively modest investment of resources and a minimum of difficulty. Both series (like the Oxford History of England) and collaborative histories (like the Cambridge Modern, Medieval and Ancient) made a great impact on the presentation of historical work in the twentieth century. Their dynamics are of interest to historians of the book and also of history-writing, as well as to those contemporary publishers who may be contemplating revisions of earlier series or new collaborative histories on the old model.

New technologies for research and publishing, on the other hand, are making it possible for more egalitarian and more widespread networks of collaboration to flourish. The deep and tangled roots of the history of the *English Historical Review* are a subject for further reflection because of what they reveal about another aspect of serialization, the appearance of historical narratives in the periodical format. Twenty years before the journal began to operate, with peer review to guarantee rigour and accuracy but without payment for authors, Macmillan, Green, Freeman and others had an alternative vision. They wanted a popular history magazine, incorporating essays, articles and reviews that engaged the public with its past in the same way as *Nature* connected serious readers with the natural world. The market may have been too small, and the newly rigorous scholars were certainly too wary of appearing to pander to a debased popular taste. Later efforts, like that of F. W. Wheeler just before the First World War, were also supplanted by the model of an academic quarterly. It would not be until 1951 and the foundation of *History Today* that there would be a periodical designed to cater to the popular audience for good strong stories of the past. By that time, the historical narratives that appeared in popular Victorian periodicals had been obscured by time and neglect. But we must remember that scholars of that era had been deeply concerned that contemporary periodicals published only popular and sketchy articles; so Mandell Creighton wrote in 1883. Surely, if they were popular, it is worthwhile to take a careful look at what those sketchy articles were about, how they were written and by whom. Periodicals were endemic – by one measure, one hundred times as much text was printed in periodical format as appeared in book format.[5] Apart from articles celebrating the foundation of the *EHR*, however, very little scholarship has focused upon the historical content of the periodicals. This is especially significant since the journal was designed to take the most highly qualified writers away from the commercial marketplace for print. The time has come to return to the popular history that Victorians read in periodical format.[6]

Finally, we need to be aware that the history of England, and the histories published in Britain, were distributed, read, taught, studied and learned throughout the world.[7] Racial and ethnic discriminations and differences were played out as lessons about long-ago defeats and in wholesale characterizations of peoples and nations. Scholars in India prepared special pamphlets of questions for Indian students based on the work of both Edith Thompson and J. R. Green. School authorities in Canada questioned Thompson's text when it seemed to contradict the teaching of the Roman Catholic Church. In the United States there were both authorized and pirated editions of Green's history in circulation.[8] The American branch of the Oxford University Press told its headquarters that that English history prior to the eighteenth century was 'the common property of English and American historians'. Readers felt that way too, not only in the United States but in the Empire and Commonwealth. The period from 1850 to 1950 was a period of migration, where the movement of peoples paralleled the traffic in print.

During the next few years of scholarship, I hope that researchers will set out to discover what history has been available to English-speaking readers (and consumed by those readers) in periodical as well as book format. Then we can begin to think about how those books and articles were understood. The time span should be longer than the century I set myself for the initial research – perhaps extending from 1700 to 2000, going back to David Hume and forward to David Starkey, back before the beginning of machine printing and forward through the social-history revolution to the age of television dons and the books that spin off from their programs.[9] With respect to books, the inventory should include all kinds of histories, good ones and bad, derivative and original – the popular, the pedagogical and the academic. It should include monographs, series and collaborative works, addressed to children and students and adults, and include titles aimed at working-class men and leisured women and their children as well as at middle-class men. As for periodicals, the inventory should also cover articles and essays in all sorts of journals and magazines.

The interests of those lower-middle class readers characterized variously as 'girls and curates' by Edward Augustus Freeman and as 'grocers and cheesemongers' by Oscar Browning have suffered too long from the condescension of posterity. So have the interests and the reading experience of labouring people, of subaltern groups in colonial situations and of women both at home and in the British world who received from print a history that was not exactly their own.

Students of book culture have made similar inventories, and asked and answered similar questions with respect to imaginative literature and to the history of science. The results are illuminating. Long-forgotten works are being resurrected and their contemporary readership reconstructed; the motivations of authors and the mediations of publishers stand revealed. Historians, however, have been slow to apply these techniques to works claiming to tell a true story of the past. Our discipline is part of both the humanities and the social sciences, on one side implicated in the intellectual culture that returns, repeatedly and creatively, to old books and reads them anew. But our training also responds to the intellectual culture and practice of science, including the social sciences, where old knowledge is routinely discarded in favour of new data and fresh interpretations. Old history books can be misleading, but we can learn how to use them. Because the unanswerable fact remains: until the advent of broadcasting, most people learned their history from books and periodicals, and they neither wished nor chose to seek out the works of academic scholars. They read books and articles published for a commercial marketplace, written by authors with a story to tell and with an economic as well as a literary interest in doing so engagingly. Those readers' experience mattered. Popular and school histories were the only accounts of the past that most people experienced, and despite the manifest deficiencies of the books and articles, readers took them seriously and remembered what they had read.

The development of history as an academic discipline did nothing to impede the composition, publication and consumption of popular histories. Readers may have been troubled by reports that history had been subject to 'revision' in academic settings, baffled by the conventions of academic writing or embarrassed at being told that it was wrong to read history with 'delight'.

Publishers meanwhile continued to review and commission manuscripts, and to produce books that were written for the common reader, not for the scholar. But we do not know enough about what such books looked like, or how they were read. An inventory of history books would allow us to ask questions about how history was conceptualized, by non-academic authors as a subject and by commercial publishers as a trade category. Which events and periods did they cover, and which historical subjects were rejected or ignored? How significant were these works in shaping a culture that claimed an Empire? And then, what happened when the same books were exported in revised editions to readers in colonial settings abroad? Scholarship in the history of science has found a way to understand popular science – largely through examining its authorship, reading and publishing.[10] Perhaps historians of history-writing can learn from historians of science how to read popular history.

Another central aspect of the history of the book, and of historical culture, is the schoolbook. School histories were the locus for the creation of national pride and the sense of ethnic and racial superiority. Despite this power, school histories have not been given the attention they deserve. Due to the wear-and-tear inherent in the genre, and because they were not collected by copyright libraries, access has been difficult and methodologies undeveloped. Influential works were hidden in the catalogues of the great copyright libraries under the obscure names of their authors. School and popular histories were sometimes regarded as ephemeral by contemporary librarians who discarded such works outright or relegated them to a supplementary catalogue. Electronic library records have made it possible to search out such works by their titles and by other key words. And projects for the digitization of books and periodicals will make possible further new techniques for research on school and popular histories.[11]

In *Past into Print* I have set about connecting historiography with the history of the book. To identify the agency and mediation of the publisher is to offer a new way of thinking about the work of influential historians, to reflect on how they conceptualized their readers from childhood to old age. It can be refreshing to turn historiography upside down, and ask what readers thought history was all about, rather than what a circumscribed and self-defined group of writers told them it should be. The mediation of publishers was crucial. A revised periodization, for example, was of great concern to the academic historians; for Lord Acton and his students, the Renaissance and Reformation were pivotal events. Seeley, however, unlike most of his peers, preferred very modern history – that is the period since the eighteenth century. Both Wright and Macmillan, with their sense of the market for works on the recent past, affected the emerging conventions on periodization. On a narrower scale, biographers and other scholars studying the intellectual culture of history-writing might learn a good deal by looking critically at the correspondence in publishers' archives, as well as at book reviews and at any 'fan mail' from readers.

Both the abstract idea of history and the material media of books and periodicals can be characterized as ingredients of the cement that held Victorian and Edwardian culture together. It was a culture that engaged with the past as a way of understanding the present and imagining the future.[12] In our own culture, history has again begun to resonate with many people. But if twenty-first-century heritage sites, museums and history-television are contemporary venues for public history, then the nineteenth- and early twentieth-century equivalent was the printed page. This was both the locale and the medium through which ordinary citizens learned about their past and shared it with their children. For some people, however, those who were not ordinary, or not fully citizens, the cement of history was experienced as a weight. In this sense, popular and school histories were the media through which even women, working-class, immigrant and colonial readers were exposed to a past that they were expected to identify as their own. The public understanding of history in the past has attracted serious scholarly attention in recent years. Bibliographical and publishing-history work can contribute to a flourishing discussion, by discovering how the narrative of England's past was mediated to what was once called 'the English common reader'.

Notes

1 Every schoolboy knows: publishing the narrative of England's liberty, 1850-1863

1 John Feather, *A History of British Publishing*, 2nd edn (London: Routledge, 2006).
2 Philip Gaskell, *A New Introduction to Bibliography* (Oxford: Oxford University Press, 1972); G. Thomas Tanselle, *Literature and Artifacts* (Charlottesville: The Bibliographical Society of the University of Virginia, 1998).
3 A few of the numerous recent works on historiography are Michael Bentley, *Modern Historiography: An Introduction* (New York: Routledge, 1999); Peter Burke, *History and Social Theory* (Oxford: Polity Press, 1992); Bonnie G. Smith, *The Gender of History: Men, Women, and Historical Practice* (Harvard University Press, 2000) and Ludmilla Jordanova, *History in Practice*, 2nd edn (London: Hodder Arnold, 2006).
4 T. W. Heyck, *The Transformation of Intellectual Life in Victorian England* (London: Croom Helm, 1982); John Kenyon, *The History Men: The Historical Profession in England Since the Renaissance* (London: Weidenfeld & Nicolson, 1983); Stephen Bann, *The Inventions of History: Essays on the representation of the past* (Manchester: Manchester University Press, 1990); A. Dwight Culler, *The Victorian Mirror of History* (New Haven and London: Yale University Press, 1985); Rosemary Jann, *The Art and Science of Victorian History* (Columbus: Ohio State University Press, 1985); Philippa Levine, *The Amateur and the Professional: Antiquarians, Historians and Archaeologists in Victorian England, 1838-1886* (Cambridge: Cambridge University Press, 1986).
5 For 'book culture' see Leslie Howsam, *Old Books and New Histories: An Orientation to Studies in Book and Print Culture* (Toronto: University of Toronto Press, 2006), pp. 12-13, 16, 41.
6 Simon Eliot, *Some Patterns and Trends in British Publishing 1800-1919* (London: The Bibliographical Society, 1994); 'Patterns and Trends and the NSTC: Some Initial Observations', *Publishing History* XLII (1997): 79-104; XLIII 1998: 71-112. See also the classic works of Richard D. Altick, *The English Common Reader: A Social History of the Mass Reading Public, 1800-1900* (Chicago: University of Chicago Press, 1957) and J. A. Sutherland, *Victorian Novelists & Publishers* (Chicago: University of

Chicago Press, 1978). A newer study is Allan C. Dooley, *Author and Printer in Victorian England* (Charlottesville: University Press of Virginia, 1992), and James Raven's *The Business of Books: Booksellers and the English Book Trade 1450-1850* (New Haven: Yale University Press, 2007) is a welcome addition to the study of the economics of publishing and bookselling.

7 The phrase 'Every schoolboy knows who imprisoned Montezuma ...' appears at the beginning of Macaulay's essay on Clive (G. O. Trevelyan, ed., *Works of Lord Macaulay* 9:186 (London: Longman, 1898). One study is Jane Millgate, *Macaulay* (London: Routledge & Kegan Paul, 1973). See also David R. Sorensen, 'Carlyle, Macaulay, and the "Dignity of History"', *Carlyle Annual* 11 (1990): 41-52.

8 One example among many is R. J. Cruickshank, *Charles Dickens and Early Victorian England* (London: Pitman, 1949): 'Macaulay's schoolboy, that classic little prig, is making outraged signals to us down the corridors of time.'

9 For the concept of a communication circuit see Robert Darnton, 'What Is the History of Books?' *Dædalus* 111, no. 3 (Summer 1982): 65-83; see also Howsam, *Old Books*, pp. 28-45.

10 For an introduction to the rich literature on religion and science in Victorian England see James Moore, *The Post-Darwinian Controversies: A Study of the Protestant Struggles to Come to Terms with Darwin in Great Britain and America 1870-1900* (Cambridge: Cambridge University Press, 1979) and Frank Turner, *Between Science and Religion: The Reaction to Scientific Naturalism in Late Victorian England* (New Haven and London: Yale University Press, 1974).

11 C. M. Yonge to A. Macmillan. 10 April 1866. BL MSS Add. 54920/152.

12 See below page 56.

13 See below page 50.

14 For a list of relevant works see Howsam, *Old Books*. In particular see D. F. McKenzie, *Bibliography and the Sociology of Texts* (London: The British Library, 1986).

15 David Cannadine, *G. M. Trevelyan: A Life in History* (London: HarperCollins, 1992), p. 224.

16 Kathleen Burk, *Troublemaker: The Life and History of A. J. P. Taylor* (New Haven and London: Yale University Press, 2000), p. 227.

17 David McKitterick, *A History of Cambridge University Press: New Worlds for Learning, 1873-1972* (Cambridge: Cambridge University Press, 2004), pp. 156-8.

18 Peter Sutcliffe, *The Oxford University Press: An Informal History* (Oxford: Clarendon Press, 1978), pp. 230-2. See below page 86.

19 See, among others, Peter D. McDonald, *British Literary Culture and Publishing Practice, 1880-1914* (Cambridge: Cambridge University Press, 1997) and Peter Shillingsburg, *Pegasus in Harness: Victorian Publishing and William Makepeace Thackeray* (Charlottesville: University of Virginia Press, 1992).

20 Cited in Sutcliffe, *Oxford University Press*, 34.

21 The authority here is Doris S. Goldstein, some of whose articles are: 'The Organizational

Development of the British History Profession 1884-1921', *Bulletin of the Institute of Historical Research* 55:132 (1982): 180-93; 'The Professionalisation of History in Britain in the Later Nineteenth and Early Twentieth Centuries', *Storia Della Storiografia* 3 (1983): 3-27; 'The Origins and Early Years of the English Historical Review', *English Historical Review* 101:398 (1986): 6-19; 'History at Oxford and Cambridge: Professionalization and the Influence of Ranke', in *Leopold Von Ranke and the Shaping of the Historical Discipline*, eds Iggers and Powell (Syracuse: Syracuse University Press, 1990). See also Reba Soffer, *Discipline and Power: the University, History and the Making of an English Elite, 1870-1930* (Stanford: Stanford University Press, 1994) and Michael Bentley, 'The Evolution and Dissemination of Historical Knowledge', in *The Organisation of Knowledge in Victorian Britain*, ed. Martin Daunton (Oxford: Oxford University Press for the British Academy, 2005).

22 E. A. Freeman, 'On the Study of History', *Fortnightly Review* 35 (1881): 326. For more on this subject see Howsam, 'Academic Discipline or Literary Genre?: The Establishment of Boundaries in Historical Writing', *Victorian Literature and Culture* (2004): 525-45.

23 P. L. Gell to L. von Ranke. 17 July 1885. OUP Archives, Letter Books 38/44.

24 A. Macmillan to E. A. Freeman. 11 September 1872. BL MSS Add. 55392/925.

25 Millgate, *Macaulay*, p. 184.

26 For 'modernism' see Michael Bentley, *Modernizing England's Past: English Historiography in the Age of Modernism 1870-1970* (Cambridge: Cambridge University Press, 2005).

27 Quoted in Boswell's *Life of Johnson* (1791).

28 James A. Secord, *Victorian Sensation: The Extraordinary Publication, Reception, and Secret Authorship of Vestiges of the Natural History of Creation* (Chicago: University of Chicago Press, 2000), 126.

29 A scholarly journal devoted to the history of textbooks is *Paradigm, the Journal of the Textbook Colloquium* (available online at http://faculty.ed.uiuc.edu/westbury/Paradigm/). See also Stephen Heathorn, *For Home, Country, and Race: Constructing Gender, Class, and Englishness in the Elementary School, 1880-1914* (Toronto: University of Toronto Press, 2000); Valerie E. Chancellor, *History for their Masters: Opinion in the English History Textbook 1800-1914* (New York: Augustus M. Kelley, 1970); G. M. D. Howat, 'The Nineteenth-Century History Text-Book', *British Journal of Educational Studies* 13:2 (May 1965), 147-59; and Howsam et al., 'What the Victorians Learned: Perspectives on Nineteenth-Century Schoolbooks', *Journal of Victorian Culture* 12 (2): 2007, 262-85.

30 Rosemary Mitchell, *Picturing the Past: English History in Text and Image 1830-1870* (Oxford: Clarendon Press, 2000), pp. 67-73.

31 See below page 20.

32 Mitchell, *Picturing the Past*, p. 36. Mitchell demonstrates that the 1823 first edition of 'Mrs Markham' was a pioneer in the field of illustration; earlier books had not been devoid of images but the

Penrose volumes incorporated illustrations that claimed to be authentic, and the authors and publishers were prepared to undertake a process of 'visual editing' to make them look right. For Elizabeth Penrose see also Mitchell's *ODNB* contribution.
33 Mitchell, *Picturing the Past*, p. 60.
34 Mitchell, *Picturing the Past*, p. 67.
35 See Brian Norton, *Freeman's Life: Highlights, Chronology, Letters and Works* (Farnborough: Norton, 1993). See also C. W. J. Parker, 'The Failure of Liberal Racialism: The Racial Ideas of E. A. Freeman', *The Historical Journal* 24:4 (December 1981): 825-46 and W. R. W. Stephens, *The Life and Letters of Edward A. Freeman* (London: Macmillan, 1895).
36 A. Macmillan to E. A. Freeman. 4 April 1870. BL MSS Add. 55390/845.
37 C. M. Yonge to E. A. Freeman. 30 August [1872]. Freeman Archive, John Rylands Library of Manchester. FA1/7/842.
38 A. Macmillan to E. A. Freeman. 8 January 1868. BL MSS Add. 55389/144.
39 C. M. Yonge to A. Macmillan. 5 November 1877. BL MSS Add. 54921/36.
40 For education in the nineteenth century see Gretchen R. Galbraith, *Reading Lives: Reconstructing Childhood, Books, and Schools in Britain, 1870-1920* (London: St Martin's Press, 1997) and Gillian Sutherland, *Elementary Education in the Nineteenth Century* (London: Historical Association, 1971).
41 Jonathan Topham, 'Publishing "Popular Science" in Early Nineteenth-Century Britain', in *Science in the Marketplace: Nineteenth-Century Sites and Experiences*, ed. Aileen Fyfe and Bernard Lightman (Chicago: Chicago University Press, 2007).
42 Charles Hastings Collette, *Rome's Jesuitical Tampering with Books of Education. Exemplified in the modern editions of Ince's Outlines of History* (London: Bateman, 1857), pp. 21-2. Gilbert's words, citing his letters to the *Morning Advertiser* where Collette's polemic had originally appeared, are found in a postscript to Collette's pamphlet.
43 In a letter to his friend Macvey Napier, Macaulay said, 'I shall not be satisfied unless I produce something which shall for a few days supersede the last fashionable novel on the tables of young ladies.' Thomas Pinney, ed., *The Letters of Thomas Babington Macaulay* (Cambridge: Cambridge University Press, 1974), IV:17.
44 David Hume's work, first published between 1754 and 1762, was reprinted many times in the nineteenth century, usually with illustrations; John Murray published *The Student's Hume* in 1859. Significantly, the work was out of copyright. See also chapter 2 ('The History of *The History of England*: The Evolution of a Standard Text and its Illustrations') in Mitchell, *Picturing the Past*.
45 See Susan Drain, 'Howitt, Mary (1799-1888)', in *ODNB*, http://www.oxforddnb.com/view/article/13995 (accessed 4 June 2007).
46 E. A. Freeman to A. Macmillan. 24 February 1867. BL MSS Add. 55049/72.
47 D. F. McKenzie, 'Trading Places? England 1689 – France 1789', in Peter D. McDonald and

Michael Suarez, eds, *Making Meaning: Printers of the Mind and Other Essays* (Amherst: University of Massachusetts Press, 2002), p. 144.

2 Quality and Profit: New Histories of England, 1863-1880

1 J. B. Bury, *An Inaugural Lecture delivered in the Divinity School, Cambridge, on January 26, 1903* (Cambridge: Cambridge University Press, 1903), pp. 41-2. 'If, year by year, history is to become a more and more powerful force for stripping the bandages of error from the eyes of men, for shaping public opinion and advancing the cause of intellectual and political liberty, she will best prepare her disciples for the performance of that task ... by remembering always that, though she may supply material for literary art or philosophical speculation, she is herself simply a science, no less and mo more.'
2 W. Stubbs to E. A. Freeman. 8 November 1857. Bod.MS.Eng.misc.e.148/7. Henry Thomas Buckle (1821-62) was a deist and rationalist, influenced by the work of Auguste Comte among others. Buckle's *History of Civilization in England* was published in two volumes 1857 and 1861 (by J. W. Parker). He argued that generalization, rather than research, is the *métier* of the historian.
3 The OUP Letter Books of the 1870s refer to various translations of Ranke's work. The Cambridge University Press considered a proposal by G. W. Prothero in the early 1880s, but declined; this was taken up by Kegan Paul & Co. In 1885 the Oxford Secretaries were negotiating with Ranke through the translator Philip Ashworth; in this case the quality of the translation was unsatisfactory.
4 Peter Novick, *That Noble Dream: The 'Objectivity Question' and the American Historical Profession* (Cambridge: Cambridge University Press, 1988), p. 222.
5 See below chapter 4.
6 D. S. Goldstein, 'The Organizational Development of the British History Profession 1884-1921', *Bulletin of the Institute of Historical Research* 55:132 (1982): 184-6. Until 1899 and the presidency of A. W. Ward, the RHS was regarded with suspicion by scholars associated with the *English Historical Review*. Creighton described it in 1889 as 'a vast fraud'. See also J. W. Burrow, 'Victorian Historians and the Royal Historical Society', *Transactions of the Royal Historical Society*: 5th series, 39 (1988), 125-40.
7 Alexis Weedon, *Victorian Publishing: The Economics of Book Production for a Mass Market, 1836-1916* (Aldershot: Ashgate, 2003), p. 57.
8 Elizabeth James, ed., *Macmillan: A Publishing Tradition* (London: Palgrave, 2002). George J. Worth, *Macmillan's Magazine, 1859-1907: 'No Flippancy or Abuse Allowed'* (London: Ashgate, 2003).
9 Asa Briggs, ed., *Essays in the history of publishing in celebration of the 250th anniversary of the House of Longman, 1724-1974* (London: Longmans, 1974). Lord Briggs's long-awaited History of Longman was published by The British Library in 2008.
10 Sutcliffe, *Oxford University Press*, p. 17.

11 McKitterick, *New Worlds*, p. 57
12 Christopher Harvie, 'Bryce, James, Viscount Bryce (1838-1922)', *ODNB*, http://www.oxforddnb.com/view/article/32141 (accessed 7 December 2005). G. P. Gooch, 'Ward, Sir Adolphus William (1837-1924)', rev. R. J. W. Evans, in *ODNB*, http://www.oxforddnb.com/view/article/36726 (accessed 24 April 2007).
13 For scholarship on Yonge see the 'Introduction' and 'Bibliography' to Clare A. Simmons' edition of Yonge's novel *The Clever Woman of the Family* (Peterborough: Broadview Press, 2001). The classic biography is Georgina Battiscombe, *Charlotte Mary Yonge: The Story of an Uneventful Life* (London: Constable, 1943). A recent article is Susan Walton, 'Charlotte M. Yonge and the "historic harem" of Edward Augustus Freeman', *Journal of Victorian Culture* 11.2 (2006): 226-55.
14 C. Kingsley to A. Macmillan 1863. BL MSS Add. 54911/113.
15 See below page 37.
16 A. Macmillan to E. A. Freeman. 23 March 1863. Freeman Archive, John Rylands Library of Manchester. 1/7/495.
17 E. A. Freeman to A. Macmillan. 16 October 1863. BL MSS Add. 55049/6.
18 E. A. Freeman to A. Macmillan. 1 December 1865. BL MSS Add. 55049/39. A close paraphrase of this passage appears in the preface to the book.
19 E. A. Freeman to A. Macmillan. 19 December 1868. BL MSS Add. 55049/99. A. Macmillan to E. A. Freeman. 30 December 1868. BL MSS Add. 55389/107.
20 Longmans, Green & Co. to E. A. Freeman. 31 January 1861. Freeman Archive, John Rylands Library of Manchester. 1/7/484. A. Macmillan to Freeman. 3 March 1863. FA1/7/493.
21 J. Bryce to E. A. Freeman. 2 December 1865. Bod. MSS Bryce. 9/82.
22 E. A. Freeman to A. Macmillan. 4 December 1865. BL MSS Add. 55049/42; 13 May 1866, f. 47.
23 A. Macmillan to E. A. Freeman. 18 February 1867. Freeman Archive, John Rylands Library of Manchester. 1/7/500.
24 See chapter 1.
25 *The Athenaeum*, 16 March 1867: 345-6. *The Athenaeum* was edited by Hepworth Dixon (1853-69), and Freeman appears to have believed Dixon wrote the review himself. However, it is attributed to John Doran (1807-78) by 'The Athenaeum Index of Reviews and Reviewers: 1830-1870' (http://www.soi.city.ac.uk/~asp/v2/home.html). See A. Macmillan to E. A. Freeman. 16 March 1867. BL MSS Add. 55387: 5. See also Freeman to Macmillan, 17 March. 555049:74. 'I appreciate the commercial value of the *Athenaeum* article; but it is grievous to one's feelings to be praised by Hepworth Dixon. It was much more satisfactory when he pronounced [my book] *Federal Government* vol. I to "show no signs of independent research". The general line of the *Athenaeum* is to run down sound scholarship in any shape.'
26 C. M. Yonge to E. A. Freeman. 11 September 1872. Freeman Archive, John Rylands Library of Manchester. FA1/7/833.
27 For more on the Historical Course for Schools see Howsam, 'Academic Discipline or Literary Genre'.

28 See John L. Kijinski, 'John Morley's "English Men of Letters" Series and the Politics of Reading', *Victorian Studies* 34:2 (1991): 205-25.
29 E. A. Freeman to J. Bryce. 30 December 1871. Bod. MSS Bryce 5/290. For Thompson see Amanda Capern, 'Anatomy of a Friendship: E. A. Freeman and Edith Thompson', *Paragon Review* 6 (1997): 25-9 and Howsam, 'Academic Discipline or Literary Genre', 536-42. One possible 'really able woman' was Mary Ward, whose interest in Spain might have been shaped into a history. Humphry Ward wrote on his new wife's behalf to ask Macmillan to release her from the semi-commitment (26 April [1880?]), BL MSS Add. 54928/3.
30 J. R. Green to E. A. Freeman. 12 November 1873. Freeman Archive, John Rylands Library of Manchester. FA1/7/279.
31 E. A. Freeman to A. Macmillan. 20 August 1877. BL MSS Add. 55051/111.
32 See Roy M. MacLeod, *The 'Creed of Science' in Victorian England* (Aldershot: Ashgate, 2000) for reprints of two essays on the important scientific periodical: 'The Genesis of *Nature*'; 'The Social Framework of *Nature* in its First Fifty Years'.
33 See Alon Kadish, 'Scholarly Exclusiveness and the Foundation of the *English Historical Review*', *Historical Research: The Bulletin of the Institute for Historical Research* 61:145 (June 1988): 183-98. See also Howsam, 'Academic discipline or literary genre'.
34 *Oxford Essays, contributed by Members of the University* was an annual published from 1855 to 1858 in London by John W. Parker and Son. A notice advertised 'Cambridge Essays' in preparation for the press, but these seem never to have appeared. The Essays were described as follows: 'not intended to advocate any particular set of opinions, theological, social, or political. Each writer is responsible for his own opinions, and for none but his own; and no attempt has been made to give a general unity of thought to the publication. The tie that unites the different contributors is not that they think alike, but that they belong to the same University.' The titles were largely historical (and classical). One in 1885 was by J. A. Froude, 'Suggestions on the best means of teaching English history'.
35 J. R. Green to E. A. Freeman (manuscript copy). 28 January 1867. Bod. MSS Bryce 73/11. E. A. Freeman to J. Bryce. 3 February 1867. Bod. MSS Bryce 5/120.
36 J. R. Green to A. Macmillan. 4 February 1870. BL MSS Add. 55058/12.
37 J. R. Green to A. Macmillan (fair copy or clean draft; no substantial alterations]. 15 June 1876. Jesus College Oxford, J. R. Green papers. Box 12. This letter does not appear among Green's letters in the Macmillan papers. See also note 39 below for correspondence on the same subject in 1870.
38 J. R. Green to A. Macmillan. [December 1869]. BL MSS Add. 55058/5. See also Anthony Brundage, *The People's Historian: John Richard Green and the Writing of History in Victorian England* (Westport, Conn.: Greenwood Press, 1994), pp. 73-99.
39 J. R. Green to A. Macmillan [undated, probably 1870]. BL MSS Add. 55058/16.

40 F. J. Furnivall to Macmillan & Co. 21 November 1874. Jesus College Oxford, J. R. Green papers/12.
41 J. Morley. Reader's report to Macmillan & Co. *c.* March or April 1874. BL MSS Add. 55933/63.
42 Sutcliffe, *Oxford University Press*, pp. 27; 33. See also Philippa Levine, *The Amateur and the Professional*, p. 138.
43 Sutcliffe, *Oxford University Press*, p. 24.
44 G. W. Kitchin to A. Macmillan. 1 February 1868. BL MSS Add. 55054/187.
45 Freeman, 'Oxford after 40 Years', *Contemporary Review* 51, 882. See also Soffer, *Discipline and Power*, pp. 100-2.
46 Reader's Report (J. Morley?) to Macmillan & Co. September 1872. BL MSS Add. 55933/17. Report on a biography of W. Carstairs by the Rev. S. Herbert Story: 'The subject is no doubt a good one – though of course not likely to attract the crowd, who like to keep to the great open road of history. It would interest historical students, and specially the Scotch.'
47 Sutcliffe, *Oxford University Press*, pp. 33-4 and A. Macmillan to E. A. Freeman. 14 May 1866. Freeman Archive, John Rylands Library of Manchester. 1/7/499: 'He [Smith] is hard on his great History of England.' Correspondence in the Macmillan archive (BL MSS Add. 55172, 1866 *passim*) confirms that Smith was at work on a History of England, which he first planned to submit to the Clarendon Press in Oxford and later intended for Macmillan. His resignation from the Oxford chair and removal to Canada put an end to the project.
48 Robert Brentano, 'The Sound of Stubbs', *Journal of British Studies* 6 (1966-7): 1-14.
49 B. Price to W. Stubbs. 6 May 1879. OUP Archives, Letter Books 20/224. No copy of this work appears to have survived in either the Bodleian Library, the British Library or the Cambridge University Library.
50 OUP Letter Books, *passim*.
51 B. Price to W. Stubbs. 8 June 1883. OUP Archives, Letter Books: 32, 252.
52 A. W. Ward to J. Bryce. 25 January [1867]. Bod. MSS Bryce 148/97. Kitchin's three-volume *History of France* had its own long and convoluted history. It first appeared in 1873-7. A third edition was required in the early 1890s, but Kitchin had become Dean of Durham and was no longer in a position to make revisions. The Clarendon Press called upon the young H. A. L. Fisher to revise volume 1 (Letter of 24 June 1890, OUP Letter Books 50/325). First volume 3 (1894) and then volume 2 (1896) were revised by Arthur Hassall. When revisions were required for a fourth edition, the Press called upon F. F. Urquhart to revise all three volumes. A letter from H. T. Gerrans to Urquhart, on 25 January 1898 (Letter Books71/68), suggests that the Press wanted only minimal revisions made, and that they expected Kitchin to give his approval, whereas Urquhart seems to have wanted to rewrite more extensively.
53 For school readers see Heathorn, *For Home, Country, and Race*.
54 G. W. Kitchin to A. Macmillan: *passim* 2 December 1867 to 2 January 1868. BL MSS Add. 55054/171-85. Macmillan to

Kitchin. 30 December 1867. BL MSS Add. 55378/823. B. Price to Macmillan. 20 January 1869. OUP Archives, Letter Books 1/313. B. Price to Miss Roberts. 7 December 1869. OUP Archives, Letter Books 2/369.
55 Sutcliffe, *Oxford University Press*, p. 24.
56 E. A. Freeman to A. Macmillan. 5 August 1869. BL MSS Add. 55049/103. Freeman excepted Stubbs and Mountague Bernard from his characterization of the Press Delegates as 'stupid old dons'. A tringle is defined by the *Oxford English Dictionary* as a 'long slender rod'. (Freeman was a student of architectural history.)
57 McKitterick, *New Worlds*, pp. 86-7. Sutcliffe, *Oxford University Press*, pp. 48-53.
58 J. R. Seeley to O. Browning. 17 March [1883?]. Browning papers, King's College, Cambridge.
59 J. R. Seeley to J. Clay. 18 December 1878. CUP.Pr.B.13.D.43-6.
60 G. W. Prothero to J. Clay. 4 March 1876. CUP.UA.Pr.B.13.A.75. Correspondence in Prothero's papers at the Royal Historical Society provides evidence that he requested, and received, advice from Stubbs as well as on the arrangements with Longman (W. Stubbs to G. W. Prothero. 21 March and 19 May 1876; 3 March [1877]. G. N. Longman to Prothero. 20 June 1876. Prothero Papers, RHS. I/3).
61 J. R. Seeley to C. Clay. 28 January [1877]. CUP.UA.Pr.B.13.A.81. See also Seeley's article 'History and Politics', *Macmillan's Magazine* 41 (1879): 27. 'There were ... no good English books on Russia in 1877; and Mr. Mackenzie Wallace told me that though he had intended to give a complete historical view of the development of Russia he had been warned that such a scheme would never succeed with the English public, and so was driven to content himself with the personal narrative we have all read, the value of which may give us some notion of how much we have lost by our own fault. Unfortunately he had no choice between presenting his historical view to the general public, which turned up its nose at such a present, and suppressing it altogether. There was no select audience of specialists to which he could present it.'
62 McKitterick, *New Worlds*, p. 36.
63 See Richard Lodge, 'Ramsay, Sir James Henry, tenth baronet (1832-1925)', rev. Marjorie Chibnall, in *ODNB*, http://www.oxforddnb.com/view/article/35662 (accessed 20 April 2007). The quotation is from Chibnall's revised contribution, but Lodge's original essay is valuable for its information on the publication between 1898 and 1913 of four volumes, in the middle section of Ramsay's long work, by Swann Sonnenschein & Co. The Clarendon Press apparently relented to publish the last two volumes and also produced an eight-volume re-issue under the general title *The Scholar's History of England* (1913).
64 J. R. Green to J. Bryce. n.d. [1882?]. Bod. MSS Bryce 73/57.
65 E. A. Freeman to G. Macmillan. 26 November 1882. BL MSS Add. 55052/183.
66 P. L. Gell to W. Stubbs. 23 October 1889. OUP Letter Books 48/475.
67 P. L. Gell to J. Ramsay. 30

December 1889; 12 February 1890. OUP Letter Books 49/136; 386.
68 P. L. Gell to F. York Powell. 22 December 1891. His wife, Edith Lyttelton Gell, was the author of the successful 'pretty little book'.
69 J. Morley to A. Macmillan. 29 June 1868. BL MSS Add. 55055/13. On Reader's Reports see Gail Chester, 'The Not So Gentle Reader: The Role of the Publisher's Reader as Gatekeeper, With Particular Reference to Macmillan and Co., 1895-1905' (MA Diss., University of London, 1996) and Linda M. Fritschner, 'Publishers' readers, publishers and their authors', *Publishing History* 7 (1980): 45-100.

3 Breaking the Drowsy Spell of Narrative, 1880-1914

1 For the *Dictionary of National Biography* see Gillian Fenwick, *The Contributors' Index to the Dictionary of National Biography, 1885-1901* (Winchester: St Paul's Bibliographies, 1989) and *Women and the Dictionary of National Biography: a Guide to DNB Volumes 1885-1985 and Missing Persons* (Aldershot: Scolar Press, 1994). J. E. Neale observed that the research culture of the Dictionary office gave A. W. Pollard 'the idea from which ultimately was to come his conception of a postgraduate seminar as a group of scholars, young and old, meeting in a library, as scientists in a laboratory, to discuss their work and aid each other by the incidental dissemination of both method and knowledge'. (Quoted in N. B. Harte, *One Hundred and Fifty Years of History Teaching at University College London* (London: University College London, 1982), 15.) Harte agrees that the co-operative scholarship involved in the *DNB* was 'the germ of the idea of the Institute of Historical Research'.
2 P. L. Gell to J. Ramsay. 27 May 1896. OUP Letter Books 65/195.
3 J. R. Seeley, *The Expansion of England*, ed. John Gross (Chicago: University of Chicago Press, 1971; originally published by Macmillan 1883), p. 139.
4 'A Historical Society', *Macmillan's Magazine* 45 (1881): 44; 46-7. Seeley was addressing the Historical Society of Birmingham, made up of University students. He asked 'who is the better for floating at ease down those delightful smooth narrations in which recent history is recorded, not for students at all, but for the general public, which must on no account be fatigued?' He wanted the Birmingham students to regard themselves as 'a sort of aristocracy of students, which may stand between the writer and the general public'. Whereas 'the realm of mere literature' was a 'democracy' (elsewhere, a 'loose democracy'), the realm of science was restricted to a select circle of knowledge and discipline.
5 See David Cannadine, *G. M. Trevelyan: A Life in History* (London: HarperCollins, 1992), pp. 27; 214-15.
6 For the politics of the tripos see Reba N. Soffer, *Discipline and Power: The University, History, and the Making of an English Elite, 1870-1930* (Stanford: Stanford University Press, 1994), 128-56.
7 See Deborah Wormell, *Sir John Seeley and the Uses of History* (Cambridge: Cambridge University Press, 1980); also Peter Burroughs,

'John Robert Seeley and British Imperial History', *Journal of Imperial and Commonwealth History* 1:2 (1973): 191-211.
8 The recommendation came from E. A. Freeman. R. T. Shannon, 'Seeley, Sir John Robert (1834-1895)', *ODNB*, http://www.oxforddnb.com/view/article/25025 (accessed 23 April 2007).
9 J. R. Seeley, *The Life and Times of Stein, or Germany and Prussia in the Napoleonic Age*, 3 vols (Cambridge: Cambridge University Press, 1878). See Wormell, *Sir John Seeley*, pp. 77-81.
10 'History and Politics', *Macmillan's Magazine* 40 (1879): 292. The four-part article appeared between August and November 1879. He addressed the theme briefly in 'Political Somnambulism' (43: 1880) and returned to it when his 1881 and 1882 addresses to the Historical Society of Birmingham were published, also in *Macmillan's*, 45 (1881): 43-56 and 47 (1882): 67-80.
11 See Howsam, 'Imperial Publishers and The Idea Of Colonial History, 1870-1916', *History of Intellectual Culture* 5:2 (2005).
12 As published, the passage reads: 'The interest of English history ought therefore to deepen steadily to the close, and, since the future grows out of the past, the history of the past of England ought to give rise to a prophecy concerning her future. Yet our popular historians scarcely seem to think so. Does not Aristotle say that a drama ends, but an epic poem only leaves off? English history, as it is popularly related, not only has no distinct end, but leaves off in such a gradual manner, growing feebler and feebler, duller and duller, towards the close, that one might suppose that England instead of steadily gaining in strength had been for a century or two dying of mere old age. Can this be right?' After four pages of exposition, Seeley observes: 'There is something very characteristic in the indifference which we show towards this mighty phenomenon of the diffusion of our race and the expansion of our state. We seem, as it were, to have conquered and peopled half the world in a fit of absence of mind.' For the excision of Green's name as an example of 'our popular historians' see J. R. Seeley to A. Macmillan. 6 September 1882. BL MSS Add. 55074: 24. 'As a matter of course I should not wish to print the passage on Green as it stands, particularly as I hear sad accounts of his health, poor fellow! You must remember that the MS was put in your hands just as it was first written – and it was not written for publication. I do not blame Green for not knowing all history equally well, though I think he may be blamed for writing on the parts he knows less well. But, if I remember aright, the passage does not blame him at all, but only his book; it only says that a History of England in which the interest steadily diminishes towards the end instead of increasing is, so far, not a good history. However I have no desire whatever to attack him; pray do not vex him by mentioning the passage to him.'
13 J. R. Seeley to G. L. Craik. 20 December [1886?]. BL MSS Add. 55074/43.
14 In addition to Macmillan, Browning corresponded with Longman, Griffith & Farran, Oxford and Cambridge University

Presses, Rivingtons, Kegan Paul Trench (Charles Kegan Paul was a friend), Cassell, Walter Scott, Edward Arnold, Methuen, Blackie, Hurst & Blackett, John Lane and others. American publishers included Harper and Brothers; one Canadian publisher with which he corresponded was the Bradley Garretson Co. Browning papers, King's College, Cambridge. See also Ian Anstruther, *Oscar Browning: A Biography* (London: John Murray, 1983).

15 Owen Chadwick, *Professor Lord Acton: The Regius Chair of Modern History at Cambridge, 1895-1902* (Grand Rapids: The Acton Institute, 1995), pp. 4-5. See also Chadwick's *Acton and History*, chapter 8.

16 *Cornelius Nepos*, with English notes by O. Browning (Oxford: Clarendon Press, 1868); 3rd edition revised by W. R. Inge, 1888. Correspondence about successive reprints and possible revisions can be found in the Clarendon Press file in the Browning papers at King's College, Cambridge and passim in OUP Letter Books 1877-9 and again in 1891 and 1898.

17 Griffith & Farran to O. Browning. 30 May and 22 December 1882. Browning papers, King's College, Cambridge.

18 Griffith & Farran to O. Browning. 29 August 1883. Browning papers, King's College, Cambridge.

19 Griffith & Farran to O. Browning. 13 January 1886. A. G. Ross to O. Browning. 1 February 1886. Browning papers, King's College, Cambridge.

20 H. Virtue to O. Browning. 16 October 1888 and 1 November 1889. Browning papers, King's College, Cambridge.

21 H. Virtue to O. Browning. 25 November 1891. Browning papers, King's College, Cambridge. Browning denied the charge and on 30 November Virtue wrote to thank him for his letter and insist they had never believed he had made 'the unfair remarks' but this was presumably face-saving on both sides.

22 Subtitled 'A Literary Journal and Genealogical Register of the United Kingdom', Vol. 2, Part 1 of a New Series of the *Historical Review* was published in 1866. No further copies are to be found in the British Library Catalogue. The editor was C. W. Glendonwyn (of Glendonwyn and Partoun) and the publishers were the Edinburgh firm Inglis & Jack and the London firm Simpkin, Marshall & Co. Strikingly illustrated, its articles discussed subjects ranging from royal lineages to trade marks.

23 M. Creighton to O. Browning. 24 February 1883. Browning papers, King's College, Cambridge.

24 O. Browning to C. Clay. 3 February 1884. CUP Archives, Cambridge University Library: CUP.Pr.B.13.C.14. J. R. Seeley to Browning. 2 February [1884]. Browning papers, King's College, Cambridge.

25 D. S. Goldstein, 'Organizational Development', 180-93.

26 M. Creighton to J. R. Seeley. 2 August 1885. J. R. Seeley Collection, Senate House Library, University of London.

27 Louise Creighton, ed., *Life and Letters of Mandell Creighton* (London: Longmans, 1904), vol. 1: pp. 333-44. Relevant letters can be found in the Acton (Cambridge University Library), Browning (King's College, Cambridge), Bryce (Bodleian Library), Freeman (John

Rylands Library) and Seeley (University of London Library) collections.
28 *The Publishers' Circular* (September 1884). See also Howsam, 'Sustained Literary Ventures: The Series in Victorian Book Publishing', *Publishing History* 31 (1992): 5-26. For series see also G. B. Neavill, 'The Modern Library Series and American Cultural Life', *Journal of Library History* 16, 1981: 241–52 and Janet B. Friskney, *New Canadian Library: The Ross-McClelland Years, 1952-1978* (Toronto: University of Toronto Press, 2007).
29 Non-resident authors were protected by US copyright, but only if the book was simultaneously published in the USA and printed in that country from type set there. See Feather, *History of British Publishing*, p. 174. For more on copyright see James J. Barnes, *Authors, Publishers and Politicians* (London: Routledge and Kegan Paul, 1974).
30 For the importance of the 'three-decker' novel see N. N. Feltes, *Literary Capital and the Late Victorian Novel* (Madison: University of Wisconsin Press, 1993) and *Modes of Production of Victorian Novels* (Chicago: University of Chicago Press, 1986). See also earlier work by Guinevere L. Greist, *Mudie's Circulating Library and the Victorian Novel* (Newton Abbot: David & Charles, 1970). For the Net Book Agreement see Feather, *History of British Publishing*, pp. 147-9; 183-92.
31 See Howsam, 'An Experiment With Science for the Nineteenth-Century Book Trade: The International Scientific Series', *British Journal for the History of Science* 33 (2000): 187-207. Macmillan worked closely with T. H. Huxley in the late 1880s on the production of a series of Science Primers.
32 Ludmilla Jordanova, *History in Practice*, 2nd edn (London: Hodder Arnold, 2006), pp. 96-7.
33 Chadwick, *Professor Lord Acton*, p. 26.
34 Howsam, 'Imperial Publishers'. See also Josef L. Althoz, 'Lord Acton and the Plan of the Cambridge Modern History', *Historical Journal* 39:3 (1996): 723-36. Earlier articles include Stanley Leathes, 'The Editorial Methods of Sir Adolphus Ward: The Cambridge Modern History', *Cambridge Historical Journal* 1:2 (1924): 219-21 and G. N. Clark, 'The Origin of the Cambridge Modern History', *Cambridge Historical Journal* 8:2 (1945): 57-64.
35 CUP.CMH1. Cambridge University Press Archives, Cambridge University Library. A facsimile of this manuscript was published under the title *Longitude 30 West: A Confidential Report to the Syndics of the Cambridge University Press by Lord Acton* (New York: Cambridge University Press, 1969) and lengthy excerpts are reproduced in R. T. Wright's account of the origin of the History (see below).
36 On the periodization 'premodern' see Jacqueline Murray, 'Introduction', in *Desire and Discipline: Sex and Sexuality in the Premodern West*, eds J. Murray and K. Eisenbichler (Toronto: University of Toronto Press, 1996), pp. xii-xiii.
37 [R. T. Wright,] *The Cambridge Modern History: An Account of Its Origin, Authorship and Production*

(Cambridge: Cambridge University Press, 1907), p. 107.
38 G. P. Gooch, 'The Editorial Methods of Sir Adolphus Ward: The Cambridge History of British Foreign Policy 1922-3', *Cambridge Historical Journal* 1:2 (1924): 222-4; Leathes, 'The Editorial Methods of Sir Adolphus Ward', 219-21.
39 One of Archbold's tasks was to work through the historical journals, preparing notes ('tickets') on bibliographical references to supplement the work of contributors. In a letter of 8 December 1897, he told Acton, 'Personally I never weary of the work. It reminds me of a balloon voyage on the military principle taking photographs without dropping the anchor.' CUL MSS Add. 6443: 52.
40 W. Archbold to Acton. 4 October 1897. CUL MSS Add. 6443/45. R. T. Wright to Lord Acton. 5 June 1897. CUL MSS Add. 8119/I/W315.
41 W. A. J. Archbold to Lord Acton. 21 December 1896. CUL MSS Add. 6443/12-13.
42 W. A. J. Archbold to Lord Acton. 14 April 1898. CUL MSS Add. 6443/68. For Maitland see H. A. Holland, *Frederic William Maitland, 1850-1906* (London: Bernard Quaritch, 1953) and G. R. Elton, *F. W. Maitland* (New Haven and London: Yale University Press, 1985).
43 W. A. J. Archbold to Lord Acton. 28 December 1896. CUL MSS Add. 6443. Fry was supporting himself by journalism, lecturing and art criticism at this period of his development as a painter.
44 Shaw was Colonial Editor of *The Times* from 1893 to 1900. See Dorothy O. Helly and Helen Callaway, 'Lugard , Dame Flora Louise, Lady Lugard (1852–1929)', in *ODNB*, http://www.oxforddnb.com/view/article/38618 (accessed April 24, 2007). Flora Shaw's name had been recommended to Acton, probably by Sir Mountstuart Elphinstone Grant-Duff.
45 See McKitterick, *New Worlds*, pp. 73-7; 156-8; 197.
46 Lord Acton to R. T. Wright. 15 July 1896. CUP CMH 1. See also a slightly different version, perhaps a draft, in CUL MSS Add. 8119 (8)/492 dated 14 July.
47 A. W. Ward to Lord Acton, 12 December 1899. CUL MSS Add. 8119/I/W127. Acton to R. T. Wright. 29 December 1899. CUP CMH 1/88. Ward to Acton. 13 February 1900. CUL MSS Add. 8119/I/W137.
48 Maitland once remarked, 'It will be a very strange book, that History of ours. I am extremely curious to see whether Acton will be able to maintain a decent amount of harmony among the chapters. Some chapters that I saw did not look much like parts of one and the same book.' (Cited in Elton, *F. W. Maitland*, pp. 88-9.)
49 Sutcliffe, *Oxford University Press*, pp. 230-1. See also correspondence dated 1929-30 in OUP Archives, Norrington correspondence files 3720 and 8820.
50 See Griest, *Mudie's Circulating Library*, pp. 97-9, 160, 209. After George Moore's three-volume novel *A Modern Lover* (1883) was censored by Mudie's and other circulating libraries, his publisher Vizetelly brought out *A Mummer's Wife* (1885) in one volume which would be affordable to readers accustomed to borrowing novels, not buying them. Moore later wrote *Literature at Nurse; or Circulating*

Morals (1885) to criticize the effect of circulating libraries on literary culture.

51 These words also appear in Acton's original proposal (CUP CMH 1). For an excerpt from his letter to the contributors see Fritz Stern, ed., *The Varieties of History from Voltaire to the Present* (New York: Vintage Books, 1972), pp. 247-9; 495-6.

52 A telling example of editorial control is Archbold's comment on A. F. Pollard, then about thirty years of age. 'He is very young & in a short talk you could see whether he would do. He is accurate, painstaking, & eminently practical. If that coupled with the fact that you can direct his reading in a way that might not be possible in the case of an older man, is sufficient well & good. The want is fire; at least that is my diagnosis. On the question of research you need have no fear.' CUL MSS Add. 6443: 94, n.d. [May 1899?].

53 Acton's initial report to the Press (CUP CMH 1, October 1896) cited in [Wright] *The Cambridge Modern History*, p. 12.

54 W. A. J. Archbold to Lord Acton. 19 January 1897. CUL MSS Add. 6443/22: 'Prothero when here [at Cambridge] was regarded as a *peacemaker*. He is not at all a violent man. I never heard of his politics, so that. ... I feel sure that there would be no danger of his putting himself into the Italian chapters.'

55 Sutcliffe, *Oxford University Press*, p. 66. For Gell see also Rimi B. Chatterjee, *Empires of the Mind: A History of the Oxford University Press in India under the Raj* (New Delhi: Oxford University Press, 2006).

56 P. L. Gell to W. Stubbs. Two letters of 24 November 1886. OUP Archives Letter Books 41/290; 369. See also Gell to A. L. Smith. 9 December 1886 and 2 March 1888. Letter Books 41/369 and 44/591.

57 Sutcliffe, *Oxford University Press*, 81. See also Oliver Elton, *Frederick York Powell: A Life* (Oxford: Clarendon Press, 1906).

58 C. E. Doble to H. Rashdall. 20 October 1890. OUP Letter Books 51/75. See also 27 April 1891 (52/457) and 25 October 1892 (56/254). For Kitchin see chapter 2 note 52. For Greswell see P. L. Gell to W. Greswell. 17 November 1888. OUP Letter Books 46/338. See also 25 June 1889 (48/18) and Gell to Greswell. 15 January 1891 (51/688).

59 P. L. Gell to Archdeacon Palmer. 14 August 1891. OUP Letter Books 53/430.

60 P. L. Gell to F. York Powell. 13 August 1891. OUP Letter Books 53/426.

61 E. A. Freeman to the Delegates of the Clarendon Press. 30 October 1891. OUP Archives. OP LB814.

62 P. L. Gell to F. York Powell. 22 December 1891: 54.

63 C. E. Doble to F. York Powell. 18 March 1890. OUP Letter Books 49/601.

64 C. E. Doble to F. York Powell. 22 August 1893. OUP Letter Books 58/264.

65 H. T. Gerrans to H. W. C. Davis. 1 February 1898. H. Milford to R. S. Rait, 23 January 1901. OUP Archives, Letter Books 71/166; 80/213. For Davis see J. R. H. Weaver, 'Davis, Henry William Carless (1874-1928)', rev. H. C. G. Matthew, *ODNB*, http://www.oxforddnb.com/view/article/32746 (accessed 7 December 2005).

66 'Herbert picked up the feeling from the school that he should

never let anyone know he used so juvenile a resource.' C. T. McIntire, *Herbert Butterfield: Historian as Dissenter* (New Haven and London: Yale University Press, 2004), p. 9.
67 Sutcliffe, *Oxford University Press*, pp. 158-62.
68 Mark Starr, *Lies and Hate in Education* (London: Hogarth Press, 1929), pp. 13; 34; 38. I am grateful to Melba Cuddy-Keane for bringing this book to my attention.

4 Historians and Publishers in an Age of War and Revolution, 1914-1929

1 Stuart Wallace, *War and the Image of Germany: British Academics 1914-1918* (Edinburgh: John Donald Publishers, 1988).
2 E. Thompson to A. Macmillan. 30 August 1916. BL MSS Add. 55078/78. In 1891, eighteen years after her book had first appeared, Thompson observed that the records showed her sales reaching 237,000 while those of J. R. Green's *Short History*, published a year after hers, were being advertised as having reached 160,000. The following figures come from copyright pages in later printings of the book. First edition 1873 (reprinted three times in 1874); 1875; 1876; 1877 (five times); 1878 (twice). Second edition [with maps added] 1878 (July); 1879 (three times); 1881; 1883 (twice); 1885; 1886; 1888; 1889; 1891; 1893; 1895; 1897. Third edition (described as 'reprinted with additions') 1901; 1903. Reprinted with corrections, Globe 8o edition 1907; 1908. New [4th] Edition 1923. There were further reprints in Canada and the United States. The 1878 printing has a note by Thompson about Freeman's sanction for adding maps (useful in schools). The 1901 edition includes a lavish description of Prince Albert which Freeman had deleted from her first text because he could not abide 'Albert worship'. The 1923 edition has Freeman's preface and Thompson's 1878 note, plus a note dated 1923, stating that she cannot obtain the sanction of the late Mr Freeman or 'benefit by his kind and thorough supervision. I cannot even venture to assert that his view of recent events would be that which I have taken' – nevertheless she trusted he would not disown her book.
3 P. A. Linehan, 'The Making of the Cambridge Medieval History', *Speculum* 57:3 (1982), 463-94.
4 Sutcliffe, *Oxford University Press*, pp. 172-3. See also Wallace, *War and the Image of Germany*, pp. 60-6.
5 For the Historical Association see Goldstein, 'Organizational Development', 188-9. The Historical Association was chiefly concerned with the teaching of history. The first president was C. H. Firth; Pollard served as assistant editor of the *Dictionary of National Biography* from 1893 to 1901. He taught in the University of London School of History (1903-31) and launched the Historical Association in 1906; he edited *History* from 1916 to 1922 and founded the Institute of Historical Research in 1921.
6 A. F. Pollard to Macmillan & Co. 14 March 1916. BL MSS Add. 55071/7. Correspondence about the journal from Pollard and his collaborator (and successor) Eliza Jeffries Davis can be found in the Macmillan papers (BL MSS Add. 55071-2). Davis later served as

Reader in the history of London at University College London from 1921 to 1941.

7 G. P. Gooch, 'Ward, Sir Adolphus William (1837-1924)', rev. R. J. W. Evans, *ODNB*, http://www.oxforddnb.com/view/article/36726 (accessed 14 May 2007).

8 A. W. Ward to Lord Acton. 6 and 19 February 1902. CUL MSS Add. 8119/I/W159-60.

9 Sutcliffe, *Oxford University Press*, pp. 195-6.

10 P. Guedalla to G. Hopkins. 23 October 1923. OUP Archives. OP2777.1941-5. Lawrence's remarks are cited in Philip Crumpton, 'Introduction to the New Edition', *Movements in European History*, D. H. Lawrence (Oxford: Oxford University Press, 1971), p. xv. The 1971 edition also contains the suppressed Epilogue. See also the 2002 edition, in the Cambridge Edition of the Complete Works of D. H. Lawrence, edited by Crumpton.

11 A. B. McKillop, *The Spinster and the Prophet: Florence Deeks, H. G. Wells and the Mystery of the Purloined Past* (Toronto: Mcfarlane Walter and Ross, 2001): published in the United States with the subtitle *H. G. Wells, Florence Deeks and the Case of the Plagiarized Text* (New York: Four Walls Eight Windows, 2002).

12 Julia Stapleton, *Sir Arthur Bryant and National History in Twentieth-Century Britain* (Lanham, MD: Lexington Books, 2006). An earlier work is Pamela Street, *Arthur Bryant: Portrait of a Historian* (Glasgow: Collins, 1979).

13 A. Bryant to S. C. Roberts. 25 November 1931. CUP.UA.Pr. A.B.1170/4. Bryant's biography of Pepys was eventually published in three volumes: 1933, 1935 and 1938.

14 Cannadine, *G. M. Trevelyan*, p. 110.

15 See above page 5. Records of the Longman Group, Records of British Publishing and Printing. Special Collections, University of Reading Library.

16 G. M. Trevelyan to A. W. Ward. 30 May 1905. CUL MSS Add. 8406/82. Trevelyan to J. R. Tanner. 25 July 1922. St John's College Library. Papers relating to the *Cambridge Medieval History* Series. Box 2. J. H. Rose to S. C. Roberts. 27 January 1927. CUP.UA.Pr.A.R.474/46. Trevelyan to Cambridge University Press. 6 March 1914. CUP.UA.Pr.A.T.429:/1.

17 A. W. Ward to Cambridge University Press. 25 August 1918. CUP.UA.Pr.A.W.146/128.

18 A. L. P. Norrington to Oxford University Press. 21 May 1929. OUP Archives. PP.2061. For Halevy see Myrna Chase, *Elie Halevy: An Intellectual Biography* (New York: Columbia University Press, 1980).

19 A. L. P. Norrington to G. N. Clark. 15 May 1929. OUP Archives. PP.2061.

20 Julia Stapleton, *Englishness and the Study of Politics: The Social and Political Thought of Ernest Barker* (Cambridge: Cambridge University Press, 1994).

21 E. Barker to H. Milford. 1 October 1942. OUP Archives. PB/ED/009576.

22 E. Thompson to A. Macmillan. 10 November 1876. BL MSS Add. 55078/5. Thompson hoped her revised book would 'get a fresh start' in the face of 'the competition of Rivingtons' and Longmans's Handbooks and

Epochs, which keep coming out so fast'.

23 James Covert, *A Victorian Marriage: Mandell and Louise Creighton* (London: Hambledon & London, 2000), pp. 155-8. Mandell Creighton served as series editor for Longman's Epochs.

24 The summary description of focus, format and price was remembered by A. L. P. Norrington in a letter to Milford: Norrington to H. Milford. 27 March 1928. OUP Archives. CP46.840. See also H. W. C. Davis to A. Johnson. 27 November 1914. OUP Archives. CP/ED/001166 and H. W. C. Davis to A. Johnson. 14 March 1916. CP/ED/001166.

25 H. W. C. Davis to A. Johnson. 14 March 1916. OUP Archives. CP/ED/001166. For Woodward's availability because he was 'invalided home' see R. Coupland to A. Johnson. 26 June 1916. R. B. Mowat to Johnson. 29 June 1916. OUP Archives. CP/ED/001166.

26 A. Johnson to H. Milford. 22 August 1916. OUP Archives. CP/ED/001166.

27 H. Milford to A. Johnson. 20 October 1916. OUP Archives. CP/ED/001166. Johnson commented to Barker: 'Milford has fears about the ladies, but I think does not know them.'

28 A. Johnson [?] to E. Barker. 27 September 1920. OUP Archives. CP46.840.

29 A. Johnson to H. Milford. 6 May 1922. OUP Archives. CP50.907.

30 A. Johnson to H. W. C. Davis. 23 February 1925. OUP Archives. CP46.840.

31 A. Johnson to A. L. P. Norrington. 10 April 1926. OUP Archives. CP46.840.

32 A. Johnson to H. Temperley. 19 June 1916. OUP Archives. CP/ED/001198.

33 *The Evolution of Prussia: The Making of an Empire*, by J. A. R. Marriott and C. Grant Robertson (1915) and *The Balkans: A History of Bulgaria, Serbia, Greece, Rumania, Turkey*, by Nevill Forbes, Arnold J. Toynbee, D. Mitrany and D. G. Hogarth (1915). Remarkably, neither work exhibits any indication of the 'Belligerents' series, although Histories of the Nations was advertised later (Fig. 4.4). Later titles covered Italy, Portugal (both 1917), Serbia, Russia and Japan (all 1918), and France (1919).

34 A. Johnson to P. E. Matheson. 3 February 1917. OUP Archives CP/ED/001198.

35 E. Barker to A. Johnson. 27 June and 3 July 1916. OUP Archives CP/ED/001200. For the story of a pioneering anthropologist, who was lecturing at Oxford and assisting the Foreign Office during this period, see David N. Collins, 'Czaplicka, Marya Antonina (1884-1921)', *ODNB*, http://www.oxforddnb.com/view/article/46557 (accessed 9 May 2007). The Mills and Boon book was *My Siberian Year* (1916), by 'Marie Antoinette Czaplicka'.

36 H. W. C. Davis to R. B. Merriman (copy). 14 June 1918. Balliol College Library, Oxford (A. L. Smith Papers), M46.

37 A. L. Smith to G. L. Beer (copy). 14 June 1918. Balliol College Library, Oxford (A. L. Smith Papers), A31.

38 C. Cannan to J. S. Mann (of Trinity College Oxford). 27 May 1919. OUP Archives. CP/ED/001201.

39 R. W. Chapman to H. Milford. 8 June 1922. OUP Archives.

CP50.907.
40 Sutcliffe, *Oxford University Press*, pp. 230-2. The relevant files in the Archives of the Oxford University Press are OHE1.P.8820 and OEH2.3720/AN.
41 G. N. Clark to K. Sisam. 30 January 1929. OUP Archives. PP 2061.
42 (R. W. Chapman?) to C. R. Cruttwell. 11 June 1929. OUP Archives. OHE1. P.8820.
43 A. L. P. Norrington to Oxford University Press. 20 March 1930. OUP Archives. OHE1. 3720/AN.
44 A. L. P. Norrington to K. Sisam. [31 May 1929]. OUP Archives. OHE1. P.8820. For Cruttwell see Geoffrey Ellis, 'Cruttwell, Charles Robert Mowbray Fraser (1887-1941)', *ODNB*, http://www.oxforddnb.com/view/article/32655 (accessed 24 April 2007).
45 H. Milford to A. L. P. Norrington. 22 September 1930. OUP Archives. OHE1. 3720/AN.
46 W. D. Hogarth to A. L. P. Norrington. 15 January 1930. Norrington to Hogarth. 25 January. OUP Archives. OHE1. 3720/AN. Norrington added that 'Godfrey Davies, of course, is an honorary American'. Davies was a research student of C. H. Firth.
47 R. W. Chapman to P. E. Matheson and others. [3 July 1929]. G. N. Clark to A. L. P. Norrington, 8 December 1929. OUP Archives. OHE1. P.8820.
48 McKitterick, *New Worlds*, p. 153 (Chapter 7, '1900-1916: a difficult period').
49 A. W. Ward. Report to Press Syndics. 25 August 1918. CUP.UA.Pr.A.W.146/128.
50 Prothero was editor of the *Quarterly Review* from 1899 until his death in 1922. The *Quarterly Review* is indexed in *The Wellesley Index to Victorian Periodicals*, Vol. 4, ed. W. Houghton et al. (Toronto: University of Toronto Press, 1987).
51 G. W. Prothero to Cambridge University Press. 4 May; 31 May 1913. CUP.UA.Pr.A.P.696/12; 30.
52 G. W. Prothero to Cambridge University Press. 9 October 1914; 22 September 1918; 26 November 1921; 22 March 1922. CUP.UA.Pr.A.P.696/21-2; 63; 93; 108.
53 J. P. Whitney to A. R. Waller. [n.d. *c*. June 1914]. CUP.UA.Pr.A.W.522/34.
54 Linehan, 'Making', 463-7.
55 A. R. Waller to Cambridge University Press. 20 November 1921. CUP.UA.Pr.A.W.S22.
56 Z. N. Brooke to J. R. Tanner. 18 November 1923. St John's College Library. Papers relating to the *Cambridge Medieval History* Series. Cambridge Medieval History. Box 1. See also Gillian Thomas, 'Weston, Jessie Laidlay (1850-1928)', *ODNB*, http://www.oxforddnb.com/view/article/38620 (accessed 12 June 2007).
57 McKitterick, *New Worlds*, pp. 151, 196.
58 E. J. Rapson to Cambridge University Press. 9 March 1914. CUP.UA.Pr.A.R.70/34.
59 E. J. Rapson to A. R. Waller. 23 February 1919. CUP.UA.Pr.A.R.70/90.
60 E. A. Benians to S. C. Roberts. 28 June 1926. CUP.UA.Pr.A.B.415/27-31 passim.
61 Vincent A. Smith, *The Oxford History of India* (Oxford: Clarendon Press, 1919). There were several revised and updated editions. H. H. Dodwell to S. C. Roberts. 30 May 1929. CUP.UA.Pr.A.D.449/40.

62 E. J. Rapson to Syndics of Cambridge University Press. 9 March 1935. CUP.UA.Pr.A.R.70/175.
63 A. W. Ward. Report to Cambridge University Press. 25 August 1918. CUP.UA.Pr.A.W.146/128. Ward to G. P. Gooch. 17 September and 31 October 1918. G. P. Gooch fonds, University of Calgary Library, Acc 333/83.30. See also Frank Eyck, *G. P. Gooch: A Study in History and Politics* (London: Macmillan, 1982).
64 S. C. Roberts, *Adventures with Authors* (Cambridge: Cambridge University Press, 1966), p. 113.
65 G. P. Gooch to S. C. Roberts. 8 June 1943. CUP.UA.Pr.A.G.336/17.
66 F. E. Adcock to S. C. Roberts. 12 November 1925. CUP.UA.Pr.A.A.64/11.
67 F. E. Adcock to S. C. Roberts. 12 July 1927. CUP.UA.Pr.A.A.64/28.
68 Maxine Berg, *A Woman in History: Eileen Power 1889-1940* (Cambridge: Cambridge University Press, 1996). See also Natalie Zemon Davis, 'History's Two Bodies', *American Historical Review* 93:2 (1988): 1-30.
69 E. Power to S. C. Roberts. 10 November [1923?]. CUP.UA.Pr.A.P.612/11.
70 Roberts, Adventures, 118-19. See also E. Power to S. C. Roberts. 7 September [1924?]. CUP.A.Pr.A.P.612/13.
71 E. Power to S. C. Roberts. 23 September 1924. CUP.UA.Pr.A.P.612/14.
72 R. Power to S. C. Roberts. 2 June 1925. CUP.UA.Pr.A.P. 614/3.
73 E. Power to S. C. Roberts. 26 September [1924]. CUP.UA.Pr.A.P.612/15.
74 E. Power to S. C. Roberts. 14 October 1926. CUP.UA.Pr.A.P.612/28.
75 H. W. V. Temperley to S. C. Roberts, 2 May 1928. UA.Pr.A.T.122/50. Arthur Grenville Bradley's book was first published by Constable in 1900, and Cambridge University Press was contemplating a revised edition.
76 A. Green to F. Macmillan. 12 September 1923. BL MSS Add. 55061/8.
77 C. H. Firth to Macmillan & Co. 25 October 1917. BL MSS Add. 55080/205. See Ivan Roots, 'Firth, Sir Charles Harding (1857-1936)', *ODNB*, http://www.oxforddnb.com/view/article/33137 (accessed 7 December 2005).
78 C. H. Firth to F. Macmillan. 5 April 1913; 28 April, 17 September 1914. BL MSS Add. 55080/175; 185; 192.
79 E. Thompson to Macmillan & Co., 17 January 1918. BL MSS Add. 55078/81-2.

5 Knowledge in the Marketplace, 1930-1950

1 Michael S. Howard, *Jonathan Cape, Publisher* (London: Jonathan Cape, 1971), p. 184.
2 Kenyon, *The History Men*, p. 216. For a critique of its gender bias see Joan Thirsk, 'The History Women', in *Chattel, Servant or Citizen: Women's Status in Church, State and Society*, ed. Mary O'Dowd and Sabine Wichert (Belfast: Institute of Irish Studies, Queen's University of Belfast, 1995).
3 H. G. Wells, *A Short History of the World* was the first Penguin reprint of a history book, number

31 of the series in 1936, followed by Elie Halevy, *A History of the European People in 1815* (1937). H. L. Beales served on the editorial board for the Pelican series of original works. The one-thousandth Pelican was a work of history, E. P. Thompson's *The Making of the English Working Class* in 1968. See Steve Hare, *Penguin Portrait: Allen Lane and the Penguin Editors 1935-1970* (London: Penguin Books, 1995). See also Tim Graham, *Penguin in Print: A Bibliography* (London: Penguin Collectors' Society, 2003).

4 Allen & Unwin Co. to H. Baerlein. 16 January 1942. Allen & Unwin Archives, AUC 130/3. Baerlein (who lived in Ambleside, Westmoreland) had submitted some translations of contemporary pamphlets on Frederick the Great, and entered into correspondence with the publisher's reader about his proposed biography. Baerlin wrote: 'Of course the chief object of the book is to point out parallelisms between Frederick's conduct and that of Hitler. This one can do over and over again.' By 12 March the book had been completed and entitled 'Hitler's Royal Ancestor'; the publisher kindly said it was interesting but that it would be difficult to obtain a substantial sale and in any case there was no paper to spare.

5 William H. McNeill, *Arnold J. Toynbee: A Life* (Oxford: Oxford University Press, 1989), pp. 159-66.

6 Martin Gilbert, *Winston S. Churchill. Vol. VI: Finest Hour 1939-1941* (Boston: Houghton Mifflin, 1983), pp. 777-9. The speech in question was the broadcast of 11 September 1940.

7 Juliet Gardiner, *Wartime Britain 1939-1945* (London: Headline, 2004), pp. 416-18. G. M. Trevelyan believed that the difficulty of getting history books reprinted, because of the paper shortage, would prevent publishers from reprinting 'old books of standard value ... good history books that [were] thus suffered to die'. Trevelyan, *History and the Reader* (London: Cambridge University Press for the National Book League, 1945).

8 G. M. Trevelyan to S. C. Roberts. 1 February 1939. CUP.UA.Pr.A.T.429/26.

9 *The Times*, 20 April 1939, p. 5 col. G. Accessed through the Times Digital Archive.

10 Z. N. Brooke to S. C. Roberts. 22 November 1931. CUP.UA.Pr.A.B.1057/27. G. G. Coulton to S. C. Roberts. 25 January 1932. CUP.UA.Pr.A.C.823/126. See also Roberts, Adventures, 116-18.

11 J. H. Clapham to S. C. Roberts. 10 October 1927. CUP.UA.Pr.A.C.440: 45.

12 D. A. Benians to S. C. Roberts. 19 October 1935. CUP.CMH(NS)/1.

13 H. Temperley to S. C. Roberts. 22 November 1935. CUP.CMH(NS)/7. See also John D. Fair, *Harold Temperley: a Scholar and Romantic in the Public Realm* (Newark: University of Delaware Press, 1992).

14 H. Temperley to S. C. Roberts. 18 March 1936. CUP.CMH(NS)/21.

15 L. M. Penson to S. C. Roberts. 10 September 1939. CUP.CMH(NS)/99.

16 L. M. Penson to S. C. Roberts. 24 January 1944. CUP.CMH(NS)/110.

17 B. Schmitt to S. C. Roberts. 24 April 1945. CUL.MSS Add. 7921/I/2.

18 H. Butterfield to S. C. Roberts. 6 June 1945. CUL.BUTT 6/2.
19 G. N. Clark to H. Butterfield. 6 June 1945. CUL.BUTT 6/2.
20 G. N. Clark to W. Hogarth. 12 June 1934. OUP Archives. PB/ED 015660.
21 J. A. Williamson (schoolmaster, Winchester) to A. L. P. Norrington. 29 October 1934; Norrington to G. N. Clark. 30 October. OUP Archives. CP46.840.
22 K. Sisam to L. Shlosberg (of Salford). 11 December 1937. OUP Archives. PB/ED 015660.
23 A. L. P. Norrington to D. M. Davin. 20 January 1949; Norrington to G. N. Clark. 3 June 1949. J. C. James (schoolmaster) to Oxford University Press. 9 April 1951. OHE2. 3720/AN.
24 G. N. Clark to A. L. P. Norrington. 2 July 1930. Norrington to Clark. 5 July. Clark to Norrington. 7 July. OUP Archives. OHE1. 3720/AN.
25 K. Sisam to H. Milford. 4 May 1937. OUP Archives. PB/ED 015660.
26 William H. McNeill, *Arnold J. Toynbee: A Life* (Oxford: Oxford University Press, 1989).
27 A. Toynbee to H. Milford. 31 December 1931. Milford to Toynbee. 1 January 1932. OUP Archives. LG29.224.
28 A. Toynbee to H. Milford. 27 June 1933. OUP Archives. LG29.224.
29 A. L. P. Norrington to H. Milford. 26 July 1934. OUP Archives. OP2777.1941-5.
30 Rockefeller Foundation (Willits) to A. J. Toynbee. 14 October 1944. OUP Archives. OP2777.19415. Boulter became Toynbee's second wife in 1946.
31 D. C. Somervell to Oxford University Press (Peacock). 6 April 1953. OUP Archives. OP2777.1941-5.
32 Henry Z. Walck (Oxford University Press, New York) to G. Cumberledge. 27 February 1947. OUP Archives. OP2777.1941-5.
33 K. Sisam to E. Barker. 30 July 1943; Barker to Sisam, 31 July; Sisam to Barker, 10 August. OUP Archives. Barker. 4853c. See also Valerie Holman, 'Carefully Concealed Connections: The Ministry of Information and British Publishing, 1939-1946', *Book History* 8 (2005): 197-226 and her *Print for Victory: Book Publishing in England 1939-1945* (London: The British Library, 2008), 220-6.
34 E. Barker to K. Sisam. 9 October 1943. OUP Archives. Barker.4853b. Paul Vaucher (1887-1966) had been chair of French history at the University of London and now served as cultural councillor and head of educational services at the French embassy; Jan Opočenský (1885-1961), served as archivist in several Czech government repositories; his research focused on the early modern period but from the mid-1930s he also served President Edvard Beneš as a diplomat; during the war he joined the Czech resistance in London and from 1946 to 1948; he was a delegate at UNESCO.
35 A. L. P. Norrington to Oxford University Press. 18 November 1943. OUP Archives. (Barker) 4853c.
36 Norrington explained to the Conference of Allied Ministers of Education that Ensor's pamphlet 'had been produced to serve a definite purpose – to give both the fighting man and the general public a short account of the origins and

events of the war. Already the Germans were saying that they were first attacked. It was important that the facts should be stated now, and that the people should know how the war really began.' Oxford University Press Draft Recommendations to Conference of Allied Ministers of Education. 5 November 1943. OUP Archives. AME/B/45. PP.6072.1.
37 R. C. K. Ensor to A. L. P. Norrington. 21 November 1943. OUP Archives. (Barker) 4853c.
38 A. L. P. Norrington to Prof. C. Falls. 24 July 1947. OUP Archives. (Barker) 4853c.
39 *Daily Sketch* (5 June 1944), 2. Clipping held in OUP Archives. PB/ED 006293.
40 For Mornet, see Richard Herr, 'Histoire Littéraire: Daniel Mornet and the French Enlightenment', *The Journal of Modern History* 24:2 (June 1952), 152-66..
41 E. Barker to K. Sisam. 11 April 1948. OUP Archives. PB/ED 006293.
42 Roger Chartier has explained that the history of the book in France gives primacy to social history, and to statistical treatments of data. 'Certain types of documents have been privileged: the inventories of books mentioned in estate inventories drawn up by notaries, the printed catalogues of public auctions ... Such sources have permitted the construction of a whole series of new cultural indicators that enable one to discover social differences.' Chartier, 'Frenchness in the history of the book: From the history of publishing to the history of reading', *Proceedings of the American Antiquarian Society* 97:2 (1987), 304.
43 Davis[?] (in absence of Norrington and Sisam) to Barker. 13 April 1948. OUP Archives. PB/ED 006293.
44 G. N. Clark to D. M. Davin. 11 January 1950. OUP Archives. PB/ED 006293.
45 E. Barker to G. P. Gooch. 13 May 1954. G. P. Gooch fonds, University of Calgary, Acc 333/83.30.
46 W. R. Richardson (Minister of Education) to E. Barker, 3 July 1950. OUP Archives. PB/ED 006293.
47 E. Barker to A. L. P. Norrington. 3 August 1951. OUP Archives. PB/ED 006293.
48 Stapleton, *Englishness and the Study of Politics*, pp. 183-4.
49 A. Bryant to C. E. Carrington. 21 May 1935. CUP.UA.Pr.A.B.1170/65. Only about seventy years passed, however, before Bryant's gloomy prophecy was fulfilled and I laughed aloud in the Cambridge University Library Manuscript Reading Room. Studies of the relations of publisher and author have become fashionable in a way Bryant could not have imagined.
50 I expanded on this theme in *Old Books and New Histories*, and in 'Book History Unbound: Transactions of the Written Word Made Public', *Canadian Journal of History* 38:4 (2003): 69-81.
51 Peter Burke, 'History of Events and the Revival of Narrative', in *New Perspectives on Historical Writing*, 2nd edition, ed. P. Burke (Pennsylvania: Pennsylvania State University Press, 2001).
52 E. A. Freeman to A. Macmillan. 2 April 1871. BL MSS Add. 55049/186.
53 E. A. Freeman to E. Thompson. 17 June 1883. Brynmore Jones Library, University of Hull.

DX/9/109.
54 See above page 75.
55 For George Allen's British Empire Series see Howsam, 'Imperial Publishers'.
56 For the circuit of communication see Darnton, 'What Is the History of Books?' For an alternative circuit, with emphasis on the material object see Thomas R. Adams and Nicolas Barker, 'A New Model for the Study of the Book', in *A Potencie of Life: Books in Society*, ed. Nicolas Barker (London: The British Library, 1993), pp. 5-43.
57 Trevelyan, *Clio: A Muse and other essays* (London: Longman, 1913), 52.
58 A prescient Kenneth Sisam of Oxford University Press remarked: 'A generation of television may alter the tastes and habits of readers, but that will be a problem for another generation than ours.' K. Sisam to G. N. Clark. 13 June 1945. OUP Archive. OHE2. 3720/KS.
59 For an interesting graphic representation of publication of history titles over time see Peter Mandler, *History and National Life* (London: Profile Books, 2002), 63-6.
60 C. Cannan (for OUP) and R. T. Wright (for CUP) to Gill & Sons. 12 February 1898. OUP Archives, Letter Books 71/314. See also a pamphlet: Transcript of the Shorthand Notes of Messrs. Cock & Kight, Rolls Chambers, 89 Chancery Lane, W.C. in the High Court of Justice Chancery Division. Royal Courts of Justice, Wednesday 24 January 1900. Before Mr Justice Stirling. The Universities of Oxford and Cambridge v. George Gill & Sons. Cambridge University Press Archives, CUR.33.8.48a.
61 For the history of reading, see *A History of Reading in the West*, ed. G. Cavallo and R. Chartier (Amherst: University of Massachusetts Press, 1999). A Reading Experience Database, managed online through the auspices of the Open University, systematically collects such records for the United Kingdom, 1450-1945.

Epilogue

1 The literature on women as writers of history includes Christine L. Krueger, 'Why She Lived at the PRO: Mary Anne Everett Green and the Profession of History', *Journal of British Studies*, 42 (January 2003): 65-90; Rohan Maitzen, '"This Feminine Preserve": Historical Biographies by Victorian Women', *Victorian Studies* (Spring 1995): 371-93; Rosemary Mitchell, '"The Busy Daughters of Clio": Women Writers of History From 1820 to 1880', *Women's History Review* 7:1 (1998): 107-34; Bonnie G. Smith, 'The Contribution of Women to Modern Historiography in Great Britain, France and the United States, 1750-1949', *American Historical Review* 100 (1995): 709-32; and Natalie Zemon Davis, 'History's Two Bodies', *American Historical Review* 93:1 (1988): 1-30.
2 For Bryce see correspondence with Freeman about the (unrealized) possibility of Kate Bryce contributing to her brother's friend's *Historical Course for Schools* (Bod. MSS Bryce/164, 266; 9/166-168, 23 October 1870-26 January 1871). For Stephen see correspondence with Macmillan about his daughter Katharine

Stephen's history of France for children (BL MSS Add. 55082/39, 41, 44, 15 November 1880 to 3 May 1881; see also a Reader's Report at MSS Add. 55935/23, 3236). The book was published under the pseudonym 'Sarah Brook' and the title *French History for English Children* in 1881 and issued again in 1899 as *French History for Schools* by Katharine Stephen.

3 W. A. J. Archbold to Lord Acton, 5 January 1897, 14 April 1898. CUL MSS Add. 6443/17, 68.

4 See above page 92.

5 John North, ed., *The Waterloo Directory of English Newspapers and Periodicals, 1800-1900*. For both print and on-line versions see www.victorianperiodicals.com.

6 My Michael Wolff Lecture to the Research Society for Victorian Periodicals (September 2005) was entitled 'Narratives and Editors: History and Historians in Victorian Periodical Research'. In 2007 I received funding from the Social Sciences and Humanities Research Council of Canada to begin research on the pervasiveness of historical narratives in Victorian periodicals.

7 For scholarship on this subject see Romila Thapar, *Somanatha: The Many Voices of History* (New York: Verson, 2005) and Antoinette Burton, 'Rules of Thumb: British History and "Imperial Culture" in Nineteenth and Twentieth-CenturyBritain', *Women's History Review* 3:4 (1994): 483-500. I am grateful to Natalie Zemon Davis for helping me to see how my research connects with the project of rethinking post-colonial histories.

8 *The Analytical History of England. Based on E. Thompson's History, with Examination Papers* (Calcutta: Behary Lall Banergee, 1880); and a second edition, revised and enlarged, also 1880 . For US piracies of Green see Alice Green to Macmillan,15 May 1887. BL MSS Add. 55059/53, and correspondence in the Green papers at Jesus College, Oxford. For problems with the New Brunswick school authorities on the statement that clerical celibacy was not practiced in the Middle Ages see Thompson to A. Macmillan. 10 and 17 August 1879. BL MSS Add. 55078/38; 40. For piracies of (or 'keys to') Green in India see the following letter (R. Lethbridge to Macmillan & Co. 12 October 1880. BL MSS Add. 55062/12): 'Just a line ... to inform you the enterprising Babus of Calcutta are pirating your Green's Readings like fun! See enclosed advertisements – & I have seen at least two or three more. These keys will injure the sale, because they generally contain the text also very fully. I should strongly recommend your prosecuting: & I would recommend also your authorising me to arrange with someone of high standing ... as they will insist on having keys, to make a key (to be approved of by me on your behalf) that cannot injure the original book's sale.'

9 For earlier periods see D. R. Woolf, *Reading History in Early Modern England* (Cambridge: Cambridge University Press, 2000) and Karen O'Brien, 'The History Market in Eighteenth-Century England', in Isabel Rivers, ed., *Books and their Readers in Eighteenth-Century England: New Essays* (London: Continuum, 2001).

10 See Bernard Lightman, *Victorian Popularizers of Science: Designing Nature for New Audiences* (Chicago: University of Chicago

Press, 2008).

11 See Patrick Leary, 'Googling the Victorians', *Journal of Victorian Culture* 10:1 (Spring 2005): 72-86 and Diana Kichuk, 'Metamorphosis: Remediation in *Early English Books Online (EEBO)*', *Literary and Linguistic Computing*, 22:3 (2007), 291-303.

12 See Mandler, *History and National Life.* Mandler works with other scholars in an inter-disciplinary Cambridge Victorian Studies Group; their research interest is in Victorian attitudes to the past.

Chronology: events, appointments and publications

1849 Macaulay, *History of England* (5 vols, 1849-61, Longmans); James Stephen Regius Professor of Modern History, Cambridge (to 1860)

1850 Public Libraries Act

1851 Great Exhibition; Palgrave, *History of Normandy & England* (Parker); Creasey, *Fifteen Decisive Battles* (Bentley); Finlay, *History of Greece* (Blackwood)

1853 Advertisement tax abolished; Oxford School of Jurisprudence and Modern History founded; Burton, *History of Scotland* (Longman)

1854 Crimean War to 1856; Working Men's College founded, London; Dickens, *Hard Times*

1855 Stamp Tax abolished and newspaper and periodical prices decline; Kingsley, *Westward Ho!* (Macmillan)

1856 Panizzi becomes principal librarian at British Museum; Froude *History of England* (12 vols, 1856-70, Longmans); critique of Roman Catholic influences in Ince and Gilbert

1857 Death of Daniel Macmillan; War of Indian independence 1857-8; Obscene Publications Act; British Museum reading room opens; Buckle, *History of Civilization* (Parker)

1858 Goldwin Smith Regius Professor of Modern History, Oxford (to 1866, succeeding Henry Halford Vaughan); OUP embarks on Oxford English Dictionary (to 1928); Macmillan moves to 23 Henrietta Street, London from 17 Trinity Street, Cambridge; Carlyle, *Frederick the Great* (6 vols, Chapman and Hall, 1858-65)

1859 *Macmillan's Magazine* begins publication; Darwin, *On the Origin of Species* (Murray); Smiles *Self-Help* (Murray); J. S. Mill *On Liberty* (Parker); death of Macaulay

1860 Charles Kingsley Regius Professor of Modern History, Cambridge (to 1869); *Essays and Reviews* (Parker)

1861 Paper duty abolished; Beeton, *Book of Household Management*; Palgrave, *Golden Treasury* (Macmillan)

1862 Revised education code begins payment by results; foundation of Chichele Professorship of Modern History, Oxford

1863 Macmillan moves to 16 Bedford Street; Alexander Macmillan becomes Publisher to the University of Oxford (to 1880); OUP starts Clarendon Press Series; Freeman, *History of Federal Government* (vol. 1, no more published, Macmillan)

1864 Early English Text Society formed; J. H. Newman, *Apologia Pro Vita Sua* (Longman)

1865 Macmillan takes George Lillie Craik into partnership; Macmillan publishes *Alice in Wonderland* and M. Arnold, *Essays in Criticism*; G. W. Kitchin joins OUP as Secretary to the School-book Committee (to 1874) then Secretary to Board of Delegates

1866 William Stubbs Regius Professor of Modern History, Oxford (to 1884; OUP Delegate 1868-84 and 1891-1901); Oscar Browning edits *Cornelius Nepos* for OUP; A. W. Ward appointed professor of history and English language and literature Owens College Manchester (to 1897)

1867 Second Reform Bill; Alexander Macmillan visits USA; in London and Oxford, preliminary conversations about an English historical review periodical

1868 Bartholomew Price becomes Secretary to the Delegates of OUP; Royal Historical Society founded; Freeman, *Norman Conquest* (6 vols, 1868-9, OUP)

1869 J. R. Seeley Regius Professor of Modern History, Cambridge (to 1895); Macmillan New York office opens with George Brett; *Nature* begins publication (Macmillan); Arnold *Culture & Anarchy* (Macmillan); Green proposes History of England to Macmillan; Freeman, *Old English History for Children* and planning of Historical Course for Schools

1870 Forster's Education Act; Stubbs *Select Charters* (OUP)

1871 Freeman, *Historical Essays* (Macmillan)

1872 Historical Course for Schools (Macmillan series; 9 volumes to 1879); Oxford School of Modern History founded; Royal Historical Society begins to publish *Transactions*

1873 CUP opens London warehouse; Edith Thompson, *History of England* (Historical Course for Schools, Macmillan); J. S. Mill, *Autobiography* (Longmans)

1874 J. R. Green, *A Short History of the English People* (Macmillan); Green starts editing Macmillan primers; George A. Macmillan joins firm; Kitchin becomes Secretary to Delegates of OUP

1875 J. R. Seeley, Regius Professor of Modern History Cambridge (to 1895), Macmillan starts publishing textbooks for India; Cambridge History Tripos (separated from Law); OUP publishes translation of Ranke's *History of England*

1876 Oscar Browning goes to King's College Cambridge (to 1909)

1877 Library Association founded; D. Mackenzie Wallace, *Russia* (2 vols, Cassell)

1878 Macmillan launches English Men of Letters (series edited by John Morley); Seeley, *Life and Times of Stein* (CUP)

1879 OUP employs C. E. Doble (to 1914); *Boy's Own Paper* begins

1880 Elementary education compulsory for ages 7-10; South African War (to 1881); end of Macmillan's term as publisher for OUP (since 1863)

1881 Death of Carlyle

1882 Further discussions of English historical review periodical; Browning starts work on English history for schools (for Griffith and Farran); foundation of *Dictionary of National Biography* (1885-1890, Smith Elder)

1883 Gardiner, *History of England* (10 vols, 1883-4, Longmans); Seeley, *The Expansion of England* (Macmillan); death of J. R. Green; Maurice Crawford Macmillan joins the firm

1884 E. A. Freeman, Regius Professor of Modern History, Oxford (to 1892); Victoria University, Manchester opens; Philip Lyttelton Gell succeeds Price as Secretary to OUP Delegates (formally takes up post June 1885; till 1898); Browning proposes an English historical review periodical to CUP

1885 Frederick York Powell becomes OUP delegate

1886 Foundation of the *English Historical Review* (Longmans); James Bryce, *Holy Roman Empire* (Macmillan); Macmillan launches Colonial Library series; death of Ranke

1887 C. P. Lucas *Historical Geography of the British Colonies* for OUP (and edits series of the same name to 1925); OUP initiate their School History of England eventually published 1901; A. W. Kinglake, *Invasion of the Crimea* (8 vols, 1863-87, Blackwood)

1888 Bury, *Later Roman Empire* (Macmillan)

1889 Longmans stop paying EHR contributors; York Powell begins to be consulted heavily by OUP; Ramsay begins work on his history of England for OUP

1890 First net book, Marshall's *Principles of Economics* (Macmillan)

1891 US agrees to end sanction of literary piracy (Chace Act); OUP initiates Rulers of India series; Browning, *Illustrated History of England*

1892 James A. Froude Regius Professor of Modern History, Oxford (to 1894); R. T. Wright Secretary CUP (to 1911)

1893 CUP starts Cambridge Historical series, edited by G. W. Prothero

1894 Frederick York Powell Regius Professor of Modern History, Oxford (to 1904)

1895 Lord Acton Regius Professor of Modern History, Cambridge (to 1902); Booksellers' Association founded; OUP opens New York branch; death of Seeley; Frederick Macmillan now chairman of a restructured Macmillan & Co.; crisis over copyright in Canada

1896 Death of Alexander Macmillan; foundation of the *Cambridge Modern History*; cinema begins at Empire Theatre; halfpenny evening newspaper *Daily Mail*

1897 Macmillan & Co. move to St Martin's Street; A. W. Ward moves from Manchester to Cambridge

1898 Charles Cannan appointed Secretary of OUP (to 1919) succeeding Gell; Macmillan acquires business of Richard Bentley; Prothero edits *Quarterly Review* (John Murray)

1899 A. W. Ward becomes president of a reorganized Royal Historical Society; G. P. Brett (of Macmillan New York) appointed American agent for CUP (to 1906); William Hunt starts editing Church History series for Macmillan (continues to 1910); Boer War to 1902

1900 Net book agreement; Humphry Milford arrives at OUP (sets up London office 1906); Frederick Macmillan President of the Publishers' Association to 1902 and 1911-13; T. F. Tout succeeds Ward at Manchester (to 1925)

1901 Macmillan opens Bombay branch; death of Stubbs (and Queen Victoria); Reginald Lane Poole editor of EHR; Leonard Whibley Assistant Secretary CUP (to 1902); OUP publishes School History of England

1902 J. B. Bury Regius Professor of Modern History Cambridge (to 1927); *Cambridge Modern History* published (to 1912); death of Acton; Prothero president of Royal Historical Society; A. R. Waller Assistant Secretary CUP (to 1911)

1903 Egerton revising Lucas's *Historical Geography* for OUP; A. F. Pollard appointed to chair of constitutional history at University College London (to 1931)

1904 Charles Harding Firth Regius Professor of Modern History at Oxford (to 1925); Methuen launches eight-volume History of England (to 1910); various publishers ask Browning for either an autobiography or a Napoleon book

1905 Times Book Club founded; Longmans launches 12-volume Political History of England, edited by W. Hunt and S. Lane Poole; Macmillan opens Melbourne branch

1906 Historical Association founded; Dent launches Everyman's Library; R. W. Chapman Assistant Secretary OUP (Secretary 1920-42); OUP World's Classics from Grant Richards; G. P. Putnam's Sons appointed CUP agents in New York; Macmillan Co. of Canada formed

1907 Macmillan opens Calcutta branch; Arthur Mee, J. A. Hammerton and A. D. Innes co-edit *History of the World* (8 vols, 1907-9, Harmsworth)

1909 George Allan & Co's British Empire series initiated

1910 Coulton proposes series of cheap monographs on medieval history to CUP (eventually includes Eileen Power's *Medieval English Nunneries* (1922)

1911 OUP publishes *History of England* for schools by C. R. L. Fletcher and Rudyard Kipling; A. R. Waller Secretary (to 1922) and S. C. Roberts Assistant Secretary CUP

1912 OUP opens a branch in Bombay; Browning *History of the Modern World* (Cassell)

1913 Firth edits illustrated Macaulay (Macmillan); Macmillan opens Madras branch; CUP begins *Cambridge History of India* (editor E. J. Rapson, published 1922-37)

1914 OUP initiates updated and improved Epochs and a new double series of English and Foreign Histories edited by Ernest Barker; OUP publishes *Why We are at War*; death of C. R. Doble; CUP has difficulty replacing 'enemy alien' contributors to *Cambridge Medieval History*

1915 John de Monins Johnson replaces Chapman as Assistant Secretary, OUP

1916 Periodical *History* launched by Historical Association (editor A. F. Pollard) replacing quarterly magazine edited by Harold F. B. Wheeler, 1912-16; OUP begins History of Belligerents series; Kenneth Sisam appointed at CUP (Junior Assistant Secretary, 1922; Secretary 1942-8); OUP receives *Dictionary of National Biography* from Smith's widow.

1917 PhD in History established at Oxford

1918 Ward's report on history books for CUP

1919 OUP's belligerents series turns into History of Nations; H. G. Wells, *Outline of History* (2 vols, 1919-20, Macmillan)

1920 Harold Macmillan joins firm; R. W. Chapman appointed Secretary, OUP (1920-42); PhD in History established at Cambridge

1921 Pollard founds Institute of Historical Research; OUP publishes *Movements in European History* by 'Lawrence H. Davison' (D. H. Lawrence); G. N. Clark becomes editor of *English Historical Review*

1922 Eileen Power, *Medieval English Nunneries* (CUP); Eliza Davis becomes editor of *History*; S. C. Roberts Secretary CUP

1923 Cambridge Historical Society founded (*Cambridge Historical Journal* from 1924); *Bulletin* of the Institute of Historical Research launched

1924 New series edited by E. Barker for OUP; Eileen Power, *Medieval People* (Methuen)

1925 H. W. C. Davis Regius Professor of Modern History Oxford (to 1928); E. A. Benians, A. P. Newton and J. H. Rose and plan a *Cambridge History of the British Empire* (8 vols, published 1929-59); J. Clapham proposes an economic history of modern England to CUP Syndics; A. L. P. Norrington becomes Junior Assistant Secretary to Delegates of OUP (Secretary 1948)

1926 Eileen and Rhoda Power, *Boys & Girls of History*; J. H. Clapham, *An Economic History of Modern Britain* (3 vols, CUP, 1926-38)

1927 G. M. Trevelyan Regius Professor of Modern History Cambridge to 1943; CUP Secretaries and Syndics discuss a revision of the *Cambridge Modern History*; J. E. Neale succeeds Pollard at University College London

1928 Maurice Powicke Regius Professor of Modern History Oxford (to 1947); OUP Epochs series launched

1929 G. N. Clark, *England in the 17th Century*

1930 Launch of Oxford History of England (published 1934-65)

1931 A. Bryant negotiates with CUP for scope of his Pepys biography (published in three volumes, 1933); Toynbee proposes *Study of History* to OUP (published 1934-54)

1932 Rhoda Power, *Great People of the Past* (CUP)

1934 Oxford History of England launched with *The Later Stuarts* by G. N. Clark; OUP undertakes abridged Toynbee by D. Somervell (published 1946; 1957); J. E. Neale, *Queen Elizabeth* (Cape)

1935 Planned new series of *Cambridge Modern History* in progress; F. R. Macmillan visits Hollywood to discuss history films

1936 Death of Frederick, Maurice and George Macmillan; Daniel de Mendi Macmillan becomes chairman

1938 Coulton *Medieval Panorama* (CUP); V. Gollanz (Left Book Club) publishes Morton, *People's History of England*; Lovat Dickson joins Macmillan

1939 CUP celebrates end of *Cambridge Ancient History* and hence of the whole series of Cambridge histories; series of Oxford Pamphlets on World Affairs

1940 Death of Eileen Power

1941 OUP (Milford) acquires Home University Library from Williams and Norgate via Thornton Butterworth

1942 Barker, *Britain and the British people* (OUP); Charles Morgan, *House of Macmillan* (Macmillan); Sisam becomes Secretary OUP

1943 George Norman Clark Regius Professor of History at Cambridge (to 1947); beginning of 'objective history of the War' project at OUP

1944 Trevelyan, *English Social History* (Longman); publishers plagued by wartime paper shortages

1945 Geoffrey Cumberlege becomes OUP Publisher in London (1945-56); plans for Butterfield and Clark to take over *New Cambridge Modern History*

1947 V. H. Galbraith Regius Professor of Modern History Oxford (to 1957); J. R. M. Butler Regius Professor of Modern History at Cambridge (to 1954); Trevor-Roper, *The Last Days of Hitler* (Macmillan)

1948 R. J. L. Kingsford appointed Secretary CUP

1949 D. M. Davin becomes Assistant Secretary OUP; end of paper rationing

1950 Problems for OUP with 'objective history' project (eventually *The European Inheritance*, 1954); schoolmasters demanding a completed Oxford History of England

After **1950** C. H. Roberts becomes Secretary OUP 1954-74

Bibliography

Works Cited

Manuscript Collections

Balliol College, Oxford
  A. L. Smith Collection

Bodleian Library, University of Oxford
  James Bryce papers in Bod. MSS Bryce
  W. Stubbs papers in Bod. MS Eng.

British Library
  Macmillan papers

Brynmore Jones Library, University of Hull
  Letters of E. A. Freeman to Edith Thompson

Cambridge University Library
  Acton Collection
  Butterfield Collection
  Cambridge University Press Archive

Jesus College, Oxford
  J. R. Green papers

John Rylands Library of Manchester
  E. A. Freeman Archive

King's College, Cambridge
  Oscar Browning papers

Oxford University Press Archives
  Letter Books
  Publishing files

Royal Historical Society
  G. W. Prothero papers

St John's College, Cambridge
  J. R. Tanner papers

Senate House Library, University of London
J. R. Seeley Collection
A. W. Pollard Collection

University of Calgary Library, Special Collections
G. P. Gooch fonds

University of Reading Library, Special Collections
Allan Unwin Archives
Records of the Longman Group

Published Primary Sources

Acton, John Emerich Edward Dalberg, Lord, *Longitude 30 West: A Confidential Report to the Syndics of the Cambridge University Press* (New York: Cambridge University Press, 1969).
Barker, Ernest, *Age and Youth: Memories of Three Universities and Father of the Man* (London: Oxford University Press, 1953).
Bury, J., Inaugural Lecture delivered in the Divinity School, Cambridge, on 26 January 1903 (Cambridge: Cambridge University Press, 1903).
Coleridge, C., *Charlotte M. Yonge: Her Life and Letters* (London: Macmillan, 1903).
Collette, Charles Hastings, *Rome's Jesuitical Tampering with Books of Education. Exemplified in the modern editions of Ince's Outlines of History* (London: Bateman, 1857).
Coulton, George Gordon, *Fourscore Years: An Autobiography* (Cambridge: Cambridge University Press, 1942).
Creighton, Louise, ed., *Life and Letters of Mandell Creighton*, 2 vols (London: Longmans, 1904).
Freeman, Edward Augustus, *The Methods of Historical Study*; Eight Lectures Read in the University of Oxford in 1884, With the Inaugural Lecture on the Office of the Historical Professor (Oxford: Oxford University Press, 1884).
'On the Study of History', *Fortnightly Review* 35 (1881).
'Oxford after 40 Years', *Contemporary Review* 51: 882.
Holden, William, ed., *Letters of William Stubbs: Bishop of Oxford, 1825-1901* (London: Archibald Constable, 1904).
Pinney, Thomas, ed., *The Letters of Thomas Babington Macaulay*, 6 vols (Cambridge: Cambridge University Press, 1974).
Macmillan, *A Bibliographical Catalogue of Macmillan and Co's Publications from 1843 to 1889* (London: Macmillan, 1891).
Nowell-Smith, Simon, *Letters to Macmillan* (London: Macmillan, 1967).
Seeley, J. R., *The Expansion of England*, ed. John Gross (Chicago: University of Chicago Press, 1971). Originally published by Macmillan 1883.
'A Historical Society', *Macmillan's Magazine* 45 (1881).
'History and Politics', *Macmillan's Magazine* 40 (1879).
Starr, Mark, *Lies and Hate in Education* (London: Hogarth Press, 1929).
Stephen, Leslie, ed., *Letters of John Richard Green* (London: Macmillan, 1901).
Stephens, W. R. W., *The Life and Letters of Edward A. Freeman* (London:

Macmillan, 1895).

Taylor, A. J. P., *A. J. P. Taylor: A Personal History* (New York: Atheneum, 1983).

Trevelyan, G. M., *An Autobiography and Other Essays* (London: Longmans, Green, 1949).

Clio: A Muse and other Essays (London: Longman, 1913).

History and the Reader (London: Cambridge University Press for the National Book League, 1945).

Wedgwood, C. V., *Literature and the Historian* (London: Oxford University Press for the English Association, 1956).

Velvet Studies (London: Jonathan Cape, 1946).

[Wright, R. T.] *The Cambridge Modern History: An Account of Its Origin, Authorship and Production* (Cambridge: Cambridge University Press, 1907).

Secondary Sources

Adams, Thomas R., and Nicolas Barker, 'A New Model for the Study of the Book', *A Potencie of Life: Books in Society*, ed. Nicolas Barker, pp. 5-43 (London: The British Library, 1993).

Altholz, Josef L., 'Lord Acton and the Plan of the Cambridge Modern History', *Historical Journal* 39:3 (1996): 723-36.

Altick, Richard D., *The English Common Reader: A Social History of the Mass Reading Public, 1800-1900* (Chicago: The University of Chicago Press, 1957).

Anderson, Amanda and Joseph Valente, *Disciplinarity at the Fin De Siècle* (Princeton: Princeton University Press, 2002).

Anstruther, Ian, *Oscar Browning: A Biography* (London: John Murray, 1983).

Ashley, Maurice, *Churchill as Historian* (New York: Charles Scribner's Sons, 1968).

Ausubel, Herman, J. Bartlet Breloner and Erling M. Hunt, eds, *Some Modern Historians of Britain: Essays in Honour of R. L. Schuyler* (New York: The Dryden Press, 1951).

Bann, Stephen, *The Inventions of History: Essays on the Representation of the Past* (Manchester: Manchester University Press, 1990).

Barnes, James J., *Authors, Publishers and Politicians: The Quest for the Anglo-American Copyright Agreement 1815-1854* (London: Routledge & Kegan Paul, 1974).

Battiscombe, Georgina, *Charlotte Mary Yonge: The Story of an Uneventful Life* (London: Constable, 1943).

Baym, Nina, *American Women Writers and the Work of History, 1790-1860* (New Brunswick: Rutgers University Press, 1995).

Beard, Charles A., *An Introduction to the English Historians* (New York: Burt Franklin, 1968).

Belanger, Terry, 'From Bookseller to Publisher: Changes in the London Book Trade, 1750-1850', in *Book Selling and Book Buying: Aspects of the 19th Century British and North American Book Trade*, ed. Richard G. Landon (Chicago: American Library Association, 1978).

Bell, Bill, 'New Directions in Victorian Publishing History', *Victorian Literature and Culture* (1994): 347-54.

'Victorian Paratexts', *Victorian Literature and Culture* (1999): 327-35.

Ben-Israel, Hedva, *English Historians on the French Revolution* (Cambridge: Cambridge University Press, 1968).

Bennett, Scott, 'Revolutions in Thought: Serial Publication and the Mass Market for Reading', in *The Victorian Periodical Press: Samplings and Soundings*, eds Joanne Shattock and Michael Wolff (Toronto: University of Toronto Press, 1982).

Bentley, Michael, *Modernizing England's Past: English Historiography in the Age of Modernism 1870-1970* (Cambridge: Cambridge University Press, 2005).

'The Evolution and Dissemination of Historical Knowledge', in *The Organisation of Knowledge in Victorian Britain*, ed. Martin Daunton (Oxford: Oxford University Press for the British Academy, 2005).

Berg, Maxine, *A Woman in History: Eileen Power 1889-1940* (Cambridge: Cambridge University Press, 1996).

Berger, Carl, *The Writing of Canadian History: Aspects of English-Canadian Historical Writing Since 1900* (Toronto: University of Toronto Press, 1986).

Bevington, Merle Mowbray, *The Saturday Review 1855-1868: Representative Educated Opinion in Victorian England* (New York: Columbia University Press, 1941).

Black, M. H., *Cambridge University Press 1584-1984* (Cambridge: Cambridge University Press, 1984).

Bolitho, Hector, *A Biographer's Notebook* (London: Longmans, Green, 1950).

Bourdieu, Pierre, *The Field of Cultural Production* (New York: Columbia University Press, 1993).

Bowler, P. J., *The Invention of Progress: The Victorians and the Past* (Oxford: Basil Blackwell, 1989).

Brentano, Robert, 'The Sound of Stubbs', *Journal of British Studies* 6 (1966-7): 1-14.

Briggs, Asa, ed., *Essays in the history of publishing in celebration of the 250th anniversary of the House of Longman, 1724-1974* (London: Longmans, 1974).

Briggs, Asa and Peter Burke, *A Social History of the Media: From Gutenberg to the Internet* (Cambridge: Polity Press, 2002).

Brooke, Christopher, ed., *A History of the University of Cambridge*, 4 vols (Cambridge: Cambridge University Press, 1988-97).

Brundage, Anthony, *The People's Historian: John Richard Green and the Writing of History in Victorian England* (Westport, Conn.: Greenwood Press, 1994).

Buckner, P. A. and Carl Bridge, 'Reinventing The British World', *The Round Table* 368 (2003): 77-88.

Burk, Kathleen, *Troublemaker: The Life and History of A. J. P. Taylor* (New Haven: Yale University Press, 2000).

Burke, Peter, 'Ranke the Reactionary', in *Leopold Von Ranke and the Shaping of the Historical Discipline*, eds Iggers and Powell (Syracuse:

Syracuse University Press, 1990), pp. 36-44.

Burroughs, Peter, 'John Robert Seeley and British Imperial History', *Journal of Imperial and Commonwealth History* 1, 2 (January 1973): 191-211.

Burrow, J. W., *A Liberal Descent: Victorian Historians and the English Past* (Cambridge: Cambridge University Press, 1981).

'Victorian Historians and the Royal Historical Society', *Transactions of the Royal Historical Society*, 5th series, 39 (1988), 125-40.

Burstein, Miriam Elizabeth, 'From Good Looks to Good Thoughts: Popular Women's History and the Invention of Modernity, ca. 1830-1870', *Modern Philology* 97 (1999): 46-75.

'"The Reduced Pretensions of the Historic Muse": Agnes Strickland and the Commerce of Women's History', *The Journal of Narrative Technique* 28:3 (1998): 219-42.

'"Unstoried in History"? Early Histories of Women at the Huntington Library, 1652-1902', *Huntington Library Quarterly* (2001).

Burton, Antoinette, 'Rules of Thumb: British History and "Imperial Culture" in Nineteenth and Twentieth-Century Britain', *Women's History Review* 3:4 (1994): 483-500.

Butterfield, H., *Lord Acton* (London: The Historical Society, 1948).

Campion, Sarah, *Father: A Portrait of G. G. Coulton at Home* (London: Michael Joseph, 1948).

Cannadine, David, 'British History as a "New Subject": Politics, Perspectives, and Prospects', in A. Grant and K. Stringer, eds, *Uniting the Kingdom? The Making of British History* (London: Routledge, 1995), pp. 12-30.

G. M. Trevelyan: A Life in History (London: HarperCollins, 1992).

Cannon, John, *The Historian at Work* (London: Allen & Unwin, 1980).

Capern, Amanda, 'Anatomy of a Friendship: E. A. Freeman and Edith Thompson', *Paragon Review* 6 (1997): 25-9.

Cavallo, G. and R. Chartier, eds, *A History of Reading in the West* (Amherst: University of Massachusetts Press, 1999).

Chadwick, Owen, *Acton and Gladstone* (London: Athlone Press, 1976).

Acton and History (Cambridge: Cambridge University Press, 1998). [Chapter 8: Professor Lord Acton.]

'Charles Kingsley at Cambridge', in *Spirit of the Oxford Movement: Tractarian Essays*, ed. Owen Chadwick (Cambridge: Cambridge University Press, 1990), pp. 105-94.

Professor Lord Acton: The Regius Chair of Modern History at Cambridge, 1895-1902 (Grand Rapids: The Acton Institute, 1995).

Chancellor, Valerie E., *History for Their Masters: Opinion in the English History Textbook 1800-1914* (New York: Augustus M. Kelley, 1970).

Chartier, Roger, 'Frenchness in the History of the Book: From the History of Publishing to the History of Reading', *Proceedings of the American Antiquarian Society* 97:2 (1987): 299-329.

Chase, Myrna, *Elie Halevy: An Intellectual Biography* (New York: Columbia University Press, 1980).

Chatterjee, Rimi B., *Empires of the Mind: A History of the Oxford University Press in India under the Raj* (New Delhi: Oxford University Press,

2006).
Chester, Gail, 'The Not So Gentle Reader: The Role of the Publisher's Reader as Gatekeeper, With Particular Reference to Macmillan and Co., 1895-1905', MA Diss., University of London, 1996.
Christianson, Gerald, 'G. G. Coulton: The Medieval Historian As Controversialist', *Catholic Historical Review* (1971): 421-41.
Clark, G. N., 'The Origin of the Cambridge Modern History', *Cambridge Historical Journal* 8:2 (1945): 57-64.
Clark, J. C. D., 'Historiographical Review: The Strange Death of British History? Reflections on Anglo-American Scholarship', *The Historical Journal* 40:3 (1997): 787-809.
Clive, John, *Macaulay: The Shaping of the Historian* (New York: Alfred A. Knopf, 1973).
Colley, Linda, *Lewis Namier* (London: Weidenfeld & Nicolson, 1989).
Collin, Dorothy W., 'Bookmaking: Publishers Readers and the Physical Book', *Publishing History* 44 (1998): 59-76.
Collini, Stefan, *Public Moralists: Political Thought and Intellectual Life in Britain, 1850-1930* (Oxford: Clarendon Press, 1991).
Connolly, G., 'The Transubstantiation of Myth: Towards a New Popular History of Nineteenth Century Catholicism in England', *Journal of Ecclesiastical History*, 35 (1984).
Covert, James, *A Victorian Marriage: Mandell and Louise Creighton* (London: Hambledon and London, 2000).
Crawley, C. W., 'Sir George Prothero and His Circle', *Transactions of the Royal Historical Society*, 5th series, 20 (1970): 101-27.
Culler, A. Dwight, *The Victorian Mirror of History* (New Haven: Yale University Press, 1985).
Dalton, Margaret Stieg, 'The emergence of the English Historical Review', *Library Quarterly* 46:2 (1976): 119-36.
The Origin and Development of Scholarly Historical Periodicals (University, Ala.: University of Alabama Press, 1986).
Darnton, Robert, 'Histoire Du Livre – Geschichte Des Buchwesens: An Agenda for Comparative History'. *Publishing History* 22 (1987): 33-41.
'What Is the History of Books?', *Dædalus* 111:3 (Summer 1982): 65-83.
Davis, Natalie Zemon, 'Gender and Genre, Woman as Historical Writers, 1400-1820', in *Beyond Their Sex: Learned Woman of the European Past*, ed. P. Labalme (New York: New York University Press, 1980), pp. 153-82.
'History's Two Bodies', *American Historical Review* 93:1 (1988): 1-30.
Dekker, George, *The American Historical Romance* (Cambridge: Cambridge University Press, 1987).
Delorme, M., '"Facts Not Options": Agnes Strickland', *History Today* 38 (1988).
Dennis, B., *Charlotte Yonge (1823-1901): Novelist of the Oxford Movement* (Lampeter: Edwin Mellen Press, 1992).
Deslandes, Paul R., *Oxbridge Men: British Masculinity and The Undergraduate Experience, 1850-1920* (Bloomington: Indiana University Press, 2005).
Dintenfass, Michael, 'Crafting Historians' Lives: Autobiographical Con-

structions and Disciplinary Discourses After the Linguistic Turn', *Journal of Modern History* 71:1 (March 1999): 150-65.

Dooley, Allan C., *Author and Printer in Victorian England* (Charlottesville: University Press of Virginia, 1992).

Dowling, Linda, 'Roman Decadence and Victorian Historiography', *Victorian Studies* (Summer 1985): 579-607.

Dunn, Waldo Hilary, *James Anthony Froude: A Biography*, 2 volumes (Oxford: Clarendon Press, 1961-3).

Eaves, Morris, 'What Is the History of Publishing', *Publishing History* 2 (1977): 57-77.

Edwards, Owen Dudley, *Macaulay* (New York: St Martin's Press, 1988).

Eliot, Simon, 'Patterns and Trends and the NSTC: Some Initial Observations', *Publishing History* XLII (1997): 79-104; XLIII (1998): 71-112.

Some Patterns and Trends in British Publishing 1800-1919 (London: The Bibliographical Society, 1994).

Elton, G. R., *F. W. Maitland* (New Haven: Yale University Press, 1985).

Elton, Oliver, *Frederick York Powell: A Life* (Oxford: Clarendon Press, 1906).

Engel, A. J., *From Clergyman to Don: The Rise of the Academic Profession in Nineteenth-Century Oxford* (Oxford: Clarendon Press, 1983).

Evans, Richard, *In Defense of History* (London: Granta Books, 1997).

Eyck, Frank, *G. P. Gooch: A Study in History and Politics* (London: Macmillan, 1982).

Fair, John D., *Harold Temperley: A Scholar and Romantic in the Public Realm* (Newark: University of Delaware Press, 1992).

Feather, John, 'Cross-Channel Currents: Historical Bibliography and L'Histoire Du Livre', *The Library*, Sixth Series, vol. 2:1 (March 1980): 1-15.

A History of British Publishing (London: Routledge, 1988).

Feltes, N. N., *Literary Capital and the Late Victorian Novel* (Madison, Wisconsin: University of Wisconsin Press, 1993).

Modes of Production of Victorian Novels (Chicago: University of Chicago Press, 1986).

Fenwick, Gillian, *The Contributors' Index to the Dictionary of National Biography, 1885-1901* (London: St Paul's Bibliographies, 1989).

Women and the Dictionary of National Biography: A Guide to DNB Volumes 1885-1985 and Missing Persons (Aldershot: Scolar Press, 1994).

Fifoot, C. H. S., *Frederic William Maitland: a Life* (Cambridge, Mass.: Harvard University Press, 1971).

Finkelstein, David, *The House of Blackwood: Author–Publisher Relations in the Victorian Era* (Pennsylvania: The Pennsylvania State University Press, 2002).

Fisher, H. A. L., *James Bryce (Viscount Bryce of Dechmont, O.M.)* (New York: The Macmillan Company, 1927).

Fitzsimons, M. A., *The Past Recaptured: Great Historians and the History of History* (Notre Dame: University of Notre Dame Press, 1983).

Fleming, Martha, 'Historic Passion: How Books Go Together and How

They Come Apart', *History Workshop Journal* (2003): 212-21.

Forbes, Duncan, *The Liberal Anglican Idea of History* (Cambridge: Cambridge University Press, 1952).

Francis, Daniel, *National Dreams: Myth, Memory, and Canadian History* (Vancouver: Arsenal Pulp Press, 1997).

Fritschner, Linda M., 'Publishers' readers, publishers and their authors', *Publishing History* 7 (1980): 45-100.

Fyfe, Aileen, 'Copyrights and Competition: Producing and Protecting Children's Books in the Nineteenth Century', *Publishing History* 45 (1999): 35-59.

Gardiner, Juliet, *Wartime Britain 1939-1945* (London: Headline, 2004).

Gaskell, Philip, *A New Introduction to Bibliography* (Oxford: Oxford University Press, 1972).

Genette, Gerard, *Paratexts: Thresholds of Interpretation* (Cambridge: Cambridge University Press, 1997).

Goldberg, Michael, 'Adventures in Publishing: Writing Scholarly History for a General Audience', *Perspectives: American Historical Association Newsletter* 33:8 (November 1995).

Goldstein, Doris S., 'History at Oxford and Cambridge: Professionalization and the Influence of Ranke', in *Leopold Von Ranke and the Shaping of the Historical Discipline*, eds Iggers and Powell (Syracuse: Syracuse University Press, 1990), pp. 141-53.

'J. B. Bury's Philosophy of History: A Reappraisal', *American Historical Review* 82:4 (1977): 896-919.

'The Organizational Development of the British History Profession 1884-1921', *Bulletin of the Institute of Historical Research* 55:132 (1982): 180-93.

'The Origins and Early Years of the English Historical Review', *English Historical Review* 101:398 (1986): 6-19.

'The Professionalisation of History in Britain in the Later Nineteenth and Early Twentieth Centuries', *Storia Della Storiografia* 3 (1983): 3-27.

'Review Essay: Not by Fact Alone', *History and Theory* 30:1 (1991): 106-12.

'The Role of Historical Journals in the Professionalization of History in England, 1886-1923', *Tijdschrift Voor Geschiedenis* [Netherlands] 99:3-4 (1986): 591-605.

Gooch, G. P., 'The Editorial Methods of Sir Adolphus Ward: The Cambridge History of British Foreign Policy 1922-3', *The Cambridge Historical Journal* 1:2 (1924): 222-4.

History and Historians in the Nineteenth Century (London: Longmans, 1928).

Grafton, Anthony, 'Is the History of Reading a Marginal Enterprise?: Guillaume Budé and His Books', *Proceedings of the Bibliographical Society of America* 91:2 (June 1997): 139-57.

Graham, Tim, *Penguin in Print: A Bibliography* (London: Penguin Collectors' Society, 2003).

Granatstein, J. L., *Who Killed Canadian History?* (Toronto: HarperCollins, 1998).

Greist, Guinevere L., *Mudie's Circulating Library and the Victorian Novel*

(Bloomington: Indiana University Press, 1970).
Gross, John, *The Rise and Fall of the Man of Letters: English Literary Life Since 1800* (London: Weidenfeld & Nicolson, 1973).
Hale, J. R., *The Evolution of British Historiography: From Bacon to Namier* (Cleveland: Meridian Books, 1964).
Hare, Steve, *Penguin Portrait: Allen Lane and the Penguin Editors 1935-1970* (London: Penguin Books, 1995).
Harrison, J. F. C., *Learning and Living: A Study in the History of the Adult Education Movement* (London: Routledge & Kegan Paul, 1961).
Harte, N. B., *One Hundred and Fifty Years of History Teaching at University College London* (London: University College London, 1982).
Haslam, Jonathan, *The Vices of Integrity: E. H. Carr, 1892-1982* (New York: Verso, 1999).
Heathorn, Stephen, *For Home, Country, and Race: Constructing Gender, Class, and Englishness in the Elementary School, 1880-1914* (Toronto: University of Toronto Press, 2000).
Heyck, T. W., *The Transformation of Intellectual Life in Victorian England* (London: Croom Helm, 1982).
Himmelfarb, Gertrude, *Lord Acton: A Study in Conscience and Politics* (London: Routledge & Kegan Paul, 1952).
Holland, Henry Arthur, *Frederic William Maitland, 1850-1906* (London: Bernard Quaritch, 1953).
Holman, Valerie, 'Carefully Concealed Connections: The Ministry of Information and British Publishing, 1939-1946', *Book History* 8 (2005): 197-226.
'The Impact of War: British Publishers and French Publications 1940-1944', *Publishing History* 48 (2000): 41-65.
Print for Victory: Book Publishing in England 1939-1945 (London: The British Library, 2008).
Holton, Sandra, 'Gender Difference, National Identity and Professing History: the Case of Alice Stopford Green', *History Workshop Journal* (2002): 119-27.
Howard, Michael S., *Jonathan Cape, Publisher* (London: Jonathan Cape, 1971).
Howat, G. M. D., 'The Nineteenth-Century History Text-Book', *British Journal of Educational Studies* 13:2 (May 1965), 147-59.
Howsam, Leslie. 'Academic discipline or literary genre?: The establishment of boundaries in historical writing', *Victorian Literature & Culture* (2004), 413-33.
'Book History Unbound: Transactions of the Written Word Made Public', *Canadian Journal of History* 38:4 (2003): 69-81.
Cheap Bibles: Nineteenth-Century Publishing and the British and Foreign Bible Society (Cambridge: Cambridge University Press, 1991).
'An Experiment With Science for the Nineteenth-Century Book Trade: The International Scientific Series', *British Journal for the History of Science* 33 (2000): 187-207.
'Imperial Publishers and the Idea Of Colonial History, 1870-1916', *History of Intellectual Culture* 5:2 (2005).
Kegan Paul, a Victorian Imprint: Publishers, Books and Cultural History

(Toronto: University of Toronto Press, 1998).

Old Books and New Histories: An Orientation to Studies in Book and Print Culture (Toronto: University of Toronto Press, 2006).

'Sustained Literary Ventures: The Series in Victorian Book Publishing', *Publishing History* 31 (1992): 5-26.

Howsam, Leslie, Christopher Stray, Alice Jenkins, James A. Secord and Anna Vaninskaya, 'What the Victorians Learned: Perspectives on Nineteenth Century Schoolbooks', *Journal of Victorian Culture* 12(2) (2007): 262-85.

Iggers, Georg G. and James M. Powell, eds, *Leopold von Ranke and the Shaping of the Historical Discipline* (Syracuse: Syracuse University Press, 1990).

Israel, Kali, *Names and Stories: Emilia Dilke and Victorian Culture* (New York: Oxford University Press, 1999).

Issitt, John, 'The Natural History of a Textbook', *Publishing History* 47 (2000): 5-30.

Jacobs, H. Edward, 'Buying Into Classes: The Practice of Book Selection in Eighteenth-Century Britain', *Eighteenth-Century Studies* 33 (1999): 43-64.

James, Elizabeth, ed., *Macmillan: A Publishing Tradition* (London: Palgrave, 2002).

Jann, Rosemary, *The Art and Science of Victorian History* (Columbus: Ohio State University Press, 1985).

Jordanova, Ludmilla, *History in Practice*, 2nd edn (London: Hodder Arnold, 2006).

Kadish, Alon, 'Scholarly Exclusiveness and the Foundation of the English Historical Review', *Historical Research* [Great Britain] 61:145 (1988): 183-98.

Kaye, Harvey J., *The British Marxist Historians: An Introductory Analysis* (New York: Basil Blackwell, 1984).

Kennedy, Dane, 'Imperial History and Post-Colonial Theory', *The Journal of Imperial and Commonwealth History* 24:3 (September 1996): 345-63.

Kent, Christopher, 'Victorian Social History: Post-Thompson, Post-Foucault, Postmodern', *Victorian Studies* (Autumn 1996): 97-133.

'Higher Journalism and the Mid-Victorian Clerisy', *Victorian Studies* (December 1969): 181-98.

Kenyon, John, *The History Men: The Historical Profession in England Since the Renaissance* (London: Weidenfeld & Nicolson, 1983).

Kijinski, John L, 'John Morley's "English Men of Letters" Series and the Politics of Reading', *Victorian Studies* 34:2 (1991): 205-25.

Krueger, Christine L., 'Why She Lived at the PRO: Mary Anne Everett Green and the Profession of History', *Journal of British Studies* 42 (January 2003): 65-90.

Lambert, Peter, 'Paving the "Peculiar Path": German Nationalism and Historiography Since Ranke', in *Imagining Nations*, ed. Geoffrey Cubitt (Manchester: Manchester University Press), pp. 92-109.

Landon, Richard G., ed., *Book Selling and Book Buying: Aspects of the Nineteenth-Century British and North American Book Trade* (Chicago: American Library Association, 1978).

Leathes, Sir Stanley, 'The Editorial Methods of Sir Adolphus Ward: The Cambridge Modern History', *The Cambridge Historical Journal* 1:2 (1924): 219-21.

Lemann, Nicholas, 'History Solo: Non-Academic Historians', *The American Historical Review* 100 (June 1995): 788-98.

Levine, Philippa, *The Amateur and the Professional: Antiquarians, Historians and Archaeologists in Victorian England, 1838-1886* (Cambridge: Cambridge University Press, 1986).

Lightman, Bernard, *Victorian Popularizers of Science: Designing Nature for New Audiences* (Chicago: University of Chicago Press, 2008).

'The Voices of Nature: Popularizing Victorian Science', *Victorian Science in Context*, ed. Bernard Lightman (Chicago and London: University of Chicago Press, 1997), pp. 187-211

Linehan, P. A., 'The Making of the Cambridge Medieval History', *Speculum* 57:3 (1982), 463-94.

McDonald, Peter D., *British Literary Culture and Publishing Practice, 1880-1914* (Cambridge: Cambridge University Press, 1997).

'Implicit Structures and Explicit Interactions: Pierre Bourdieu and the History of the Book', *The Library*, Sixth Series 19:2 (June 1997): 105-21.

McIntire, C. T., *Herbert Butterfield: Historian As Dissenter* (New Haven: Yale University Press, 2004).

McIntire, C. T. and Marvin Perry, eds, *Toynbee: Reappraisals* (Toronto: University of Toronto Press, 1989).

McKenzie, D. F., *Bibliography and the Sociology of Texts* (London: The British Library, 1986).

Making Meaning: Printers of the Mind and Other Essays, eds Peter D. McDonald and Michael Suarez (Amherst: University of Massachusetts Press, 2002).

'The Sociology of a Text: Orality, Literacy and Print in Early New Zealand', *The Library*, Sixth Series 4 (1984): 333-65.

McKillop, A. B., *The Spinster and the Prophet: Florence Deeks, H. G. Wells and the Mystery of the Purloined Past* (Toronto: Mcfarlane Walter & Ross, 2001).

McKitterick, David, *A History of Cambridge University Press: Scholarship and Commerce, 1698-1872* (Cambridge: Cambridge University Press, 1998).

A History of Cambridge University Press: New Worlds for Learning, 1873-1972 (Cambridge: Cambridge University Press, 2004).

MacLeod, Roy M., *The 'Creed of Science' in Victorian England* (Aldershot: Ashgate, 2000).

McNeill, William H., *Arnold J. Toynbee: A Life* (Oxford: Oxford University Press, 1989).

McNiven, Peter, 'Handlist of the Papers of Edward Augustus Freeman in the John Rylands University Library of Manchester', *Bulletin of the John Rylands University Library of Manchester* 72:2 (Summer 1990): 27-71.

Maitzen, Rohan. '"This Feminine Preserve": Historical Biographies by Victorian Women', *Victorian Studies* (Spring 1995): 371-93.

Mandler, Peter, *The English National Character: The History of an Idea from Edmund Burke to Tony Blair* (New Haven: Yale University Press, 2007).

History and National Life (London: Profile Books, 2002).

Markus, Julia J., *Anthony Froude: The Last Undiscovered Great Victorian* (New York: Scribner, 2005).

Marwick, Arthur, 'Knowledge and Language: History, the Humanities, the Sciences', *History* (2002): 3-17.

Mathew, David, *Lord Acton and his Times* (London: Eyre & Spottiswode, 1968).

Matthew, H. C. G. and Brian Harrison, eds, *Oxford Dictionary of National Biography* (Oxford: Oxford University Press, 2004).

Melman, Billie, *The Culture of History: English Uses of the Past 1800-1953* (New York: Oxford University Press, 2006).

'Under the Western Historian's Eyes: Eileen Power and the Early Feminist Encounter With Colonialism', *History Workshop Journal* (1996): 147-68.

Michie, Michael, *An Enlightenment Tory in Victorian Scotland: The Career of Sir Archibald Alison* (Kingston: McGill–Queens University Press, 1997).

Millgate, Jane, *Macaulay* (London: Routledge & Kegan Paul, 1973).

Scott's Last Edition: A Study in Publishing History (Edinburgh: Edinburgh University Press, 1987).

Mitchell, Rosemary, '"The Busy Daughters of Clio": Women Writers of History From 1820 to 1880', *Women's History Review* 7:1 (1998): 107-34.

Picturing the Past: English History in Text and Image 1830-1870 (Oxford: Clarendon Press, 2000).

Mittal, S. C., *India Distorted: A Study of British Historians on India*, 3 vols (New Delhi: MD Publications PVT, 1995-8).

Moore, James, *The Post-Darwinian Controversies: A Study of the Protestant Struggles to Come to Terms with Darwin in Great Britain and America 1870-1900* (Cambridge: Cambridge University Press, 1979).

Morbey, C. C., *Charles Knight: An Appreciation and Bibliography of a Great Victorian Publisher* (Birmingham: Birmingham Polytechnic Department of Librarianship, 1979).

Morgan, Charles, *The House of Macmillan (1843-1943)* (London: Macmillan, 1943).

Mumby, Frank, *Publishing and Bookselling: A History From the Earliest Times to the Present Day* (London: Jonathan Cape, 1949).

Murray, K. M. Elisabeth, *Caught in the Web of Words: James Murray and the Oxford English Dictionary* (New Haven: Yale University Press, 1977).

Norrington, A. L. P., *Blackwell's 1879-1979: The History of a Family Firm* (Oxford: B. H. Blackwell, 1983).

North, John S., ed., *Waterloo Directory: The Waterloo Directory of English Newspapers and Periodicals, 1800-1900* (Waterloo: North Waterloo Academic Press, 1997–. (Series 1, vols 1-10; Series 2, vols 1-20; See also directories of Irish (1986) and Scottish (2 vols, 1989) newspapers and periodicals, and the on-line edition www.victorianperiodicals.org).

Norton, Brian, *Freeman's Life: Highlights, Chronology, Letters and Works* (Farnborough: Norton, 1993).

Novick, Peter, *That Noble Dream: The 'Objectivity Question' and the American Historical Profession* (Cambridge: Cambridge University Press, 1988).

O'Brien, Karen, 'The History Market in Eighteenth-Century England', in Isabel Rivers, ed., *Books and their Readers in Eighteenth-Century England: New Essays* (London: Continuum, 2001).

Olabarri, Ignacio, 'The Development of Review Articles in English-Language Historical Journals: Significance and Consequences', *Storiografia* 1 (1997): 225-30.

Osborne, John W., 'The Endurance of "Literary" History in Great Britain: Charles Oman, G. M. Trevelyan, and the Genteel Tradition', *Clio* 2 (1972): 7-17.

Palmer, William, *Engagement with the Past: The Lives and Works of the World War II Generation of Historians* (Lexington: University Press of Kentucky, 2001).

Parker, C. J. W., 'The Failure of Liberal Racialism: The Racial Ideas of E. A. Freeman', *The Historical Journal* 24:4 (1981): 825-46.

Parker, Geoffrey, 'George Norman Clark 1890-1979', *Proceedings of the British Academy* [Great Britain] 66 (1980): 407-25.

Patten, Robert and David Finkelstein, 'Editing Blackwood's; or, What Do Editors Do?' in D. Finkelstein, ed., *Print Culture and the Blackwood Tradition, 1805-1930* (Toronto: University of Toronto Press, 2006).

Penguin Books [written by William Emrys Williams], *The Penguin Story 1935-1956* (London: Penguin, 1956).

Plumb, J. H., *The Making of An Historian: The Collected Essays of J. H. Plumb* (Athens, Georgia: University of Georgia Press, 1988).

Pope-Hennessy, Una, *Agnes Strickland, Biographer of the Queens of England, 1796-1874* (London: Chatto & Windus, 1940).

Porter, Roy, 'Reading Is Bad for Your Health', *History Today* (1998): 1-9.

Price, Richard, 'Historiography, Narrative, and the Nineteenth Century', *Journal of British Studies* 35 (April 1996): 220-56.

Rauch, Alan, *Useful Knowledge: The Victorians, Morality, and the March of Intellect* (Durham and London: Duke University Press, 2001).

Raven, James, *The Business of Books: Booksellers and the English Book Trade 1450-1850* (New Haven: Yale University Press, 2007).

'The Promotion and Constraints of Knowledge: The Changing Structure of Publishing in Victorian Britain', in *The Organisation of Knowledge in Victorian Britain*, ed. Martin Daunton (Oxford: Oxford University Press for the British Academy, 2005).

Readman, Paul, 'The Place of the Past in English Culture, *c*. 1890-1914', *Past and Present* 186 (2005): 147-99.

Rein, Gustov Adolf, ed., trans. John L. Herkless, *Sir John Robert Seeley: A Study of the Historian* (Wolfeboro, New Hampshire: Longwood Academic, 1987).

Roberts, S. C., *Adventures with Authors* (Cambridge: Cambridge University Press, 1966).

The Evolution of Cambridge Publishing (Cambridge: Cambridge University Press, 1956).

Roscow, James P., 'The Common Ground: Crossing Over Between History and Publishing', *Public Historian* 4:2 (1982): 29-34.

Rose, Jonathan, *The Intellectual Life of the British Working Classes* (New Haven: Yale University Press, 2001).

Rosenberg, J. D., *Carlyle and the Burden of History* (Oxford: Clarendon Press, 1985).

Rothblatt, Sheldon, *The Revolution of the Dons: Cambridge and Society in Victorian England* (New York: Basic Books, 1968).

Rowse, A. L., *Froude the Historian: Victorian Man of Letters* (Gloucester: Alan Sutton, 1987).

St Clair, William, *The Reading Nation in the Romantic Period* (Cambridge: Cambridge University Press, 2004).

Schorske, Carl E., *Thinking with History: Explorations in the Passage to Modernism* (Princeton: Princeton University Press, 1998).

Schuettinger, Robert L., *Lord Acton: Historian of Liberty* (LaSalle, Illinois: Open Court, 1976).

Scott, Christina, *A Historian and his World: A Life of Christopher Dawson 1889-1970* (London: Sheed & Ward, 1984).

Secord, James A., *Victorian Sensation: The Extraordinary Publication, Reception, and Secret Authorship of Vestiges of the Natural History of Creation* (Chicago: University of Chicago Press, 2000).

Shattock, Joanne, *Politics and Reviewers: the Edinburgh and the Quarterly in the Early Victorian Age* (Leicester: Leicester University Press, 1989).

Shea, Donald F., *The English Ranke: John Lingard* (New York: Humanities Press, 1969).

Sher, Richard B., *The Enlightenment and the Book: Scottish Authors & their Publishers in Eighteenth-Century Britain, Ireland & America* (Chicago: University of Chicago Press, 2006).

Shillingsburg, Peter, *Pegasus in Harness: Victorian Publishing and William Makepeace Thackeray* (Charlottesville: University of Virginia Press, 1992).

Simmons, James C., 'The Novelist as Historian: An Unexplored Tract of Victorian Historiography', *Victorian Studies* (March 1971): 293-305.

Slee, Peter, *Learning and a Liberal Education: The Study of Modern History in the Universities of Oxford, Cambridge and Manchester, 1800-1914* (Manchester: Manchester University Press, 1986).

Smith, B. G. 'The Contribution of Women to Modern Historiography in Great Britain, France and the United States, 1750-1949', *American Historical Review* 100 (1995): 709-32.

The Gender of History: Men, Women, and Historical Practice (Cambridge, Mass.: Harvard University Press, 1998).

Smith, David C., *H. G. Wells: Desperately Mortal, a Biography* (New Haven: Yale University Press, 1986).

Soffer, Reba, *Discipline and Power: The University, History and the Making of an English Elite, 1870-1930* (Stanford: Stanford University Press, 1994).

Sorensen, David R., 'Carlyle, Macaulay, and the "Dignity of History"',

Carlyle Annual 11 (1990): 41-52.

Stapleton, Julia, *Englishness and the Study of Politics: The Social and Political Thought of Ernest Barker* (Cambridge: Cambridge University Press, 1994).

Sir Arthur Bryant and National History in Twentieth-Century Britain (Lanham, MD: Lexington Books, 2006).

Steadman, C., '"The Mother Made Conscious": The Historical Development of a Primary School Pedagogy', *History Workshop Journal* 26 (1985).

Steedman, Carolyn, 'Culture, Cultural Studies, and the Historians', in *Cultural Studies*, eds Lawrence Grossberg, Cary Nelson and Paula Treichler (New York: Routledge, 1992), pp. 613-22.

Street, Pamela, *Arthur Bryant: Portrait of a Historian* (London: Collins , 1979).

Sutcliffe, Peter, *The Oxford University Press: An Informal History* (Oxford: Clarendon Press, 1978).

Sutherland, John, 'The Institutionalisation of the British Book Trade to the 1890s', in *Development of the English Book Trade, 1700-1899*, eds Robin Myers and Michael Harris (Oxford: Oxford Polytechnic Press, 1981), pp. 95-105.

'Publishing History: A Hole at the Center of Literary Sociology', in *Critical Inquiry* 14 (Spring 1988): 574-89.

Victorian Novelists & Publishers (Chicago: University of Chicago Press, 1978).

Tanselle, G. Thomas, *Literature and Artifacts* (Charlottesville: The Bibliographical Society of the University of Virginia, 1998).

Thapar, Romila, *Somanatha: The Many Voices of History* (New York: Verso, 2005).

Thompson, F. M. L., 'The Best Club in England', [Institute of Historical Research] *The Historian* 1985 (8): 3-8.

Topham, Jonathan, 'John Limbird, Thomas Byerley, and the Production of Cheap Periodicals in the 1820s', *Book History* 8 (2005), 75-106.

'Publishing "Popular Science" in Early Nineteenth-Century Britain', in *Science in the Marketplace: Nineteenth-Century Sites and Experiences*, ed. Aileen Fyfe and Bernard Lightman (Chicago: Chicago University Press, 2007).

Tosh, John, *The Pursuit of History*, 3rd rev. edn (London: Pearson Education, 2002).

Tulloch, Hugh, *Acton* (New York: St Martin's Press, 1988).

Turner, Frank, *Between Science and Religion: The Reaction to Scientific Naturalism in Late Victorian England* (New Haven: Yale University Press, 1974).

Contesting Cultural Authority: Essays in Victorian Intellectual Life (Cambridge: Cambridge University Press, 1993).

Vincent, David, *Bread, Knowledge and Freedom: A Study of Nineteenth-Century Working Class Autobiography* (London and New York: Methuen, 1981).

Literacy and Popular Culture: England 1750-1914 (Cambridge: Cambridge University Press, 1989).

Wallace, Stuart, *War and the Image of Germany: British Academics 1914-1918* (Edinburgh: John Donald Publishers, 1988).

Walton, Susan, 'Charlotte M. Yonge and the "historic harem" of Edward Augustus Freeman', *Journal of Victorian Culture* 11.2 (2006): 226-55.

Wang, Q. Edward and Franz L. Fillafer, *The Many Faces of Clio: Cross Cultural Approaches to Historiography* (New York: Berghahn Books, 2007).

Watson, George, *Lord Acton's History of Liberty: A Study of His Library* (Aldershot: Scolar Press, 1994).

Weaver, J. R. H., *Henry William Carless Davis 1874-1928: A Memoir* (London: Constable, 1933).

Weedon, Alexis, *Victorian Publishing: The Economics of Book Production for a Mass Market, 1836-1916* (Aldershot: Ashgate, 2003).

Weedon, Alexis and Michael Bott, *British Book Trade Archives, 1830-1939: A Location Register* (Oxford: History of the Book-on-demand series, 1996).

White, H., *Metahistory: The Historical Imagination in Nineteenth Century Europe* (Baltimore: Johns Hopkins University Press, 1973).

Wiener, Joel H., *Innovators and Preachers: the Role of the Editor in Victorian England* (Westport, Connecticut: Greenwood Press, 1985).

Wilkinson, L. P., *Kingsmen of a Century 1873-1972* (Cambridge: King's College, 1981).

Winstanley, D. A., *Later Victorian Cambridge* (Cambridge: Cambridge University Press, 1947).

Woolf, D. R., *Reading History in Early Modern England* (Cambridge: Cambridge University Press, 2000).

Wormell, Deborah, *Sir John Seeley and the Uses of History* (Cambridge: Cambridge University Press, 1980).

Worth, George J., *Macmillan's Magazine, 1859-1907: 'No Flippancy or Abuse Allowed'* (Aldershot: Ashgate, 2003).

Wright, Anthony, *R. H. Tawney* (Manchester: Manchester University Press, 1987).

Index

Acton, John Emerich Edward Dalberg-Acton, 5, 24, 62-71, 75, 79, 81-2, 93, 103, 122-4, 127
Adcock, F. E., 95
agency of the publisher, 3, 5-6, 63-4, 117
Alfred, king of England, 4, 11, 32, 119
Allen, George (publisher), 117, 152n55
American Historical Review, 77
Archbold, W.A., 65, 68, 123, 142n39
archives of publishers, 2, 8, 47, 82, 120-1, 128
archives used by historians, 6, 25, 32, 70, 81, 94
Ashton, T. S., 101
Athenaeum, The, 32, 134n25
Austria (history of), 84, 86; Austrian historians, 92

Barker, Ernest, 77, 81-6, 102, 107-13
Bateson, Mary, 65, 92, 122
Bell, George & Sons (publishers), 61, 87-8
Belligerents, Histories of the (series), 77, 84-6, 90, 146n33
bibliography, 1-2, 5, 23, 114
Blennerhassett, Charlotte, 65, 122
book culture, 2, 126, 129n5
book history. *See* history of the book
Book of the Month Club, 107
Book Society, 80
Bradley, A. G., 96, 148n75
Brewer, J. S., 20
Brooke, Zachary N., 92, 123
Browning, Oscar, 32, 50, 54-9, 64, 82, 119, 126, 139n14, 140n21
Bryant, Arthur, 8, 80, 101, 113, 115, 120, 145n25, 151n49
Bryce, James, 27, 30-1, 35, 46, 59-60, 79, 82, 122
Bryce, Kate, 33, 152n2
Buckle, H. T., 24, 133n2
Bury, J. B., 24, 50, 80, 95, 133n1
Butterfield, Herbert, 75, 104, 116

Callcott, Maria, 10-13
Cambridge Historical Series, 90-1, 115
Cambridge histories, collaborative, 73, 81, 89, 92-5, 102-4, 113, 117, 123-4. *See also Cambridge Modern History*; India, history of
Cambridge Modern History, 5, 22, 25, 49, 62-71, 83, 88, 123; *The CMH, An Account of its Origin* (1907), 64-7; *New Cambridge Modern History*, 89, 104
Cambridge University Press, 5, 25, 27, 44-7, 80, 87, 89-96, 99, 101
Cambridge, University of, 24, 50, 54, 57
Canada, 125; history of, 72-3
Cannan, Charles, 75, 86
Cape, Jonathan (publishers), 100
Carrington, Charles, 114
Cassell, Petter & Gilpin (publishers), 45, 61, 71
Chartier, Roger, 151n42

children, histories for, 3-4, 8, 10-17, 28, 30-5, 80, 95-6, 120, 125-6. *See also* school histories
Churchill, Winston, 87-8, 99, 101
Clapham, John, 101, 104
Clarendon Press Series, 40-1, 44
Clarendon Press. *See* Oxford University Press
Clark, G. N., 87-8, 104-6, 112-13, 123
collaboration, 5-6, 25, 68-70, 103, 111, 122-4
Collette, Charles Hastings, 16, 132n42
Collingwood, R. G., 117
Collins, William (publishers), 115
colonies: as market, 43, 50, 98,127; histories of, 53-4, 65, 70, 81, 83, 89, 93
Conference of Allied Ministers of Education, 107-9, 150n36
Constable (publishers), 98
copyright, 61, 72
Coulton, George, 102, 113
Creighton, Louise, 82
Creighton, Mandell, 59-61, 82, 122, 124, 133n6
Cruttwell, Charles, 88
Czaplica, M. A., 84, 123, 146n35

Daily Sketch, 111-12
Darnton, Robert, 3, 6. 130n9. 152n9
Davin, D. M., 112
Davis, H. W. C., 75, 82-3
Dictionary of National Biography, 49, 98, 138n1
Dodwell, H. H., 93-4
Doran, John, 32

editorship of historical series, 82, 93, 123-4. *See also* series format
Edwards, Owen M., 73-5, 105
Eliot, Simon, 2, 7
Elizabeth, queen of England, 4
English Historical Review, 22, 35, 37, 49, 59-60, 104, 119, 124. *See also* historical review (planned periodical)
English Men of Letters (series), 33, 61
Ensor, R. C. K., 105-6, 109-11, 117
Epochs (series), 80, 82-6, 146n23
European Inheritance, The, 107, 109-13
Everyman's Library (series), 20

Firth, C. H., 98
Fisher, H. A. L., 88, 94-6, 136n52
Fletcher, C. L. R., 74-5
format, 6-7, 9, 26, 47, 59-62, 69, 86, 90, 115-19, 124-5
France, history of, 33-4, 41, 72, 111, 116, 152n2
Frederick the Great, 101, 149n4
Freeman, E.A., 7, 13, 20-2, 24, 28-35, 40-1, 44, 46, 72-3, 79, 119. *See also* Historical Course for Schools
Freeman, Margaret, 30, 33, 122
Froude, J. A., 26-7, 32, 39, 41
Fry, Roger, 65

Gell, P. L., 46-7, 49, 71-3, 138n68
Germany, 7, 76, 92; history of, 41, 52, 76, 79
Gilbert, James (publisher), 13-17, 20
Gill, George & Sons (publisher), 20, 120, 152n60
Gladstone, William, 52
Goldsmith, Oliver, 15, 17
Gooch, G. P., 94, 103
Grant, A. J., 90
Green, Alice, 50, 98
Green, J.R., 6, 8, 26-8, 33, 54, 87, 139n12; editorship of planned historical review, 35-7, 59; *Short History of England* (1874), 37-40, 46, 49-51, 62, 80-1, 89, 98, 125, 144n2, 153n8
Greswell, W. P., 72
Griffith & Farran (publishers), 56-7, 61

Haig, Wolseley, 93
Halevy, Elie, 81
Hassall, Arthur, 136n52

Historical Association, 77, 98, 144n5
Historical Course for Schools (series), 13, 33, 46, 76, 82, 93, 116, 123-4, 134n26
historical review (planned periodical), 35-7, 59-61, 77
Historical Review (periodical circa 1860), 73-4
History (periodical), *see* Historical Association
history as academic discipline, 1-2, 4-5, 6, 22
history curricula, 50, 52, 57
history of the book, 5-6, 23, 117-18, 127
Hitler, Adolf, 101
Hogarth, William, 88
Home University Library (series), 106
Howitt, Mary, 20-1
Hume, David, 6, 10, 20, 62, 125

illustrated histories, 11, 50-1, 57, 80, 96, 98-9
Ince, Henry, 13-17, 20
India: history of, 53-4, 89, 92-4; school histories for, 22, 33, 98, 139, 153n8
Italy (history of), 70

Johnson, J. de M., 82-4, 123
Johnson, Samuel, 8
Jordanova, Ludmilla, 62

Kenyon, John, 100-1
Kingsley, Charles, 27-30, 33, 52
Kipling, Rudyard, 74-5
Kirkpatrick, A. F., 90
Kitchin, G. W., 40-3, 72, 136n52

Lane, John, 101
Lane-Poole, Austin, 105
Lawrence, D. H., 79-80, 96
life cycle of the reader, 2-5, 10, 122
Linehan, P.A., 92
literary replication, 9, 18, 20
Little Arthur, *see* Calcott, Maria
Longman, Robert, 5
Longmans (publisher), 8, 26-7, 31, 45, 60-1, 80-4, 87, 115

Macaulay, T.B., 3, 8, 18, 26-7, 47, 50-2, 80, 98-9
McKenzie, D. F., 23
McKillop, A. B., 80
McKitterick, David, 27, 89
Macmillan & Co. (publisher), 26, 76-7, 79-80, 96-8. *See also* Alexander Macmillan
Macmillan, Alexander, 13-16, 20, 26-40, 43-62, 115, 122, 128. *See also* Historical Course for Schools
Macmillan, Daniel, 26
Macmillan, Frederick, 98
Macmillan's Magazine, 35, 52
Maitland, F. W., 65, 68
Manchester University, 65, 79, 89
Markham, Mrs. *See* Penrose, Elizabeth
materiality of history books, 3, 9-10, 69, 81, 114-17
Maunder, Samuel, 15
Merriman, R. B., 84
Methuen (publisher), 82-4, 87, 95, 105
Milford, Humphrey, 83, 88, 106, 123
Miller, William, 90
Mitchell, Rosemary, 13
Morley, John, 33, 39
Mornet, Daniel, 111-12
Mrs Markham (*History of England*), 10-21, 28, 30, 123
Murray, John (publishers), 10-11, 46

Nature, 27, 35, 124
Neale, J. E., 100-1
New Cambridge Modern History, *see Cambridge Modern History*
Norgate, Kate, 50
Norrington, A. L. P., 84-5, 87, 105-12
nursery histories, *see* children, histories for

objectivity, 25, 69-70, 119. *See also*

European Inheritance, The
Oxford Essays, 35-6
Oxford History of England, 73, 81, 86-8, 99, 104-6, 117
Oxford School History of England, 73-5, 82, 105
Oxford University Press, 27, 31, 40-8, 69, 71-5, 77, 81-8, 96, 104-13, 123
Oxford, University of, 31, 41, 60

Palgrave, Francis, 10
Parker, John W. (publisher), 28, 40
part-publication, 9, 50, 57
Payne, E. J., 41, 90
Penson, Lillian M., 103, 123
Pepys, Samuel, 80, 101, 113-14
periodicals, 9, 35-7, 47, 59-61, 122, 124-6, 128. *See also English Historical Review*
Pinnock, William, 13-17
Pitt Press, *see* Cambridge University Press
Pogson Smith, W. G., 75
popular history, 6-9, 24, 37, 43, 52-4, 57, 59, 69, 80-2, 96, 101, 118, 124-8
Postan, M. M., 101
Powell, F. York, 47, 72-3, 82
Power, Eileen, 95-7, 100-1, 119
Power, Rhoda, 95-7, 101
Previté-Orton, Charles, 92
Prothero, G. W., 45, 63, 72, 90, 133n3, 137n60, 143n54

Ramsay, James, 8, 45-7, 49, 72
Ranke, Leopold von, 7, 25, 70, 133n3
Rapson, E.J., 93-4
Rashdall, Hastings, 72
Richardson, G. Noel, 74-5
Richardson, W. R. (minister of education), 113
Roberts, Margaret, 42-3
Roberts, S. C., 80, 94-6, 102-4
Robertson, Grant, 85
Roman Catholicism, 16, 40, 80, 125
Royal Historical Society, 25, 77

Saturday Review, 28
Schmitt, Bernadotte, 103-4
school histories, 3, 5, 9, 15-16, 30-1, 37-43, 56-7, 79-80, 82-3, 98, 120, 127. *See also* Historical Course for Schools, *Oxford School History of England*
science, 9, 18, 61; history as a science, 6-8, 24-6, 28-30, 37, 49-53, 111
Scotland (history of), 33, 136n36
Scott, Walter, 52
Secord, James, 9, 18
Seeley, J. R., 7, 24, 32, 44-5, 59-61, 70, 72, 118, 128, 138n4, 139n12; *Expansion of England*, 50-4
series format, 6, 9, 47-8, 61-2, 82-6, 115-19, 123-4. *See also* Belligerents, Histories of the; Cambridge Historical Series; Cambridge Modern History; Clarendon Press Series; English Men of Letters; Epochs; Everyman's Library; Historical Course for Schools; Home University Library; Oxford History of England
Shaw, Flora, 65, 123
Sisam, Kenneth, 87, 105-6, 109, 152n58
Smith, A. L., 72
Smith, Goldwin, 28, 30-1, 41, 136n47
Smith, Vincent, 94
Somervell, David C., 107-8, 113
Stapleton, Julia, 113
Starr, Mark, 75
Stephen, James, 122
Stephen, Katherine, 152n2
Stubbs, William, 24, 32, 41, 111, 137n60; as advisor to OUP, 41-2, 46, 72; *Select Charters*, 41, 72
Sutcliffe, Peter, 27, 44, 69, 71, 72

Tanner, J. R., 92, 113
Tawney, R. H., 101
Taylor, A. J. P., 5
Temperley, Harold, 84, 96, 103
textbooks, *see* school histories

Thompson, Edith, 9, 33-4, 76, 92, 98, 116, 122, 125, 144n2
Topham, Jonathan, 15
Toynbee, Arnold, 101, 106-8
transpersonal replicability, 25, 119
Trevelyan, G. M., 5, 50, 80-1, 90, 101-2, 118-20, 149n7
Tripos, *see* history curricula

United States, 20, 61, 87-8, 96, 103, 125; history of, 83, 86, 104
Urquhart, F. F., 136n52

Vaucher, Paul, 109, 112, 150n34
Victoria, queen of England, 28, 75
Virtue & Co. (publishers), 56-9

Waller, A. R., 90, 95
Warbeck, Perkin, 4
Ward, A. W., 27, 41, 52, 65, 68, 79, 81, 89-90, 94-5, 124
Ward, Marcus (publisher), 28
Ward, Mary, 135n29
Weedon, Alexis, 26
Wells, H. G., 79-80, 115
Weston, Jessie, 92-3, 123
Wheeler, Harold F. B., 77, 124
Whibley, Leonard, 95
whig history, 8, 24
Whittaker, G. & W.B. (publishers), 15, 17
Why we are at War, 77
William the Conqueror, 20, 32
women as historical subjects, 15, 126
women historians, 8-10, 33, 65, 70, 80, 92-3, 98, 103, 122-3, 146n27
Woodward, Llewellyn, 83
Wright, Richard T., 62, 64-71, 86, 93, 102, 123, 128

Yonge, Charlotte M., 9, 13, 15, 27-9, 32-4, 119, 124